Matt Fuller claims he has wr  10 years – and after readin The result is not a dry comi would rather avoid, but a thoroughly practical preacher's guide that tackles the 'law/grace' issues that Deuteronomy forces us to wrestle with, while relentlessly pointing us to Christ ('He took the curse for us!'). Matt's pointers for application at the end of each chapter are very realistic, making this one of the most useful books for preachers I have come across. Deuteronomy needs to be preached (it's as much about 'heart' as 'law'), and preachers will not find a better guide.

Jeremy McQuoid
Teaching Pastor, Deeside Christian Fellowship,
Aberdeen, Scotland
Chair of Council, Keswick Ministries

Books encouraging people to preach consecutively through long Old Testament books and giving help to do so are always to be welcomed. It is a pleasure to commend *Teaching Deuteronomy* by Matt Fuller. He gives a very helpful analysis of the whole book and his comments on individual passages are penetrating and concise and never lose sight of practical application. I hope this will lead to many more sermons on this magnificent but often neglected book.

Bob Fyall
Former Senior Tutor at Cornhill Scotland & author of
several books

As I read *Teaching Deuteronomy*, there was no doubt in my mind Matt Fuller has taken Deuteronomy's message

– to love the Lord with all your heart – deeply into his own, and the fruits of this are clear on every page. In teaching Deuteronomy to theological students preparing to be pastors and preachers, I've only found a handful of resources to recommend wholeheartedly, that hold together theological and exegetical depth, with real-life pastoral and practical insight. I'll be recommending *Teaching Deuteronomy* to them, not only as an extremely helpful guide for preparation, but for personal edification and engagement with God through this foundational part of his Word.

Dan Wu
Old Testament Lecturer, Moore Theological College,
Sydney, Australia

Brimming with pastoral insight and helpful suggestions for preachers. But what I love most is how the overarching purpose of Deuteronomy reverberates throughout.

Denesh Divyanathan
Senior Pastor of The Crossing Church, Singapore
President of Project Timothy Singapore & Chairman of the
Evangelical Theological College of Asia

Deuteronomy was—and still is—a passionate burst of preaching. Matt Fuller's book provides the warm and wise insights that preachers need and love. It's exegetically faithful, thoroughly applied and leaves you convinced of Deuteronomy's key place in the Bible's big message.

Kirk Patston
Director of the Centre for Preaching and Pastoral Ministry,
Sydney Missionary and Bible College, Sydney, Australia

TEACHING DEUTERONOMY

From text to message

MATT FULLER

PT RESOURCES

CHRISTIAN
FOCUS

All Scripture quotations, unless otherwise indicated, are taken from the ESV® Bible (*The Holy Bible, English Standard Version®*), copyright © 2001 by Crossway Bibles, a publishing ministry of Good News Publishers. Used by permission. All rights reserved.

Scripture quotations marked NIV are taken from *The Holy Bible, New International Version®* NIV®. Copyright © 1973, 1978, 1984, 2011 by Biblica, Inc.™ Used by permission of Zondervan. All rights reserved worldwide.

Copyright © Proclamation Trust Media 2022

Paperback ISBN: 978-1-5271-0900-1
Ebook ISBN: 978-1-5271-0988-9

10 9 8 7 6 5 4 3 2 1

Published in 2022
by
Christian Focus Publications Ltd.,
Geanies House, Fearn, Ross-shire,
IV20 1TW, Scotland, Great Britain
with
Proclamation Trust Resources,
116-118 Walworth Road, London, SE17 1JL
England, Great Britain.
www.proctrust.org.uk

www.christianfocus.com

Cover design by Moose77.com

Printed by Bell & Bain, Glasgow

All rights reserved. No part of this publication may be reproduced, stored in a retrieval system, or transmitted, in any form, by any means, electronic, mechanical, photocopying, recording or otherwise without the prior permission of the publisher or a license permitting restricted copying. In the U.K. such licenses are issued by the Copyright Licensing Agency, Saffron House, 6-10 Kirby Street, London, EC1 8TS www.cla.co.uk.

Contents

For Ceri,
for encouraging me constantly
(even to write books …)

ACKNOWLEDGEMENTS

All books have many voices sitting behind the author. I would want to give thanks to James Robson, who was the first to open up Deuteronomy to me so that I wasn't completely bewildered.

Thanks to Christopher Ash, who first encouraged me to write on Deuteronomy, and then told me to slow down and give it 'a little more time in the oven, so that it's cooked'. I hope ten years was enough time.

Thanks to the faculty of Sydney Missionary Bible College. Without the invitation to lecture on Deuteronomy at the college, I would never have done the work to complete this book.

Thanks to the congregations at Christ Church Mayfair. I'm very thankful that you desire to hear the 'full counsel of God' taught.

Thanks to Jon Gemmell, Stephen Boon and the team at the Proclamation Trust for encouragement and suggestions.

Thanks to the eternal God who is our refuge and keeps his everlasting arms beneath us (Deut. 33:27).

How to Use This Book

This book aims to help the preacher or teacher understand the central aim and purpose of the text in order to preach or teach it to others. Unlike a commentary, therefore, it does not go into great exegetical detail. Instead, it helps us to engage with the themes of Deuteronomy, to keep the big picture in mind, and to think about how to present it to our hearers.

'Introducing Deuteronomy' examines the purpose, tone, themes, and structure of Deuteronomy, and gives some suggestions for possible preaching series in the book.

The remainder of the volume contains separate chapters on each preaching unit identified in the introductory chapter. The structure of each chapter is the same. It begins with a brief introduction to the unit. This is followed by 'Listening to the text', which outlines the context and structure of the unit and takes the reader through a section-by-section analysis of the text. Under the heading 'From text to message', a main theme and aim for the preaching unit is suggested, as well as ideas for application. Each chapter concludes with suggestions for preaching, and some questions that could form the basis for a group Bible study.

Introducing Deuteronomy

Getting our Bearings in Deuteronomy

On a wedding day you promise your spouse, 'I will love you.' It's hopefully easy to do on *that* day. Yet it is a promise that, after a honeymoon, you will love them on Monday in how you talk, on Tuesday in serving them, on Wednesday in remembering what is important to them. Not perfectly – no one loves perfectly – but it is possible as a default setting, as an orientation of life.

Deuteronomy is the call to choose 'today' to love God with unswerving loyalty. To love him 'with all your heart and with all your soul and with all your strength'. To love God as a response to his grace. To love him with very practical obedience. To love him on a Monday and then again on a Tuesday and every day. It's fundamentally a call to love him from the heart and yet that love will be demonstrated in obeying him in the practical details of life. Not perfectly – no one loves the Lord perfectly, but it's possible as an orientation of life.

For the Christian reader, Deuteronomy is a vivid, urgent and passionate call to love Jesus Christ in response to his grace and demonstrate that love in obedience to him.

Deuteronomy is probably not the first book any preacher would choose to preach. For many years, I was scared of Deuteronomy and didn't know what to do with it, and yet I knew it was too important to ignore. It is the climax of the Pentateuch. It explains the fundamental categories of blessing and curse which explain the rest of Israel's history up until exile and return. It reveals what exactly it means for Jesus to become our curse (Gal. 3).

Along with Psalms, it is Jesus's favourite book! He quotes it regularly in the gospels. When asked which is the greatest commandment, Jesus famously answers, 'You shall love the Lord your God with all your heart and with all your soul and with all your mind and with all your strength' (Mark 12:30). This is clearly a crucial command, yet the only place it appears in the Pentateuch is in Deuteronomy (6:5; 11:1; 13:3; 30:6).

However, in my entirely unscientific search of the internet, it appears to be one of the least preached books in our churches. Now, there are some natural reasons that might be the case:

- *Exegetical:* There are a variety of genres within the one book – there is history, poetry, law and prophecy. That is hard for both the preacher and the congregation.

- *Apologetical:* There is the *apparent* command to commit genocide, and we may think that too unpalatable for a modern audience. That's before we engage with laws within a patriarchal society that may sit uncomfortably today.

- *Relevancy:* There are a lot(!) of laws and we may think that Jesus has abrogated all of them so that they have no relevance. Or maybe we think that they are too complicated or boring to explain. (I really would want to disagree: wait until, for example, 14:26 is read: 'Spend the money for whatever you desire ... wine or strong drink, whatever your appetite craves.' The congregation will wonder what it means for them, but I don't think they'll say it's a dull command!)

- *Applicatory:* Perhaps above all, we wonder how to preach Deuteronomy as Christian scripture. It is obvious that Moses preaches obedience for Israel as a response to God's grace (Deuteronomy will not allow works righteousness; see 9:4-6). And yet it is equally obvious that Israel will fail and fall under God's curse. We wonder: how does that apply to Christians? Happily, we will see that God's grace triumphs.

What is Deuteronomy?

There ought to be no great debate about the authorship of Deuteronomy. Moses is declared to be the author of the three speeches and a song which compose the majority of the book, with occasional comments from an editor.

We are not served well by the Greek title of *Deuteronomos* ('second law') as it stresses the law code in the book. In fact, only a little over a third of the book is actually law, overwhelmingly found in chapters 12–26. The title in the Hebrew Torah is probably more helpful: *Debarim* – 'The words' which Moses spoke. The editor's introduction tells us what is happening in the book: 'Moses undertook to explain (or expound) this law' (1:5).

Deuteronomy is Moses's final chance to preach to Israel before his death and so he further applies the meaning of the law and preaches – with passion, urgency, authority and colour – the need to love and obey the LORD.

The purpose of Deuteronomy

In his final few sermons before his death, Moses presses the choice upon Israel (11:26-28):

> See, I am setting before you today a blessing and a curse: the blessing, if you obey the commandments of the LORD your God, which I command you today, and the curse, if you do not obey the commandments of the LORD your God, but turn aside from the way that I am commanding you today, to go after other gods that you have not known.

A similar summary of the entire book comes in the crucial and climactic chapter 30. The whole chapter is key for rightly interpreting the book. The summary comes in verses 19-20:

> I call heaven and earth to witness against you today, that I have set before you life and death, blessing and curse. Therefore choose life, that you and your offspring may live, loving the LORD your God, obeying his voice and holding fast to him, for he is your life and length of days, that you may dwell in the land that the LORD swore to your fathers, to Abraham, to Isaac, and to Jacob, to give them.

This has many of the repeatedly emphasised themes of the entire book and is the climactic appeal:

- 'Today': fifty-eight times in the book, Moses refers to the decision they must make 'today'. It's used in a similar sense to Psalm 95 and Hebrews 3–4; 'today' is every day. Each new day is a day to choose to follow the LORD.

- The stark choice: life or death, blessing or curse.
- The fundamental call to love the LORD (cf. 6:5) seen in obedience and holding fast to him.

So, at its most simple, the purpose of Deuteronomy for Israel was an urgent call from the departing Moses to choose to love the LORD and obey him in response to his grace 'today'.

Adding further detail, this fundamental choice is made in the heart and will be seen in the details of life in the promised land. It will be seen in their loyalty to the LORD and in the way they treat their fellow Israelites. This love and obedience will be a striking witness to the nations looking on.

Importantly, Israel is to make this choice despairing of their own ability and dependent upon God's mercy. Heaven and earth are called as witnesses against her, because she will undoubtedly fail.

The tone of Deuteronomy

Two melodies flow throughout the book – those of optimism and pessimism. Often as one ebbs the other flows. In places, they are disconcertingly next to one another and it feels jarring, like switching between the theme from *Superman* and Chopin's 'Funeral March'. Yet Moses is explicit in numerous places that Israel *will* fail; it is not a matter of 'if' but 'when':

- *When* you are in tribulation, and all these things come upon you in the latter days [the curses for

disobedience], you will return to the LORD your
God and obey his voice' (4:30).

- *When* all these things come upon you, the blessing
  and the curse, which I have set before you, and you
  call them to mind among all the nations where the
  LORD your God has driven you ...' (30:1).

- The LORD said to Moses, "Behold, you are about to
  lie down with your fathers. *Then this people will* rise
  and whore after the foreign gods among them in the
  land that they are entering, and they will forsake me
  and break my covenant'" (31:16).

- 'This song may be a witness for me against the people
  of Israel. For when I have brought them into the
  land ... they *will* turn to other gods and serve them,
  and despise me and break my covenant' (31:19-20).

- 'I know that after my death *you will surely* act corruptly and turn aside from the way that I have commanded you' (31:29).

Alongside this, the shadow of Moses's death hangs over the
book. On the one hand, this is neutral and Deuteronomy is
an answer to the question, 'What will we do without Moses?'

Yet it also contributes to the pessimistic tone, especially
in the opening and closing chapters (1:37; 3:23-27; 4:21-22;
31:2; 32:48-52; 34:4). It creates this atmosphere: If *even*
Moses was not able to demonstrate obedience to the LORD,
what chance did the nation have?

However, although failure is presented as inevitable,
there are certain strands of optimism too:

- When Israel remembers who their God is, they do
  manage to obey him. Moses encourages them early

on with the conquests of Sihon and Og (2:26–3:11). They can, at times, remember who their God is and so obey him.

- Far more importantly, God has *promised* the patriarchs that Israel would enter the land of Canaan and this land is wonderful! The LORD will provide generously and abundantly.

- Even though failure is inevitable, there is more grace for Israel. The LORD has made a binding promise, so although Israel can lose his blessing and experience his curse in one generation, they can never lose his love completely. This reaches a climax in 30:1-10 with the promise that God would circumcise their hearts. Grace will triumph.

The heart of the problem

Deuteronomy is not primarily concerned with external law obedience. If we teach that, we are viewing the law in the same mistaken way as the Pharisees of Jesus's day, believing that obedience leads to righteousness. The great call of Deuteronomy is to love the Lord your God from *the heart*.

We will distort the meaning of the book if we suggest that the law in Deuteronomy is only for external obedience, especially when the Ten Commandments include 'Do not covet.'

There are close to fifty references to the heart in the book, with the highest density in chapters 4 (four times), 6 (four times), and 30 (eight times). In the Old Testament, only the wisdom literature of Psalms, Proverbs, Song of Songs and Ecclesiastes has a greater density (and only Ephesians and 1 John in the New Testament). Deuteronomy *really* cares about the heart.

The central command in the book,[1] which Jesus later highlights as summarising the law is

> You shall love the LORD your God with all your heart and with all your soul and with all your might. (6:5)

But Israel has a problem with their hearts:

> Oh that they had such a heart as this always, to fear me and to keep all my commandments, that it might go well with them and with their descendants forever! (5:29)

> But to this day the LORD has not given you a heart to understand or eyes to see or ears to hear. (29:4)

They could not take external words and bring them into their hearts. They could not make themselves obey God. No one could then and still no one can naturally do so today. What was required was for God to act, to change their hearts and give them a heart to understand and eyes to see and ears to hear. He promises to do so in the key chapter 30:

> And the LORD your God will circumcise your heart and the heart of your offspring, so that you will love the LORD your God with all your heart and with all your soul, that you may live. (30:6)

Here is the blessing of a new heart that will be taken up further in Jeremiah 31:31-34 and Ezekiel 36:26-27. It is

---

1. Most commonly 'the commandment' (singular) is a reference to the *Shema* of Deut. 6:4-5, in contrast to the details of chapters 12–26, although at other times it seems more likely to be a reference to the entire law (e.g. 17:18-20).

seen ultimately on the Day of Pentecost when the ascended Lord Jesus pours out his Spirit in an unprecedented fashion.

Although Israel could not know this new covenant blessing fully, they could cling to God's promise. See the notes on chapter 30 for a full explanation, but a true Israelite believer would declare, '*I know that in the future we as a nation will fail you and we will fall under curse, but today I choose to love you and obey. I trust in the promises you made to the patriarchs and that you have provided a sacrificial system at Sinai so that there is forgiveness. Today, I don't fully understand how forgiveness works. Today, I don't understand how I can have a circumcised heart, but I know my only hope is you.*'

It is like someone using a credit card to purchase forgiveness, knowing that he can't pay but that, at some future point, God would pay off the cost. The power to put an Old Testament believer right was drawn from Christ through faith in God's promise of forgiveness through Israel's sacrificial liturgy.

The conclusion of the Pentateuch

On a first reading of Deuteronomy, we might think that Moses is teaching a 'works righteousness', that it is Israel's obedience alone that wins them God's blessing. If we listed all of the verses which declare, 'Do this and live,' they would probably outnumber the references to 'Trust in what the LORD has promised.' If you spent a week of private devotions in chapters 12–26 it would certainly have the 'feel' of justification by works. Yet that would be to ignore the centrality of the appeal to the heart in Deuteronomy and also make no sense of what has come before in the Pentateuch. Remembering what has come before will prevent us from falling into that mistaken thinking.

Crucially, standing behind the covenant in the plains of Moab are the promises that God made to Abraham back in Genesis. God reminds Israel sixteen times that he has promised to bless them (only Psalms and Hebrews refer to God promising more frequently).[2] In a book which expects Israel to fail, here is the source of their hope – the promises of God!

When you read through the legal section of 12–26, it is striking how many references there are to the events of Exodus. *Remembering* what life was like and how God rescued them is a crucial factor in empowering their obedience. The imperative 'remember' comes fourteen times in the book, half of them in the law code of chapters 12–26. It is also striking what answer a father is to give to his son when asked, 'What's the point of the law?':

> When your son asks you in time to come, 'What is the meaning of the testimonies and the statutes and the rules that the LORD our God has commanded you?' then you shall say to your son, 'We were Pharaoh's slaves in Egypt. And the LORD brought us out of Egypt with a mighty hand … and the LORD commanded us to do all these statutes, to fear the LORD our God, for our good always, that he might preserve us alive, as we are this day. And it will be righteousness for us, if we are careful to do all this commandment [singular – probably, in context, a reference to 6:5] before the LORD our God, as he has commanded us.' (6:20-25)

---

2. 1:11; 6:3; 6:19; 9:3; 9:28; 11:25; 12:20; 15:6; 18:2; 19:8; 23:23; 26:18-19; 27:3; 26:68; 29:13.

Moses keeps reminding them that they must be shaped by the story of what the LORD has done for them. Before we draw up any kind of systematic theology from Deuteronomy, we must take seriously its message that Israel's call can only be understood within the story of God's activity for them.

We will also need to be careful in reading Deuteronomy to let the text define what it means by 'righteousness'. Many preachers are most familiar with forensic righteousness that is by faith (as the apostle Paul expounds) and may be a little thrown by the language here. Yet throughout the Old Testament, believers do appeal to their righteousness,[3] so they are either:

1. appealing to their merit (which cannot be the case given Deuteronomy 9:4-6) or

2. sinners pleading a consistency of life with what God has revealed. Their primary delight is in the LORD who is their refuge. They trust in his promises and not their own goodness, so they repent of their sins and then seek to live in obedience as the fruit of their faith.

It is in this sense of a life of integrity, consistent with what God has revealed, that Deuteronomy uses the term 'righteousness'. Blessings could still come to the disobedient *if* they were fundamentally loyal to the LORD and trusting in the provision for forgiveness.[4]

---

3. Most obviously seen in the over 200 references to a righteous person in Psalms and Proverbs.

4. Christopher Ash has written a very helpful article titled "'According to My Righteousness': Do the Psalms Teach Justification by Works?' which explores further how the psalmists use the language of righteousness in this way, in about sixty different psalms. Online:

In comparison to Leviticus, Deuteronomy clearly spends less time on sacrifices for forgiveness and more time on what a life of obedience looks like. Yet Deuteronomy assumes the sacrificial system that has already been described in detail in Leviticus, just as Leviticus assumes that the LORD is still acting in line with the promises given to Abraham (despite this covenant only receiving one mention in Leviticus 26:42).

The fundamental call to choose between two paths, which is so stressed in Deuteronomy, has already been given in Leviticus 26:

> If you walk in my statutes and observe my commandments and do them, then … [a long list of blessings from vv. 4-11] …. And I will walk among you and will be your God, and you shall be my people. I am the LORD your God, who brought you out of the land of Egypt, that you should not be their slaves. (vv. 3-13a)

> But if you will not listen to me and will not do all these commandments … then … [a long list of curses from vv. 16-32] …. And I will scatter you among the nations, and I will unsheathe the sword after you, and your land shall be a desolation, and your cities shall be a waste. (vv. 14-33)

The message of the two books is the same and so it would be a misstep to think that, because Deuteronomy has very few references to sacrifices for sin, Moses was now encouraging them to trust in their own righteousness. On the contrary, Moses keeps reminding them that they are stubbornly sinful and need a mediator (especially in 9:25-29). Similarly, at one climactic point, ahead of reciting the list of curses and blessings,

---

https://www.desiringgod.org/articles/according-to-my-righteousness.

the need for an altar and sacrifices is reiterated (27:5-7). The only way to come before the LORD is through sacrifice!

What precisely is the choice they must make?

The fundamental choice that is stressed in Deuteronomy is loving the LORD or following other gods. This is the choice that sets Israel off down one of two paths.

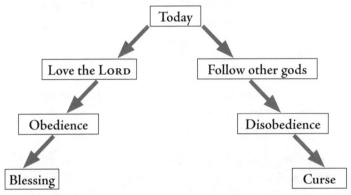

Deuteronomy contains more references to 'other gods' than any other book in the Bible.[5] In the Pentateuch, Exodus only mentions other gods in chapter 20 during the Ten Commandments, and there are no mentions of other gods in Genesis, Leviticus or Numbers. This stress shows that *here is the great threat* for Israel in Deuteronomy: being drawn after other gods. This is what will lead to them suffering God's curse:

> You shall not go after other gods, the gods of the peoples who are around you – for the LORD your God in your

5. There are references in 5:7; 6:14; 7:4; 8:19; 11:16, 28; 13:2, 6, 13; 17:3; 18:20; 28:14, 36, 64; 29:26; 30:17, 18; and 31:20 (and there are additional references to 'strange gods', 'new gods' and 'no gods'). Indeed, apart from Jeremiah, it has at least four times the frequency of any other book.

midst is a jealous God – lest the anger of the LORD your
God be kindled against you, and he destroy you from off
the face of the earth. (6:14-15)

And if you forget the LORD your God and go after other
gods and serve them and worship them, I solemnly warn
you today that you shall surely perish. (8:19)

All the nations will say, 'Why has the LORD done thus
to this land? What caused the heat of this great anger?'
Then people will say, 'It is because they abandoned the
covenant of the LORD, the God of their fathers, which he
made with them when he brought them out of the land
of Egypt, and went and served other gods and worshiped
them, gods whom they had not known and whom he had
not allotted to them. (29:24-26)

Then my anger will be kindled against them in that day,
and I will forsake them and hide my face from them, and
they will be devoured .... And I will surely hide my face
in that day because of all the evil that they have done,
because they have turned to other gods. (31:17-18)

The summary in 29:24-26 is particularly striking. When
the curse comes, the question is asked, why? The answer is
idolatry. This also explains what is, to our ears, the unusual
severity of the penalty for idolatry. Anyone who enticed
an Israelite to serve another god was to suffer the death
penalty (13:5, 9, 15; 17:5; 18:20). The fate of the nation
rests upon preventing their hearts being drawn away.

When we come to the climactic chapter 30, we'll
see that the choice is not a simple 'obey' or 'disobey'. It
is 'Choose to love the LORD, as seen in your obedience,
or serve other gods.' Or, as Paul Barker summarises,
'It is not a simple choice to obey. Rather Israel is being

asked to choose Yahweh and his grace which will enable obedience.[6]

Then, finally, in the song which is given as a 'witness' against Israel (31:26) the main charge is that of turning to other gods (32:12, 15-18, 37-44).[7]

It is inevitable that the nation will fail eventually. But each individual and each generation had to make their choice: love the LORD or follow other gods. And they had to make that choice 'today'.

To clarify, although pessimism hangs over the book with regard to Israel's obedience, it is overly simplistic to say that Israel could not ever keep the law. Elsewhere it is evident that Israel *could* keep the law acceptably *for a time*, even though ultimately her failure was inevitable. For example:

> Israel served the LORD all the days of Joshua, and all the days of the elders who outlived Joshua and had known all the work that the LORD did for Israel. (Josh. 24:31)

It also seems obvious that at least some individuals such as Joshua and Caleb were able to obey the LORD (Deut. 1:34-38) as well as a whole group of Israelites at Baal Peor (4:4), and so we see the beginnings of the concept of a faithful remnant.

This matters deeply, because the call to love the LORD and obey him was not a meaningless one. Israel's obedience

---

6. Paul Barker, *The Triumph of Grace in Deuteronomy* (Milton Keynes: Paternoster, 2012), 212.

7. From the beginning of the third speech to the end of the book, it becomes increasingly obvious that covenant breaking is clearly expressed in terms of idolatry: 29:15-18, 25; 30:17-18; 31:16-18, 20; 32:12, 15-18, 17, 37-49.

could never be better than fleeting and imperfect, but there was the possibility that they could serve him loyally for periods, throwing themselves upon his grace when they failed.

In 4:4, the language of obedience is that they 'held fast', the same term used in Genesis 2:24 of a man leaving his parents and holding fast to his wife. No husband is perfect! But they can be fundamentally loyal and faithful.

So, there is a fundamental choice to be made between loyalty to the LORD or following other gods. Yet we must not conflate loyalty with perfection. A basically faithful Israelite was still sinful! One feature of Deuteronomy's long list of laws is that it prevents any sense of smugness, even for the faithful Israelite. They still require sacrifices for their sin. The faithful Israelite never trusts in their loyalty to God. They trust in him and his promises. Again, a discerning and faithful Israelite in the plains of Moab would have thought, 'I can see that the LORD requires perfect obedience and I can't provide it. I have to trust in him to resolve this problem.'

What is the place of obedience?

A question we must face in Deuteronomy is whether the promised land is a gift of God or conditional upon obedience. In Deuteronomy, it is described as *both* a gift and also as a reward for obedience. Sometimes, I have heard people teach that Israel entered the land by God's grace but remained by obedience. But that won't do as they are required to obey in order to enter:

> And now, O Israel, *listen to the statutes* and the rules that
> I am teaching you, *and do them, that* you may live, *and go*

> *in and take possession of the land* that the LORD, the God
> of your fathers, is giving you. (4:1)

> And you shall do what is right and good in the sight of
> the LORD, that it may go well with you, and *that you may
> go in and take possession* of the good land *that the LORD
> swore to give to your fathers.* (6:18)

Yet while obedience is required for entry, this entrance has
also been promised:

> And when the LORD your God brings you into the land
> that *he swore to your fathers*, to Abraham, to Isaac, and to
> Jacob, to give you … (6:10)

> And the LORD said to me, 'Arise, go on your journey
> at the head of the people, so that they may go in and
> possess the land, which *I swore to their fathers to give
> them.'* (10:11)

According to 9:4-6, possession of the land is *not* because
of any merit, and Moses is clear that they will only enter
because the LORD is fighting for them:

> When the LORD your God brings you into the land that
> you are entering to take possession of it, *and clears away
> many nations before you.* (7:1)

So *entry* is both promised by the LORD and dependent
upon Israel's obedience. The same is true of *possessing* the
land. Perhaps this is nowhere clearer than in 4:40:

> Therefore you shall keep his statutes and his
> commandments, which I command you today, that it
> may go well with you and with your children after you,
> and that you may prolong your days in the land that the
> LORD your God is giving you for all time.

Israel is responsible for prolonging life in the land
and yet the Lord has given it for all time. We need to
take both seriously and not allow one to displace the
other. God gave the land to Israel as a nation, but every
generation had to accept that gift. The gift was embraced
by loving the Lord, demonstrated in obedience. Hence
this generation, addressed by Moses, did indeed enter
the land and enjoy it, but there was always a provisional
nature to the ongoing possession of the land. I like James
Robson's pithy summary: 'Failure to trust and obey
cannot invalidate the promise but it can mean exclusion
from its benefits.'[8]

Continuity and discontinuity

To state the obvious, we are not Israelites in the plains of
Moab. The temptation for preachers is that we remember
that in 'difficult' texts and work hard to show it, yet forget
this fact in 'easy' texts and so apply without going through
God's final revelation in Christ. Without being wooden, we
always want to show our congregations how Deuteronomy
is being read in the light of the coming and work of Christ.

In doing so we will keep returning to the need to
avoid two opposite positions in teaching Deuteronomy as
Christian Scripture:

1. We must not preach flatly and imply that Joe Israelite
    in Moab is the same as a born-again Christian in the
    twenty-first century. There are enormous differences
    between their experience and ours, chiefly that we
    have awareness of definitive forgiveness through
    the work of Christ (once-for-all) and the Spirit

---

8. James Robson, *Honey from the Rock* (Nottingham: Apollos, 2013), 43.

indwelling us. These are new covenant blessings[9] (cf. Heb. 8:6-13 and the summary and conclusion to the central section of Hebrews found in 10:15-18).

2. We must avoid suggesting that God offered salvation by works in the Old Testament. Israel was to respond to the LORD's *prior* grace by loving him, choosing him, being loyal to him. This was seen in their obedience.

To put this in other terms, we must be wary of overstressing either continuity or discontinuity. I imagine those reading this will place themselves on a variety of points on this spectrum and all of us bring our presuppositions and systematic thoughts to our study of Deuteronomy. I find McConville's warning salutary here: 'The combination of … the book's ambiguity and the interpreter's theological preference is potent, and while the last one is in a sense unavoidable, any reader of the Bible needs to be aware of the excessive role it can play.'[10]

So, on the one hand, I really enjoy Dan Block's arresting use of the title *The Gospel According to Moses*,[11] as it

---

9. Personally, I am averse to using the language of 'born again' regarding Old Testament believers being indwelt by the Spirit. 1 Peter 1:3 seems clear that this is a blessing that can only come after the resurrection: 'He has caused us to be born again to a living hope *through the resurrection of Jesus Christ* from the dead.' Of course, no one can be a true Israelite apart from the grace of God, but I think we need to maintain a distinction, using language such as 'the Spirit acting *upon*' the faithful Israelite, rather than 'the Spirit dwelling *within*'. The Spirit in the Old Testament *dwells within* the Tabernacle and then the Temple, not the individual.

10. J. G. McConville, *Grace in the End: A Study in Deuteronomic Theology* (SOTBT; Carlisle: Paternoster Press, 1993), 24.

11. Dan Block uses this title for his *excellent* book *The Gospel according to Moses: Theological and Ethical Reflections on the Book of Deuteronomy*

helpfully stresses continuity between the covenants. Yet it perhaps has the unintended drawback of suggesting that the gospel preached in Moab was *identical in content* to that preached in the book of Acts.

Moses preaches a covenant of grace, yet it is administered in a far more legal fashion than on the lips of Christ. We must not flatten revelation and neglect the fact that it is progressive. To put it practically, the Christian rests far more comfortably upon the work of Christ than even the 'true' Israelite would have done in Moab. While all of Moses's preaching is underpinned by an appeal to God's promise to the patriarchs, Deuteronomy is less clear on grace than Paul! In colloquial language, we read Deuteronomy and at points it 'feels more works-y'. Sometimes it seems that, in an attempt to stress an essential continuity within the covenants, we might downplay the fact that the gospel in the Old Testament is one of shadows and types, lacking the clarity we find in the New.

However, at the other end of the spectrum, I don't think Deuteronomy allows us to say, 'The covenant at Horeb was conditional whereas the new covenant is unconditional. The two are radically different.'

This is because *all* covenants have conditions attached. Look at these examples in the New Testament:

- Q: What must we do to be saved? A: Repent and believe. (e.g. Acts 2:37-28; 16:30-31)

(Eugene: Cascade, 2012). Of course, I'm fully aware that this is entirely justifiable biblically. As Paul writes, 'The Scripture, foreseeing that God would justify the Gentiles by faith, *preached the gospel* beforehand to Abraham, saying, "In you shall all the nations be blessed."' (Gal. 3:8.)

- 'You who once were alienated ... he has now reconciled ... IF indeed you continue' (Col. 1:21-23).

- 'Let what you heard from the beginning abide in you. IF what you heard from the beginning abides in you, then you too will abide in the Son and in the Father' (1 John 2:24).

- Jesus teaches that his sheep receive eternal life as a gift that can never be lost (John 10:28-29) and also that only if you obey his commandments will you abide in his love (John 15:10). Those who have received the gift demonstrate that fact through their obedience.

The sensible question to ask is: What role do the conditions within the covenant play? Are they meritorious or non-meritorious?[12] Are they contributing to salvation or demonstrating it? With the repeated warning not to flatten scripture between the old and new covenants, obedience in both is a sign of the people of God.

It is the mark of genuinely converted Christians that they love God and want to live lives that please and obey him. As John puts it, 'If we say we have fellowship with him while we walk in darkness, we lie and do not practise the truth' (1 John 1:6). Christians are not perfect this side of heaven, but if we are born again, then we try to live lives of obedience. That's the orientation of our lives.

At the risk of being very simplistic, let me use the comments on possession of the land in Deuteronomy 4 to illustrate points of continuity in comparison with Hebrews.

---

12. With thanks to Garry Williams for this clarifying question which helped this preacher's thinking.

Life in the promised land	Israel	Christians
It's God's free gift	'The land that the LORD your God is giving you for all time' (4:40).	'We have confidence to enter the holy places by the blood of Jesus' (Heb. 10:19).
It belongs to those who obey	'Keep the commandments ... so that ... you may live long in the land' (4:2, 5, 14, 40).	'See that you do not refuse him who is speaking ... much less will we escape if we reject him who warns from heaven' (Heb. 12:25).
And yet ... the overall 'mood' is different	Pessimism: even though God will never forget the nation (4:31), many generations will fail and exile is inevitable (4:26-27).	Optimism: a few will fall away but the Christian has a new heart moving them to obey. They have confident assurance in the finished work of Christ.

There is continuity in that both Israel and Christians indicate their genuine faith by living lives of obedience to God's word. But do not flatten biblical revelation! There is a discontinuity in assurance. Deuteronomy predicts that although individuals may be faithful, the nation overall will eventually fail. There is a mood of pessimism that hangs over Deuteronomy because of the hard hearts of the Israelites.

So, again at the risk of being simplistic, the discontinuity is also stark:[13]

---

13. The writer to the Hebrews seems to give this emphatic summary of the difference between the two covenants in 10:16-17. Having already quoted Jeremiah 31, he emphasises by repetition two aspects of the new covenant: (1) the Spirit dwelling within a believer to write the 'law on their hearts' and (2) definitive, once-for-all forgiveness.

Israel	Christians
Their acceptance by God is uncertain in any given generation.	The individual Christian has full assurance that they are justified and accepted because of Christ.
Israel as a nation will stand trial and be found guilty. The law will be a witness against them, as will heaven and earth and the Song of Moses (Deut. 31:21, 26, 28).	The Christian already possesses a 'not guilty' verdict upon them. Rather, they are positively righteous (e.g. Rom. 8:1-4).
They must obey the Deuteronomic law as a demonstration of their trust in God's promise.	Christians will obey the law only as it is 'translated' by Jesus and 'filtered' through his work, not directly.
Individuals do not have the indwelling Spirit and so lack the expectation of change.	Christians have the Spirit dwelling within and so have the hope of progressive sanctification.

So, preach Deuteronomy to Christians!

Summing up our thoughts so far, we will preach Deuteronomy as an urgent and passionate call to love the Lord wholeheartedly in response to the grace he has shown us in Jesus Christ. We must choose to love him each and every day:

- We must press home the need to <u>remember</u> that, like Israel, the Lord has chosen us and made us his treasured possession *despite* our unworthiness. Yet he has shown Christians far greater love and grace than Israel knew, as we know and look back to the sacrifice that Jesus made.

- We must recognise that, like Israel, we will fail to
  love the Lord with all our heart and so will need to
  repent and cling to the promises that God has made
  that he will not forsake us. Yet, again, we have a
  much clearer understanding of how wonderfully
  perfect and sufficient our mediator is and so have
  greater confidence than any Israelite to come before
  the throne of God.

- Like Israel, we must *respond* to his grace with a
  delight in the Lord and love for him. The fruit
  of this delight will be seen in lives of obedience.
  Again, Christians do so with a much greater sense
  of assurance. Every new covenant believer has a
  new heart (unlike every Israelite) and so, while imperfect, we have the ability to live more consistent
  lives of obedience.

Preachers will want to show that the call for Israel to love
the LORD in response to his grace has now become the
call to Christians to respond to the gospel of Jesus Christ
with 'the obedience of faith for the sake of his name
among all the nations' (Rom. 1:5). There is a fundamental
continuity there. And yet, we will also need to stress the
far greater privileges that Christians have, in a deeper
sense of assurance that comes from a cleansed conscience;
the wonder of having a new heart as God's Spirit now
dwells within us; and the joy of knowing a mediator and
high priest whose name is Jesus (Heb. 8–10). We know
that he took our curse and we live in his blessing. We are
far more privileged than any of Moses's hearers in the
plains of Moab.

The Structure of Deuteronomy

At one level, Deuteronomy is dominated by three speeches by Moses, with some editorial touches in between, followed by a song and a blessing.

> Editor (1:1-5)
> > Moses's first speech (1:6–4:40)
> Editor (4:41–49)
> > Moses's second speech (5:1–28:68)
> Editor (29:1)
> > Moses's third speech (29:2–30:20)
> Editor (31:1-29)
> > Moses's song (31:30–32:47)
> Editor (32:48-52)
> > Moses's blessing (33:1-29)
> Editor (34:1-12)

There is also evident within the book a large chiastic structure:

A 'These are the words ...' (learning from failure in the past in 1:1–4:44)

> **B** 'Moses summoned all Israel and said ...' (the fundamental covenant demands in chs. 5–11)

> > **C** Blessing or curse (11:26)

> > > **D** 'These are the statutes and rules that you shall be careful to do ...' (12:1)
> > > The detailed covenant stipulations (chs. 12–26)

> > > **D'** 'This day the LORD your God commands you to do these statutes and rules ... (26:16)

> > **C'** Blessing or curse (27:12-13)

> **B'** 'These are the words ...' (29:1) / 'Moses summoned all Israel and said ...' (29:2)

A' Looking to failure in the future (30:1–34:12)

However, this large chiasm shouldn't blind us to observing that Moses does move to a climax. The overwhelming curses of chapter 28 underscore the inevitability of Israel's failure and yet the final dramatic appeal of chapter 30 *both* demands that Israel choose 'today' and yet also promises God's future grace beyond exile.

So, a more helpful outline of the structure looks something like this:

First speech (chs. 1–4) Learn from past failure so that you listen now.	• Introduction: Moses is expounding the torah (1:1-5). • Success and failure so far (1:6–3:22). • Moses forbidden to enter the land (3:23-29). • Application of sermon one – 'Listen to the one and only God so it goes well with you and the nations may see wisdom' (4:1-43).

Second speech (chs. 5–28)
 Love the LORD with all your heart, soul and might.
	• The fundamental commandments (chs. 5–11).
	  ○ The Ten Words (ch. 5).
	  ○ Love the LORD (ch. 6).
	  ○ Threats within their heart (chs. 7–10).
	  ○ Make your choice (ch. 11).
	
	 • The detailed stipulations (chs. 12–26).
	  ○ Rejoicing before the LORD: the more exhortatory laws (chs. 12–18).
	  ○ Life in the land: the more detailed statutes (chs. 19–26).
	
	 • Set before you blessings and curses (chs. 27–28).

Third speech (chs. 29–30) Learn about future failure so that you choose life now.	• You don't have a heart to understand and your future is exile (ch. 29). • God will give you a circumcised heart and the far future is blessing (30:1-10). • Make your choice (30:11-20).
A song and a blessing (chs. 31–34) Learning to live without Moses.	• A new leader in Joshua (ch. 31). • A song of witness against you (ch. 32). • Moses's final blessing (ch. 33). • Longing for a prophet like Moses (ch. 34).

Why Should We Preach and Teach Deuteronomy

It deepens our understanding of the work of Christ

He is the one who deals with the curse of the law

Paul's explanation of curse bearing, in Galatians 3:10-13, draws heavily from Deuteronomy:

> For all who rely on the works of the law are under a curse; for it is written, 'Cursed be everyone who does not abide by all things written in the Book of the Law, and do them' [Deut. 27:26]. Now it is evident that no one is justified before God by the law, for 'the righteous shall live by faith.' But the law is not of faith, rather 'The one who does them shall live by them.' Christ redeemed us from the curse of the law by becoming a curse for us – for it is written, 'Cursed is everyone who is hanged on a tree' [Deut. 21:23].

The sensitive Christian believer will find it impossible to read the long list of curses in chapters 27–28 without giving thanks to Jesus. They are a vivid, alarming and threatening list – a loving warning from the Lord not to drift into idolatry for the consequences are horrific. For the Christian, they give a stronger sense of what Christ endured as he bore God's wrath in our place.

The faithful Israelite knew that they related to God through the law/torah which contained both rules and sacrifices. They were to keep the rules but recognise that they could never do so perfectly and so had faith in God's sacrifices to remove sin. Yet with the coming of Christ, the sacrificial system is ended and all that's left are the statutes and rules. If you relate to God on that basis, if you *'rely on'* works of the law, rather than faith in God's promises, then you are under a curse.

Relying on law-keeping could never secure entry into the promised land, even in the plains of Moab. It was always a response to God's promises and the way to life.

Relying on your works, or self-reliance, still places you under the curse. The Christian knows that Jesus has taken the curse for us. He 'became' a curse. The curses of Deuteronomy make us shudder in horror and give thanks to him once again.

THE Israelite with perfect obedience

It is striking that when Jesus responds to Satan's temptations, he does so by quoting Deuteronomy three times (Deut. 8:3 in Matt. 4:4; Deut. 6:16 in Matt. 4:7; Deut. 6:13 in Matt. 4:10). Why Deuteronomy and why *only* Deuteronomy? It seems probable that Jesus is identifying himself with Israel in the plains of Moab on the borders of the promised land of Canaan. Jesus is the faithful one who can take us into the promised land of heaven.

The route of salvation in Deuteronomy is presented as 'choosing life' – that is, an active faith in God's promises. Yet the incredible detail of the decrees and laws reveals that the perfect God also requires perfect obedience.[14] Moses is close to being this perfect one, yet falls short. God's people were always waiting for one who could live a perfectly obedient life on their behalf. The faithful Israelite in Moab may have lacked the language to express this, but somewhere in his embryonic understanding of salvation, there would have been the thought that 'I need someone to perfectly obey for me.' What a privilege we have to be able to name and know the better Israelite, the better Moses, the better sacrifice, who is Jesus.

He must have our exclusive worship

One of the primary ways that the New Testament applies Deuteronomy is to make the point that the Lord, the one true God that you're to love with all your heart, soul and strength, is, in fact, Jesus.

One of the most obvious drumbeats throughout Deuteronomy is the requirement that the Lord is to be worshipped alone. There is no other name under heaven given among men by which we must be saved – only Jesus (Acts 4:12).

A prophet like Moses

Chapters 17–18 teach that, to replace Moses, a whole new system was required, including prophets, priests and

---

14. With particular thanks to Stephen Boon for pushing me to express this more clearly.

king. The descriptions we're given of their character and behaviour provide varied language in which to explain the character and work of Christ. The book ends with the sad comment: 'There has not arisen a prophet since in Israel like Moses' (34:10). Not until John and Peter declare that the prophet like Moses is Jesus (John 1:22ff; Acts 3:22-26).

It deepens our understanding of the New Testament more generally

To take the book of Romans as one example, Paul turns to Deuteronomy to explain:

- the necessity of God circumcising the heart if you are to obey him (Rom. 2:29, from Deut. 30:6);

- righteousness by faith (Rom. 10:6–8, from Deut. 30:12–14);

- that the Ten Words explicate what loving your neighbour looks like (Rom. 13:9, from Deut. 5);

- that we should not take vengeance ourselves (Rom. 12:19, from Deut. 32:35);

- that it was always the plan to include Gentiles in the people of God (Rom. 15:10, from Deut. 32:43).

The urgent need to choose 'today' between two paths

Deuteronomy claims to be expository preaching: 'Moses brought out the meaning of the torah' (1:5). What is striking is the urgent and passionate manner in which he does this. He uses vivid imagery, both enticing and horrific. He anticipates their response and repeatedly

forces upon them the need to decide to follow the Lord
– the importance of choosing to do so. For preachers, it
is a wonderful biblical model of preaching and within
the regular diet of expository preaching has a great role
in forcing choice upon congregations. While the decision
to become a Christian years ago was wonderful and the
zeal and sacrifices for Christ when we were younger were
admirable, what of today? Will you choose to trust today?
Yet this urgent need to resolve each day to follow the
Lord is balanced within the book by the reminder of the
underpinning of God's promises – of our great need for
him to act and show us grace.

While we cannot apply Deuteronomy directly to a
modern audience without filtering Moses through Christ,
we must not lose the homiletical directness of 'Choose
today!' (cf. 1 Cor. 9:9–10; 1 Cor. 10:11).

As an added encouragement to preachers, in the course
of preaching the book, chapter 4 is a really helpful chapter
to explain to congregations more of what we hold true
about scripture generally and the need to gather together
to hear it preached. There is a great stress upon the fact
that access to the Lord is through his voice and that this
voice is vivid, overwhelming and contemporary. He is
speaking 'today'.

Moses preaches very practically
to the idols of our hearts

After the call to love the Lord wholeheartedly in 6:4,
Moses warns of three challenges to their love of God –
affluence, a desire for conformity, and hardship causing
them to wander. Don't those sound familiar? He then
pursues those in chapters 7–9 with the threefold 'Do not

say in your heart …': we can't resist the culture; look at what
I've achieved; look at my righteousness. To put it simply:
preach Deuteronomy because it's already a collection of
brilliant sermons!

Alongside diagnosing our hearts, Deuteronomy presents us with an overwhelming, terrifying and glorious
vision of the LORD. This is the one who should be first in
our hearts. He is 'a jealous God' who can 'destroy you from
off the face of the earth' (6:15), 'the Rock' whose 'work is
perfect, for all his ways are justice' (32:4). He 'came from
the ten thousands of holy ones, with flaming fire at his right
hand' (33:2). 'The eternal God is your dwelling place, and
underneath are the everlasting arms' (33:27). Deuteronomy
gives us an awesome God to replace our small idols.

Deuteronomy delivers us from a nebulous self-defined love of God and reminds us that obedience to God's law matters

The New Testament is very clear that love is still demonstrated in obedience: 'This is the love of God, that we keep
his commandments. And his commandments are not
burdensome' (1 John 5:3). Of course they *are* burdensome if
you try to *rely upon* works of the law for your righteousness.
But if you know the law as the way of response to a gracious
God, then it is a delight. Certainly the psalmists think so:

- 'Blessed is the man … [whose] delight is in the law of
  the LORD' (Ps. 1:1-2).

- 'The law of the LORD is perfect, reviving the soul'
  (Ps. 19:7).

- 'Oh how I love your law! It is my meditation all the
  day' (Ps. 119:97).

It is worth reviewing the questions asked about the law within the text of Deuteronomy itself.

Question of chapter 4:

'When [the pagan nations] hear all these statutes [they] will say, 'Surely this great nation is a wise and understanding people.' For ... what great nation is there, that has statutes and rules so righteous as all this law that I set before you today?' (4:6-8).

The law evidently has a missiological purpose – it attracts unbelievers to the LORD. There is clearly something about the law that is universal and not purely limited to Israel; other cultures will look on and declare, 'Wow, this is wisdom!'

Question of chapter 6:

'What is the meaning of the testimonies and the statutes and the rules that the LORD our God has commanded you?' (6:20).

Answer: 'We were Pharaoh's slaves in Egypt. And the LORD brought us out of Egypt with a mighty hand. ... And the LORD commanded us to do all these statutes, to fear the LORD our God, for our good always, that he might preserve us alive, as we are this day' (6:21-24).

The law is a good gift graciously given to a redeemed people so that they know how to live a life of righteousness. Allowing myself an anachronism, it teaches 'evangelical obedience': obedience in response to the joy of salvation.

It is striking that our Puritan forebears thought it essential to teach regularly on the Ten Commandments, so that roughly two-fifths of the Westminster Shorter Catechism is explicating them. A teaching series on the

Ten Words is profoundly helpful in giving guidance on Christian living. I certainly now regret not teaching them more regularly in our church context. In a culture where Christians may be chasing after 'guidance', here is a book full of wisdom on how to live for God, and working through chapters 12–26 will shape us in a similar fashion to working through the book of Proverbs.

When we rightly understand how the laws of Deuteronomy apply – that is, we filter them through Jesus – then we have greater cause to obey them than Israel. We receive them knowing that Christ has taken the curse of the law for us and that, as Spirit-filled believers, we have a far greater capacity to obey than an Israelite did.

Planning to Preach on Deuteronomy

Deuteronomy can appear a daunting book at first, but I hope you'll see that there are certain natural units with a clear uniting theme and aim. If you are coming to the book for the first time, I think it probably best to preach an overview series to ensure that you understand the movement of the whole book: the urgency to choose, the pessimistic note of failure for Israel and the optimism that God's grace will triumph.

An alternative, to ease your way into the book, would be to take one key section, such as chapter 4 or chapters 29–30, and preach a mini-series of three or four from it. This would force you to grapple with key issues of interpretation and application while actually preaching shorter texts.

In general, a number of the passages will probably require you to fillet the reading during a church service; otherwise, you'll be left with ten-minute (or longer) readings. I think that's quite possible to do, with the encouragement that people read the whole thing before-hand or afterwards.

In an overview series, I think the minimum number of sermons would be seven:

1. Trust in the Lord who fights for you (chs. 1–3)
2. Listen to the voice from the fire (ch. 4)
3. One Lord, one love, one loyalty (chs. 5–6)
4. The murmurings of the heart (chs. 7–11)
5. Responding to God's grace with obedience (chs. 12–26)
6. Failure for Israel – God must circumcise hearts (chs. 27–30)
7. Despair of yourselves but trust in the Lord (chs. 31–34)

There is a great deal of rich preaching throughout the book though and at some point, I imagine, preachers will want to have a more in-depth attempt at bringing Moses's preaching to a modern audience.

A full teaching series could look like this in sixteen sermons:

1. Trust in the Lord who fights for you (chs. 1–3)
2. A voice from the fire (ch. 4)
3. Walk in all of God's ways (ch. 5)
4. One Lord, one love, one loyalty (ch. 6)
5. The murmurings of the heart (chs. 7–9)
6. The need for a mediator (chs. 9–11)
7. Worship him rightly (chs. 12–14)
8. Sabbath generosity (chs. 14–16)
9. Being worthy of honour (chs. 16–18)

10. No murder or adultery (chs. 19–23)

11. No stealing, lying or coveting (chs. 23–26)

12. Curses and blessings (chs. 26–28)

13. A poisonous heart (ch. 29)

14. A new heart (ch. 30)

15. A song to shape you (chs. 31–32)

16. Life beyond Moses (chs. 31–34)

Most preachers will find it easier to preach the 'frame' of 1–11 and 27–34 where we are expounding Moses's sermons. So, you could also preach the book in two series: a longer first series on the frame and then returning to the trickier chapters, 12–26.

Another alternative would be to preach the frame in one series and then return for a second series where you take the Ten Words for a series of ten and use the relevant sections of chapters 12–26 to illustrate each of the Ten Words.

A few mini-series for a weekend away or other setting:

There is none like him

1. Who has a God like this? (4:1-8)

2. Assemble the people (4:9-13)

3. Watch yourselves carefully (4:14-31)

4. There is no other (4:32-40)

Murmurs of the heart

1. Love the Lord with all you've got (6:1-25)

2. Don't say 'The obstacles are too great' (7:1-26)

3. Don't say 'Look at *my* success' (8:1-20)

4. Don't say 'I'm better than you' (9:1–10:11)

5. (Optional) What does the Lord require of you? (10:12–11:32)

The heart of the matter

1. The danger of a faltering heart (ch. 29)

2. The necessity of a new heart (30:1-10)

3. The possibility of obedience (30:11-20)

1.

Learning from Past Mistakes
(Deuteronomy 1–3)

Introduction

Almost everything in chapters 1–3 has already been recorded in Numbers and Joshua, but Moses gives the gathered Israelites a history lesson in order to confront them with a choice. In the distant past when 'they' doubted God, it led to failure. More recently, when they have obeyed God, then they have known success. Moses reminds them of this to impress upon them the choice they now face – obedience or doubt. Success or failure.

Listening to the text

Structure

Moses's first sermon runs from 1:6–4:40, although most commentators run the section to 4:43 to include the cities of refuge.

> 1:1-5   Prologue: Setting and explanation of Moses' activity
>
> 1:6–3:29   God's grace and human failure from Horeb to the edge of the promised land

4:1-40   God's reminder of how he spoke to them and warning not to forget

4:41-43 Cities of refuge

Chapters 1–3 form the broad frame to the book (along with chapter 34) with their emphasis upon the death of the disobedient wilderness generation and the death of Moses. At various points in teaching Deuteronomy we need to bring out the fact that although Israel could have great optimism because the LORD had promised them the land, there is a constant tragic tune in the background of the book, occasionally coming to the forefront. It's the theme of failure. Israel will fail. Even Moses failed. Yet God's promise will prevail despite these deaths. Ultimately, it will prevail through the death of Jesus, who was cast out into the wilderness so that we could enter into the promised land.

Working through the text
1:1-5

The book begins with crucial historical and geographical markers. Straight away, here is a mixture of pessimism and optimism. Verses 1–3 point out that forty years ago the nation was at Mount Sinai (Horeb). Only now are they on the outskirts of the promised land. (Undoubtedly, a map showing the locations of Horeb, the plains of Moab and a lot of wandering around in between is a helpful visual to show people.) A journey that should have taken eleven days took forty years. Chapter 1 will explain why.

Yet, alongside this tragic failure, there is encouragement in that Israel had known a few victories (v. 4). So, from the outset, Israel is presented with a choice: When they trust God's promises, it leads to success. When they doubt God's promises, it leads to failure.

We're also told what the book of Deuteronomy is: a sermon designed to move the people to choose to serve the Lord.

1:1 'These are the words'

1:3 'Moses spoke to the people of Israel according to all that the Lord had given him in commandment to them'

1:5 'Moses undertook to explain [or expound] this law [torah]'. The verb 'explain' is found only here, Deuteronomy 27:8 and Habakkuk 2:2 in the Old Testament. The other times it is translated as 'make plain'. Literally it is that Moses undertook 'to explain the torah/instruction'. There is actually no legal vocabulary in 1:1-5.

In Deuteronomy, Moses speaks not so much as lawgiver but as prophet (18:15; 34:10). The torah in Deuteronomy is pastoral instruction and exhortation. 'Deuteronomy is thus 'preached law' – that is, law explained with prophetic urgency, divine authority and a preacher's clarity.'[1] Moses is not merely giving information. He is seeking to teach and persuade.

1:6-18

The little section 1:6-8 introduces the theme of 'turning' that will dominate chapter 2. After revisiting the failures of the past in chapter 1, the Lord says it is now time to 'turn' and take possession of the land.

It is not immediately obvious why we get the section on leadership in verses 9-18. Moses seems to highlight that it had been important 'at that time' (v. 9 and v. 18). It certainly gives prominence to the importance of justice and legal

---

1. Christopher Wright, *Deuteronomy* (NIBC; Peabody: Hendrickson, 1996), 21.

administration in Israel. There is a connection being drawn between the giving of the law and its implementation. The quality of Israel's leadership will determine the level of her faithfulness.

Pastors may want to dwell personally upon verses 16-17. It's good to ask occasionally if we're guilty of the sin of partiality. The principles of impartiality in how we treat people at church – whether great or small, 'useful' or not, intimidating or unimpressive – remain timeless (James 2).

Olson also makes the sensible suggestion that even at this early stage, Israel is being prepared to enter the land without Moses. Other leadership will suffice: 'It is the first stroke of the theme of Deuteronomy: the dying of the old voice of Moses and the rising of the living voice of God for a new generation.'[2]

The failure that comes from disobeying God (1:19-46)

The events at Kadesh Barnea only took two weeks, yet they take up about a quarter of 1:6–3:29, which covers forty years.

'Go up'– the LORD is giving you the land (1:19-25)

The key command actually comes in verse 8: 'See, I have set the land before you. Go in and take possession of the land that the LORD swore to your fathers… to give to them.' The land had been promised but possession was not automatic for any particular generation; it required faith.

Verses 19 and following recall the history of Numbers 13–14. Israel was told to 'go up' (v. 21). They are encouraged

---

2. Dennis T. Olson, *Deuteronomy and the Death of Moses: A Theological Reading* (Eugene: Wipf & Stock, 1994), 25.

that God has given them the land and so they really do not need to fear or be dismayed.

It's worth noting that the Lord is the 'God of your fathers' (1:21). This phrase or 'the promises made to your fathers' occurs repeatedly in the book as Moses views the generation he is addressing as in covenant solidarity with the patriarchs (1:11; 4:1, 31; 6:3, 10; 7:12; 8:18; 9:5; 12:1; 19:8; 26:3, 7; 27:3; 29:13, 25; 30:5, 9, 20).

No comment is made on whether it was a lack of faith that caused spies to be sent (v. 22). Moses is happy to say it seemed good to him (v. 23). Despite it being good land, the report from the spies led to Israel's rebellion.

The first rebellion: we're too scared to obey God (1:26-33)

'You would not go up' (v. 26). 'You'? Strictly speaking, Moses's audience in the plains of Moab were not guilty of the events of Numbers 13–14. They are the little ones of 1:39. In what sense can Moses say 'you' (as he also does in 4:9-10; 5:3)? It is because the covenant was not a one-off event; it was for those in Moab too. Later, in 29:10-13, Moses is clear that those in Moab are entering into the same covenant that was made with their ancestors. Indeed, it is the same covenant made with Abraham, Isaac and Jacob. This covenant also stretches into the future, with those 'not here today' (29:14-15).

It seems as if the rebellion started with murmuring and then saying out loud, 'The Lord hates us!' (v. 27). Wow! The Lord who delivered you from Egypt, parted the Red Sea and gave you food and water every day in the desert – he hates you?

'Where are we 'going up?' (v. 28). Three things had made their hearts melt: the people were too tall, the walls were too high and the giants (the Anakim were known for their physical prowess) will destroy us.

Moses responds with three countertruths: (1) The LORD is with you; (2) he will fight for you, like he did in Egypt; (3) he will care for you, just as he fathered you in the wilderness (vv. 29-31). This last is a particularly lovely picture of an exhausted small child being carried on the shoulders of his strong dad. Preachers need to make these truths hit home: believing these produces obedience. Not just knowing the truth but believing the truth.

'Yet in spite of this word you did not believe the Lord your God, who went before you' (vv. 32-33). Israel had every good reason to trust the LORD, given his past performance and his promises. But they forgot who their God was and looked at who their enemies were.

So Israel was returned to the wilderness (1:34-40)

The LORD is angry and so swears that none of that generation, except Caleb and Joshua, shall enter the land. In fact, Israel suffered a sort of anti-exodus as they went back to the wilderness and the Red Sea. A significant note is also introduced in verse 37 – that Moses will not enter the land.

God has, of course, promised that Israel will inherit the land and his promise cannot be broken. However, it will not be the generation at Kadesh Barnea that experiences blessing; it will be those listening to Moses in the plains of Moab. 'Failure to trust and obey cannot invalidate the promise but it can mean exclusion from its benefits.'[3]

---

3. Robson, *Honey from the Rock*, 43.

*The second rebellion: we expect the
Lord to fight for us (1:41-46)*

Ah, we don't like that news, say Israel, so we will 'go up'
after all. The Lord is very clear about the consequences
(v. 42). They are not to 'go up' because God is not with
them; they will be defeated. How ironic that they now
rebel by doing the very thing that they had previously
refused to do. Their rebelliousness is emphasised by the
piling up of three verbs in verse 43 – 'not listen', 'rebelled',
'presumptuously went up'. It is this last which explains
the rebellion: they were presumptuous or arrogant. They
have not learned anything about listening to the Lord and
trusting his word.

The consequence was utter defeat and, after that, the
crushing line: 'You returned and wept before the Lord,
but the Lord did not listen to your voice or give ear to you'
(v. 45). The Lord is not interested in their tears. He wants
their obedience. Christians can be guilty of presumption too.

They remained at Kadesh 'many days'. Indeed thirty-
eight years – or 13,880 days!

God is powerful to give victory (2:1–3:29)

Things change dramatically in chapter 2. In 2:1, Moses
recalls that we 'turned'. Chapter 2 is dominated by the
language of movement. Rather than going around in circles
(in chapter 1, and even in 2:1–3 twice they're described
as wandering around), now, in chapter 2, the Israelites
pass through the land (vv. 4, 8, 13, 14, 18, 24) and take
possession (vv. 5, 9, 12, 19, 21, 22).

Why is this? It is because the Lord had promised (1:8).
Even in the wilderness, he has been keeping his promise
to sustain them (2:7).

Much of chapter 2 emphasises that God is faithful – even to promises to other nations. Along with that, it gives evidence that God is powerful. When you obey him, victory follows!

Your brothers conquered the 'giants' (2:1-23)

The LORD tells Israel not to fight three near neighbours: Seir/Edom, who are descended from Esau (vv. 4-8); and Moab (vv. 9-15) and Ammon (vv. 16-23), both descended from Lot. The LORD cares for other families and nations besides Israel, but Israel is meant to be a blessing to other nations.

Yet the other striking thing emphasised about Israel's relatives is that *they* managed to conquer the Canaanite nations (or more accurately, the LORD conquered their enemies). Even the mighty Anakim, whom Israel had feared, fell to their cousins (vv. 11-12, 21-22). The point is this: 'Israel, if your cousins – who do not have the same Abrahamic promises given to them as you do – if they can defeat Anakim, so can you!' The LORD is powerful to conquer.

Now your conquest begins (2:24–3:11)

Verse 24 has six imperatives: Israel is to 'rise up', 'set out', 'go over', 'begin', 'take possession' and 'contend'. It's a time for movement! But all this action is based upon two promises of God: 'I have given' (v. 24) and 'I will begin to put... dread' (v. 25).

The result is that Israel conquered Sihon, king of Heshbon, in chapter 2 and Og, king of Bashan, in chapter 3.

In the defeat of Sihon, the repeated word is 'all' in verses 32-37. Sihon and 'all his people' were defeated so that 'all' the cities and 'all' the land was captured. The LORD's success is total.

What a contrast between 1:28, when Israel said pathetically, 'The cities are… fortified up to heaven', and here in 3:5, where we're told again that the cities 'were fortified with high walls'. This time, they trusted the Lord God who was with them and so he gave all sixty cities into their hands.

In 3:1, Israel 'went up' (as they should have done forty years earlier). Moses dwells upon the size of Og's bed – it was about 6 feet by 13 feet. We may in the twenty-first century have king-sized and super-king-sized beds, but no one has an Og-sized bed. Moses tells Israel, 'Go to Rabbah and see it in the Ammonite museum – you'll be encouraged when you remember that in God's strength we can conquer giants.'

There is a key precedent established here. Israel can conquer, if they trust in the Lord. On top of this description in chapter 3, the story is recounted in 1:4; 4:46–47; 29:7–8; 31:4 (and a further twelve times in the Old Testament). They should be encouraged. Notice again how God's role is emphasised repeatedly: 'I have given' (2:31, 33, 36; 3:2, 3, 18, 20).

Israel needed the promise of 3:2 and 3:22, 'God had given their enemies into Israel's hands.' There is no need to be afraid when the Lord your God fights for you. It's a familiar truth for Israel: 'Trust the promise and you'll obey the command.'

Preachers need to drive home that the Lord has kept his promises thus far. WE can trust that he'll keep them in the future.

The allocation of land to the eastern tribes (3:12-22)

The Reubenites, Gadites and half-tribe of Manasseh are each allotted their portion of the land in the Transjordan.

However, they are only able to enjoy it after they have fought with the rest of Israel to conquer lands west of the Jordan river.

The exclusion of Moses from the land (3:23-29)

Moses surprisingly states that he was excluded 'because of you' in verse 26 (also in 4:21). We would not have picked that up from the book of Numbers. It is not mentioned in the account of the rebellion in Numbers 13–14 where the LORD offers to start over with Moses (Num. 14:12), while in Numbers 20:10-13, the problem is normally viewed as Moses's arrogance or failure to obey the LORD precisely. Later, in Deuteronomy 32:48-52, it is clear that it is this latter incident at Meribah when Moses broke faith with the LORD and did not treat him as holy.

So, how can Moses tell the people that he was excluded 'because of you'? Deuteronomy tends to compress historical events and so, perhaps here, Moses is viewed as being in solidarity with the people who deserved their exclusion. Yet, it seems to me very normal to think that, although Moses is responsible for his own actions, the constant grumbling of the Israelites had worn him down and so they share some responsibility for his exclusion. Pastors need to be aware of being led into sin when dealing with grumbling people (Gal. 6:1). God's people can have a significant impact upon the life and ministry of their pastors (Heb. 13:17).

The exclusion of Moses from the land is, remarkably, stressed three times in this opening sermon in chapters 1–4 (1:37; here in 3:23-29; 4:21-22). 'The death of Moses outside the land hangs like a pall over the entire book.'[4]

---

4. Daniel Block, *Deuteronomy* (NIVAC; Grand Rapids: Zondervan, 2012), 108.

From text to message

Getting the message clear: the theme

There are plenty of interesting details, but the focus is the contrast between rebellion (which leads to failure) in chapter 1 and obedience (which produces success) in chapter 2.

Within the failure of chapter 1, there are two different types of rebellion. They refuse to 'go up' when told to do so. Then they 'go up' when told not to do so. The first rebellion is due to fear: they forget who God is and focus upon the obstacles. The second rebellion is presumption: they assume that God will bless them even if they disobey him.

Getting the message clear: the aim

The aim is that we should obey God! Remember how he has treated us in the past and kept his promises, so that we can trust him today.

A way in

The challenge of the first sermon in any series of expositions is to introduce the book and yet also the passage being preached on. Here, it's easier than some, as chapters 1–3 call upon the people to choose, which is the purpose of the whole book.

It's easy to promise to love someone on your wedding day. The challenge comes weeks, months and years later – to keep on loving them, not just with words but in the details of life. Each and every day of marriage you effectively decide to repeat your wedding vows and love you spouse. To love them with unswerving loyalty, to love them for better or worse, to love them in the details of life. The book of

Deuteronomy is Moses imploring the people to love the LORD unswervingly in all the details of their life. In chapters 1–3 he encourages them by reminding them of how badly things go when they do not love and trust the LORD, yet how well they go when they do love and trust him.

Ideas for application

- **The two rebellions:**
  1. Israel forgot who their God was, what he had done and what he had promised because they focused on their problem (tall people and high walls). Christians can easily do the same. We may not be facing Anakim, but we might be facing massive bank loans, bullying at work, unemployment, loneliness or exhaustion. Christians can ask, 'How can I trust the Lord when my problems are massive?' We can be tempted to grumble 'in our tents' and say that the Lord has abandoned us. The antidote is to remember that God is a Father who is with us, will fight for us, and will carry us when we're tired.

  2. We can presume upon the Lord's blessing, similarly to Israel. Their plan seems spiritual but it is disobedient. The Lord wants our obedience not just our tears. There is a world of difference between regret ('I don't like this …') and repentance ('I will change my life'). Regret says, 'Sorry, Lord,' but repentance says, 'I'm sorry and will now do what you say.'

- **Reasons to hope:**
  1. Moses reminds Israel that God has promised the land and that he is powerful to give it to them.

The Lord has not promised Christians conquest of Canaan, but, broadly, we can expect God's blessing if we obey him and, narrowly, we can be confident of the promised land of heaven if we trust his promises in Christ. That trust will be seen in obedience.

2. The preacher has to decide how often to mention the sombre note of failure that hangs over the book. It is never the quality of our obedience that guarantees our entry into the promised land. Even the great Moses did not trust the LORD at Meribah. But our hope is in the faithfulness of God seen in Jesus Christ. He was obedient in the wilderness (and so deserves to enter the land) and was so for us. At the cross, he was banished to the wilderness (for our disobedience) so that we don't face banishment. The death of Moses was a solemn warning to Israel, but, by contrast, the death of Jesus is a source of great hope for us.

Suggestions for preaching

Unless you're going for a long series in Deuteronomy, this is a natural unit to take in one sermon. However, it would be quite possible to do one sermon on chapter 1 and a second sermon on chapters 2 and 3.

Failure came when 'you' disobeyed God (ch. 1)

- The first rebellion: trusting in what they can see and doubting what God has said
- The second rebellion: presumptuously expecting God to bless them despite disobedience

Success came when you trusted God (chs. 2–3)

- You can conquer giants (2:24–3:11)
- But failure is never far away (3:23-29)
- ⇨ Trust God's promises and character and you'll be able to obey his commands

Questions to help understand the passage

1. Why is Moses preaching to Israel? What is this sermon described as? What does God want his people to do (1:1-8)?

2. What can we learn about the importance of leadership by the fact that this paragraph is included here (1:9-18)?

3. What was the basic command given to Israel (1:21)?

4. How did they respond (1:26)? Why was that their response (1:26-28)?

5. How did Moses address these concerns (1:29-33)?

6. So, what was their punishment (1:34-40)?

7. What was the second way in which Israel rebelled? What was the nature of this rebellion and what exactly was wrong with their action (1:41-43)?

8. What was the outcome (1:44-46)?

9. What do we learn from the language of movement in these verses (2:1-8)?

10. What is Israel reminded of (2:7-8)?

11. What was Israel meant to learn from the conquests of the Moabites, Horites and Ammonites (2:9-23)? How had these three related nations conquered (2:9, 12, 19)?

12. What encouragement was there here for the Israelites? What happened when they trusted and obeyed the LORD (2:24–3:11)?

13. What was Israel meant to learn about the solidarity of God's people (3:12-22)?

14. How does the failure of Moses to enter the land (3:23-29) affect the mood of this opening section in chapters 1–3?

Questions to help apply the passage

1. Israel refused to trust the Lord because they were scared (1:26-32). Can you think of examples of fear leading to disobedience for Christians?

2. Can you think of occasions when that has been true of you?

3. How do we stop 'murmuring' our doubts and fears so that they grow within us?

4. Moses told Israel that God was with them, would fight for them and carries them through adversity. How are those things true for the Christian? How does Christ do those things for us?

5. Why did Israel decide to 'go up' and fight (1:41)? Had they repented of disobedience here (1:42-43)?

6. Israel sinned by presuming that God would bless them despite their disobedience. How might Christians think the same?

7. What is wrong with Israel's tears in verse 45? Why were they crying and so why did the LORD not listen?

8. What promises of the Lord are we currently struggling to believe? How does reading about his

power and faithfulness to keep all his promises encourage you?

9. Moses was excluded from the land because of his sin and that of the Israelites. Why was Jesus excluded from the land in his death (Heb. 13:11-13)? What does that mean for us?

2.

A Voice from the Fire

(Deuteronomy 4)

Introduction

The exhortation moves from the implicit command for obedience in chapters 1–3 to more explicit demand here in chapter 4. This chapter is the application of the history lesson of chapters 1–3: 'Choose today' (vv. 4, 8, 26, 38). Moses is forcing the choice upon Israel and the preacher must press the choice upon their listeners: 'Choose to love the LORD – today.'

It is a rich passage, particularly important for a biblical theology of God's word and preaching. Gary Miller describes it as 'the most profound chapter in the book'.[1] It is clear that you cannot separate the preaching of Deuteronomy from God's revelation at Mount Sinai. The word spoken there was still God's word for the people in the plains of Moab. In fact, anyone hearing a sermon on Deuteronomy 4 will be listening to a sermon (Sunday morning) about a sermon (in Moab 3,000 years ago) about a sermon (given at Sinai forty years before that). The wonder is that, in a sermon about a sermon about a sermon, God will address us personally.

---

1. J. Gary Millar, *Now Choose Life: Theology and Ethics in Deuteronomy* (NSBT; Leicester: Apollos, 1998), 73.

It also throws up some of the recurring tricky issues in Deuteronomy:

- Is the land a gift or must it be earned?
- What is the function of the word 'today' in the book?

These need to be addressed at some point in a sermon series. I think that here – and especially in chapter 30 – it is particularly important to drive home the call to respond 'today'. However, the issue of land could be addressed at numerous points in a series.

Listening to the text

Structure

This is the climax to Moses's opening speech 1:1–4:40. Chapter 4 has close links with chapters 29 and 30:

- Bowing down and serving gods of the nations that have been allotted to those nations (4:19; 29:25)
- Calling heaven and earth as witnesses against them (4:26; 30:19)
- A vision of national disaster being followed by restoration (4:29-31; 30:1-10)

It seems that chapter 4 forms one frame to the book along with chapters 29–30. The more narratively focused chapters 1–3 and 31–34 form the outmost frame.

Chapters 5–28 are bracketed by an obviously pessimistic view of Israel's future obedience, albeit one rescued by God's grace. One important way that we read these chapters in their original context is **not** as the way for Israel to succeed **but rather** as the legal charge that God brings against them, summoning heaven and earth as witnesses against Israel.

This failure will not be because the law is bad or God lacks faithfulness, but because Israel has a problem with their stubborn hearts.

There is a movement in the use of the second person 'you' in the chapter. In verses 1-28 they are plural, seemingly addressing individual Israelites and stressing that faith and ethics must be applied personally. In verses 29-40 they are singular, seemingly referring to Israel collectively as a nation in the future. Yet in verses 23-26 they alternate, placing a focus upon this section and the warning against idolatry.

The bulk of the chapter is constructed around the threefold warning:

- 'Take care and keep your soul diligently, lest you forget the things your eyes have seen' (v. 9)

- 'Therefore watch yourselves very carefully' (v. 15)

- 'Take care, lest you forget' (v. 23)

All of these are reinforced by an appeal to history.

There are also links between 4:1-8 and 4:32-40:[2]

- 'Great' occurs eight times in the chapter but only in these sections (vv. 6-8, 32, 34, 36-38).

- Eyes seeing is prominent in verse 3 and verse 34.

- 'Rhetorical questions that stress the incomparability of Yahweh, the uniqueness of Israel's historical experience and the excellence of the law itself.'[3] Verses 1-8 stress the uniqueness of Israel among the nations; verses 32-40 stress the uniqueness of Yahweh among the gods.

---

2. I owe this clarity to James Robson (lecture notes from 2008).

3. Wright, *Deuteronomy*, 45.

So 4:1-8 bookend the chapter along with verses 32-40, while the central section is a warning against idolatry.

4:1-8   Learn from the past so that you listen
4:9-14   Remember the LORD spoke from the fire
4:15-22   So don't make an idol
4:23-31   But when you forget, the LORD will not
4:32-40   There is none like him; choose him today

Working through the text

Verse 1 adopts a more sermonic tone with the transition 'And now, O Israel, listen'. There is an obvious emphasis upon statutes and rules (4:1, 5, 8, 14, 45) and the need to teach them (vv. 1, 5, 11, 14).

Hear and respond to embrace life and impact the watching world (4:1-8)

There are two smaller sections here: both start with a call to obey and seek to encourage that obedience with an example from Israel's history.

Hear and respond because that is the way to embrace life (4:1-4)

There is the command in 4:1a to listen and do, followed by the motive in 4:1b ('that you may live, and go in'). Then the command is reinforced in verse 2 (Do not add or take from it) and the motive is reinforced in verses 3-4 (you've seen destruction and life).

The formula 'Listen ... and do ... that you may live' is a frequent one in Deuteronomy (5:33; 8:1; 11:9; 16:20; 30:6, 16) and reaches its conclusion in 30:19-20 with 'Choose life, that you and your offspring may live.'

We'll see there that to 'choose life' means to choose the LORD. Fundamentally it is where your loyalty lies. Moses is not calling for perfection but loyalty which is seen in obedience.

Listen to the 'statutes and the rules' comes in verse 1 (also in vv. 5, 8, 14, 45 and see comments at 5:1). There is a primary reference to the Decalogue (ch. 5) but then also to their practical outworking in the whole of life.

Statutes/decrees are instructions given by a superior. Rules/laws are judgments or divine case law. They are divine decisions from the judge who runs the world.

'Do not add or subtract' (v. 2) will be amplified in the rest of the chapter, but immediately, the issue of authority is raised. Is the word of God your authority or will you remove the parts which are too challenging and make some additions to fit your preferences?

Peor was the place where the historical narrative ended in 3:29. It is just east of the Jordan River on the edge of the promised land. Back in Numbers 25, Israel had reached Peor and worshipped the local baal ('lord') by sacrificing to him in the context of ritual sex with religious prostitutes. It was an appealing message: worship me by having sex with prostitutes and then life will go well with you. Yet it leads to God's judgment and the death of 24,000.

Why give this example? The guts of the chapter in verses 9–31 is a warning against idolatry. Moses is saying, 'You know how badly life goes when you reject the LORD and follow pagan gods.'

By contrast some of you here 'held fast' (v. 4) to the LORD. Some Israelites *were* loyal. They *did keep* the covenant. Not the whole nation, but there was always a remnant; they were not perfect but they were loyal. We need to keep stressing this. It was *not* that the LORD had set a standard impossible to keep. Israelites back in Numbers 25 had held fast to him; they had been loyal to him; they had loved him. It *was* possible to do because they had previously done it! (But not many would in the future).

The command to hold fast is repeated in Deuteronomy as the fundamental loyalty required by the LORD (10:20; 13:4; 30:20). It is the Hebrew verb *davaq* – the same as in Genesis 2:24 where it says, 'A man shall leave his father and mother and *hold fast* to his wife.' It is a covenant loyalty that is called for, not sinless perfection. Some Israelites had achieved it in Peor, and Moses was calling this generation to demonstrate that same loyalty again (see also comments on 30:20).

'Thus his point is made: Just as obedience to the Lord in the past resulted in life, so obedience in time to come would guarantee ongoing life. Obviously the converse was equally true. Those who fell short of the Lord's expectations of them would die (cf. 8:1; 30:19).'[4] This is 'evangelical obedience' – that is, obedience in response to the saving grace of the LORD, not obedience to win his favour.

There's an interesting tangent for preachers here: Moses does not simply say, 'Do this because the LORD commands you to.' He also says that holding fast to the LORD works (v. 4)! Those who did it are still here and can testify. Moses insists that they must obey and shows them in their experience that law-keeping works. Of course it does; following the creator's wise instruction is always going to be the best way of living. Obedience to God is good for us!

---

4. Eugene H. Merrill, *Deuteronomy* (NAC; Nashville: B&H, 1994), 116.

Excursus: Is the promised land a gift of God or is life in the land conditional upon obedience?

In Deuteronomy, it is described as both a gift and also as a reward for obedience. We need to take both seriously and not allow one to displace the other. The text in 9:4-6 can also insist that possession of the land is not meritorious. God gave the land to Israel as a nation, but every generation had to accept that gift. The gift was embraced by loving the LORD, demonstrated in obedience. Hence, this generation addressed by Moses did indeed enter the land and enjoy it, but there was always a provisional aspect to the ongoing possession of the land (see notes in 'Getting Our Bearings').

By way of simplistic illustration, I have been given free membership of my local gym by the owner. It was indeed a gift. However, the gym does have certain rules (there is outrage if someone uses their phone to take a call while exercising) and, if I flout the rules, I am abusing the owner's gift. If I offend repeatedly, he may well kick me out.

That's far from perfect, as I'm only one person and not a nation, yet it captures something of the provisional nature of the gift Israel received.

Hear and respond to impact the watching world (4:5-8)

These are important verses in terms of Israel fulfilling the promise given to Abraham that his descendants would be a blessing to the nations (Gen. 12:1-3). Israel is to keep God's statutes and rules so that the nations looking on will recognize them as a 'great nation' (three times in vv. 6, 7, 8). Israel is in the middle of a watching world. Their reputation will be evident to all.

What is greatness? It's not in the size of your military, population or GDP. It's not in the extent of your boundaries or the number of Nobel prize winners you have:

- According to verse 7, greatness is that God is near. The commentaries describe statues of pagan gods who have massive ears carved on them to indicate that they listen. The nations recognised that Israel had a God who listened.

- According to verse 8, greatness is in being given righteous rules which they keep (v. 6). Israel demonstrated that they were close to God by their obedience. Presumably, the watching nations could only tell that Israel was close to their God by the fact that they did what he said.

So, there is something about God's law that is universally recognizable as good. Not always; sometimes believers will be vilified. Yet the watching world may also recognize the behaviour of Christians as good (1 Pet. 2:12). When we reach chapters 12–26, there is much there which could make a watching world sit up and think: 'Those people live differently and it's impressive.'

So, the important application here is that God's people need to live transformed lives of obedience in order to have an impact upon the watching world. We really shouldn't be surprised; it is when Christians demonstrate love for one another that the world will know that we are disciples of Jesus and that he is near to us (John 13:35). Our evangelism will rarely be effective if it is not accompanied by a church community which demonstrates the reality of God in their lives of sacrificial obedience to him: 'The world will see no reason to pay any attention to our claims about our invisible God, however much we boast of his alleged nearness to us in prayer if it sees no difference between the lives of those who make such claims and those who don't.'[5]

Remember the LORD spoke from the fire (4:9-14)

The first of the three warnings comes in verse 9 (with the others in vv. 15 and 23). A woodenly literal translation would be as follows: 'Be extremely careful to guard your souls from forgetting.'

Verse 9 could be referring to the things that this generation saw in the defeat of Sihon and Og (3:21), but the emphasis of remembering in verse 10 is the events of Exodus 19 at Mount Sinai (or Horeb). (Deuteronomy commonly uses Horeb but is not averse to using the name Sinai, as in 33:2.)

The emphasis falls on the command 'Gather the people to me, that I may let them hear my words' (v. 10). The people are to be gathered to hear the word of God. Reading an account of Israel gathering at Mount Sinai we might make the mistake that the most significant thing was the fire and smoke (v. 11) but the stress is upon the words: 'You heard the sound of words but saw no form; there was only a voice' (v. 12).

Literally it translates as 'You saw no form, a voice.' At one level it's nonsensical to say, 'You saw ... a voice'; but Moses is stressing how vivid, how powerful and how overwhelming the voice of God was. The point is that, even though Israel was no longer at Sinai, they could still have the same experience as that generation because they still had the voice of God.

---

5. Christopher Wright, *The Mission of God* (Leicester: IVP, 2006), 380.

The torah which Moses was preaching in the plains of Moab was a portable Sinai experience. God's word is immediate and contemporary – it is like a 'volcanic experience'.

We are forced to notice the relationship between the generations:

- 'The day that *you* stood before the LORD your God at Horeb' (v. 10)
- '*You* came near … the mountain'(v. 11)
- 'The LORD spoke to *you*' (v. 12)
- 'He declared to *you* his covenant' (v. 13)
- 'The LORD commanded me … to teach *you*' (v. 14)
- 'You saw no form on the day that the LORD spoke to *you*' (v. 15)

Moses is addressing Israel as if they were all at Mount Sinai, but the adult generation of Sinai has nearly all died out (1:35-36). Yet the point is that as God's word was proclaimed to them, they share in the same experience that the generation of Mount Horeb had. They were not physically at Mount Sinai forty years earlier, but the same God was addressing them in the same words in Moab. The Lord spoke then (Sinai) from the fire and he was speaking then (Moab) through Moses, and he speaks to us today (church) as we assemble the people together to hear God's word.

So don't make an idol (4:15–22)

'Since you saw no form … beware lest you act corruptly by making a carved image for yourselves, in the form of any figure' (v. 15). Verses 16-18 reverse the order of creation of Genesis 1: 'Idolatry not only corrupts God's redemptive achievement for God's people (v. 20), but perverts and turns upside-down the whole created order.'[6]

The contrast here is not simply between the visible and invisible but between idols that are visible and the LORD who is audible. The difference is ultimately between who is in control. When you make an image, be it animal (v. 17), stars (v. 18) or human you are asserting your control; you are projecting your thoughts and desires onto your creation. Whereas when the LORD speaks, he is in control.

We are not at liberty to make a god who fits our image – one who conforms to our desires and our moods. He is the living and speaking God and he will *not* fit our agenda. We do not form him as we desire. We listen to him as he is.

If we do, then we image God to the watching world. The strange reference in verse 20 to Israel being brought out of an 'iron furnace' may be making the point that, by contrast with a false image emerging from a furnace, Israel emerged from Egypt to display a true image of God. They will show the world what the LORD is like if they listen to him and are careful to keep his statutes and laws.

The surprising return to the death of Moses in verses 21-22 is probably making the point that, if Moses was excluded, so too might they be. They must be careful.

But when you forget, the LORD will not (4:23-31)

Here is a clear anticipation of exile in the future. Even though Moses speaks of future generations (v. 25) he still addresses Israel as a unity. The failure will be one of idolatry. Israel will be sent into exile to 'serve gods of wood and stone, the work of human hands' (v. 28). There they

---

6. Wright, *Deuteronomy*, 50.

will discover the utter impotence of the gods they desired to follow.

Despite the certainty of failure, there is also hope (v. 29). Hope rests upon two truths – the LORD is merciful (v. 31) and, alongside that, he 'will not ... forget the covenant' that he made with their fathers.

What a striking contrast between the threefold imperative 'Don't forget, Israel' (vv. 9, 15, 23) and the wonderful indicative: The LORD will not forget. Ultimately, the law does not supply the basis for the relationship between God and the people. They *will* disobey but he *will not* forget his covenant (v. 31).

The LORD *is* merciful and patient. A natural reading of verse 26 would assume a very short tenancy in the land, yet in Israel's history the LORD is remarkably patient with idolatrous kings and people.

Yet, it is clear that repentance is necessary – Israel must seek the LORD (v. 29). They must search after him with their heart and soul. They must return (see notes on chapter 30) to the LORD and obey his voice (v. 30).

There is none like him, choose him today (4:32-40)

Moses concludes his first sermon with this strong demand to worship the LORD alone. He stresses that *now* is the moment of decision. They must decide 'today' (vv. 4, 8, 39 and 40).

For Moses, Israel lives in a series of perpetual 'todays'. Whenever you hear or read this passage you must respond with faith and obedience. Although the physical journey of the Israelites ended when they entered the promised land, their spiritual journey did not. This is of course picked up on in Psalm 95 and then Hebrews 3 and 4. 'There is a sense in which the people of God are constituted by the preached word of God, which comes to every generation in the continual, "Today".[7]

When preaching Deuteronomy we must press home that a choice needs to be made 'today' to listen and obey the Lord. This need to choose is brought to the fore with the use of imperatives: 'ask' (v. 32), 'know' (v. 39) and 'keep' (v. 40).

Although Moses moves here to his conclusion, it's worth observing that even in this climax, the bulk of the text remains on telling the story of what has happened.[8] Israel has a unique God who has provided a unique revelation (v. 33) and a unique redemption (v. 34). He is incomparable (v. 35). If Israel is going to obey, they need to know what their God has done for them. Christians are no different.

It seems natural to rephrase this section with the greater revelation that the New Testament brings:

> *Has any god come and lived among his people like Jesus Christ? Has any god experienced the frustration and known the pain of this world like Jesus? Has any god shown love and tenderness like Jesus? Has any God died to rescue people like Jesus? Has any god conquered death like Jesus? Has any god come and dwelt within his people like Jesus has by his Spirit? He has done these things so you might know – there is No Other.*
>
> *So now hear him as he says, 'If you love me you will obey what I command' (John 14:15).*
>
> *There is no other – listen to his voice and obey.*

---

7. Robson, *Honey from the Rock*, 46.

8. Block counts 163 words, of which 109 tell the story, 26 reflect theologically and 26 are words of application (*Deuteronomy*, 201).

Cities of refuge (4:41-43)

This is a strange anti-climax to the first speech. It obviously anticipates the section on cities of refuge in 19:1-13. Is it one example of publicly demonstrating the greatness of Israel with her righteous laws (4:8)? It is certainly an attempt to limit the spiral of vengeance that a murder can unleash.

From text to message

Getting the message clear: the theme

Listen to and obey your God, for he is unique and there is no other. No other God speaks like him, is supremely present by his word like him, or addresses us with a contemporary word like him.

Getting the message clear: the aim

The aim is that we should choose to love and obey God today!

A way in

'On Wednesday morning, I woke as normal, made a cup of tea and then God spoke to me: He addressed me and told me to rejoice! He rebuked me for being a little joyless recently. He commanded me to rejoice and help my family to rejoice and praise him for all he has given us recently. He was overwhelming and challenging and I could barely think of anything else for the rest of the day. How did this happen? I had spent thirty minutes reading and reflecting on Deuteronomy 12.

What a blessing that the Lord spoke to me, addressed me, commanded me, encouraged me. What a God, that he does that when we open his word. There is no other like him.'

Ideas for application

- **God is present by his voice, so keep listening.** There is a recurrent emphasis in Deuteronomy to pass this truth on to the next generation (e.g. 4:9-10). Never take the word of God for granted. Never assume that everyone knows what he says. Unless we keep listening to his voice in the scriptures, we will make an idol of him in our minds and lives. We have never had enough Bible teaching. We must keep returning to his word. It is when we listen that we 'will not forget' (vv. 9, 15, 23). It's when we fail that God's word provides hope (vv. 25-31). This passage makes clear that if you want a real encounter with the living God, you listen to his word. You cannot separate this real encounter with him from his word.

- **We need to be careful not to drift into idolatry.** Not many in the West in the twenty-first century are carving idols, but the temptation to form a mental image of God which conforms to our whims and desires is as strong as ever. All around us are people following idolatrous forms of God who are content with their sin. If you have a god who dislikes all the people and issues in the world that you do, while loving all the people and morals of the world that you do, be careful! Either you have been wonderfully conformed to Jesus or you have created a form of god in your image. It's worth asking how we might be drifting towards constructing our own god.

- **We need to listen to and obey God's law to have an impact upon the unbelieving world.** We should expect the people around us to have a growing acceptance that Christianity is true because of the way we live and the wisdom of pursuing a biblical lifestyle. But this will only happen if they actually see it.

- **Has any God redeemed like Jesus?** 'Has any god come and lived among his people like Jesus Christ? Experienced and felt the frustration and pain of this world like Jesus? Shown love and tenderness like Jesus? Died to rescue people like Jesus? Conquered death like Jesus? Come and dwelt within people like Jesus by his Spirit? He has done these things so you might know there is No Other. So now hear him as he says, "If you love me you will obey what I command" (John 14:15). There is NO OTHER saviour like him – listen to his voice and obey him.'[9]

Suggestions for preaching

This chapter is an important one for a biblical theology of preaching, of the land and of the uniqueness of God. It can prove really helpful to preach a little series of four on it:

There is none like him

1. Who has a God like this? (4:1-8)

- Listen and do so that you may live (vv. 1-4)
- Listen and do so that the world is wowed (vv. 5-8)

2. Assemble the people (4:9-14)

- Gather God's people (vv. 9-10)
- Listen to his words (vv. 11-14)

---

9. This paragraph came via the suggestion of Dan Block (*Deuteronomy*, 148).

3. Watch yourselves carefully (4:15-31)

- Don't make an idol, listen to him (vv. 15-19)
- Don't make an idol, reflect God's character (v. 20)
- Listen to the exact image of the Father (Heb. 1:1-3)

4. There is no other (4:32-40)

- Does any God speak like the LORD? (v. 33)
- Does any God save like the Lord Jesus? (v. 34)
- There is none like him, so choose today (vv. 35-40)

However, if you are preaching this as part of one series on Deuteronomy, it makes sense to structure a sermon around the threefold 'Don't forget':

- Remember the LORD who spoke from the fire (vv. 9-14)
- SO, don't make an idol (vv. 15-22)
- When you forget, the LORD will not (vv. 23-31)
⇨ Choose the LORD today! (vv. 32-40)

Questions to help understand the passage

1. What is the threefold warning given to Israel in the chapter (vv. 9, 15, 23)?
2. What motivations are given to Israel to 'hear and follow' the laws (vv. 1-4)?
3. What makes a people great, according to verses 5-8?
4. What will stop the people forgetting (vv. 9-10)?
5. What did the people see and, by contrast, what did they hear (vv. 11-14)?

6. What is the mistake that Israel is likely to make (vv. 15-22)?
7. What is going to happen in the future to Israel (vv. 23-28)?
8. What is their only hope (vv. 29-31)?
9. What is unique about Israel's God (vv. 32-38)?
10. What is the appropriate response (vv. 39-40)? When does this decision have to be made (vv. 4, 8, 26, 39, 40)?

Questions to help apply the passage

- Do we expect the watching world to be impressed with the Christian community? Why or why not?

- In what ways are we likely to make an idol of God? Where have you seen people physically make idols? How in our minds do we create something in our image rather than listen to God's word?

- What about the culture around us? How does that tend to make an image of God? What does he look like?

- In what areas are you personally tempted not to listen to what God says but substitute your own view of what God should be like?

- When do we have to decide to follow the Lord? What days might we be tempted to stop listening to him and make a god who fits into our lives more easily? (cf. Heb. 3:12-14)

3.

Walk in All of God's Ways
(Deuteronomy 5)

Introduction

We begin Moses's second sermon, which runs from chapter 5 through to the end of chapter 26. It clearly breaks down into these sections:

- Introduction (4:44-49)
- The fundamental covenant demands of chapters 5–11
- Detailed covenant stipulations of chapters 12–26

Chapter 5 recalls the giving of the Decalogue to Israel at Sinai/Horeb and establishes its central role as shaping the people of God. Craigie is typical of commentators in suggesting that 'the Decalogue is at the heart of the message of Deuteronomy.'[1]

It is quite possible to preach chapter 5 on its own or together with chapter 6 (if preaching a shorter series on the whole book). However, many will want to take the

---

1. Peter Craigie, *The Book of Deuteronomy* (NICOT; Grand Rapids: Eerdmans, 1995), 149.

Decalogue as a separate sermon series and there are a few pointers to that here. Personally, I had never preached a series on the 'Ten Words' before 2019 and I now categorically consider that a mistake.

While some, such as Block, take chapters 5–11 as an exposition of the first commandment, I prefer Wright's comparison of chapters 5–11 with the Beatitudes at the start of the Sermon on the Mount – they describe a whole-life stance and orientation towards God and others, before we get the detail (in chapters 12–26).[2] There is a sense in which chapters 5–11 are an expansion of the ideas of Exodus 19:4-6:

> You yourselves have seen what I did to the Egyptians, and how I bore you on eagles' wings and brought you to myself. Now therefore, if you will indeed obey my voice and keep my covenant, you shall be my treasured possession among all peoples, for all the earth is mine; and you shall be to me a kingdom of priests and a holy nation.

Moses is seeking to inspire Israel to keep God's word, with a mixture of remembering what God has done and looking forward to his blessing in a wonderful land, as well as warning that his displeasure will be incurred if they are disobedient.

Listening to the text

Structure

        4:44-49 Introduction to the law
        5:1-5   Prologue
        5:6-21   The Ten Words

---

2. Wright, *Deuteronomy*, 61.

5:22-31 The appeal for a mediator
5:32-33 Summary exhortation

Working through the text

Introduction to the law (4:44-49)

Commentators are divided on whether 4:44–49 is another conclusion to the first speech or introduces the second. This is hard to decide, but 4:44 is *probably* a superscription beginning a new section (cf. 1:1; 6:1; 12:1; 29:1).

It begins with 'This is the law … These are the testimonies, the statutes, and the rules' (vv. 44-45). At points in the book, it seems that the recurrent phrase 'statutes and rules' is a reference to the whole of Moses's teaching in Deuteronomy and seems to be synonymous with 'the commandment' (singular). Although at other points (e.g. 6:1), it reads more naturally as though 'the commandment' (singular) refers to the basic demand for loyalty, as in 6:25.

The expression 'statutes and rules' has already been used five times in chapter 4, but now seems to frame chapters 5–11 and 12–26 (5:1, 31; 6:1, 20; 7:11; 11:32; 12:1; 26:16, 17).

This is not 'law' as Western ears tend to hear it though. Clearly, in chapter 5, the Decalogue is not mere statutes – it has pithy prohibitions, lengthier explanations for the behaviour of some commandments, and detailed motivation, like avoiding God's jealousy and embracing his love (vv. 9-10), and long life in the land (v. 16). Crucially, the Decalogue appeals to the heart. The Tenth Word on coveting is not something that can be ruled on in a courtroom! Those who want to suggest that the Old Testament was concerned with external conformity and not internal transformation are siding with the Pharisees of Jesus's day. Moses is preaching to stimulate a love for the LORD which is in the heart.

Like the introduction to the first speech in 1:1-5, these verses provide a summary of the story detailed in chapters 1–3. Law is always embedded in story in Deuteronomy. Only if you know who God is and what he has done, will you respond rightly with obedience.

The prologue to the law (5:1-5)

The section begins 'Hear, O Israel' (also 6:3; 6:4; 9:1; 20:3; 27:9), not merely in the sense of sound hitting eardrums, but in obedience. These verses give an important framing of the law and help reveal its purpose and impact. We cannot skip over these quickly if we are to understand the purpose of the Decalogue and its importance:

- The Decalogue is for training (v. 1). Israel is to 'learn' these laws. They are not simply to be obeyed but these are principles which will train and shape the people in right living.

- The Decalogue is contemporary (vv. 2-3). Here again is the surprising emphasis that the covenant was *not* made with our fathers but with *us*. 'Our fathers' is best understood as the generation before rather than the patriarchs, following the same emphasis in chapter 4. McConville expresses it well: 'We have here the clearest expression in Deuteronomy of one of its main contentions, namely that Israel in all its generations stands in principle once again at Horeb, confronted with the covenant commands as if about to be given for the first time.'[3]

---

3. J. G. McConville, *Deuteronomy* (AOT; Leicester: Apollos, 1992), 124.

- The Decalogue is direct (vv. 4-5). At first glance, verse 4 seems to contradict verse 5 (and also 4:12): 'they saw no form.' Yet the emphasis is upon the immediacy and directness of the revelation they received. It is the same truth, on a national level, that Moses knew: he could not see the LORD's face and live (Exod. 20:20) and yet he spoke with the LORD face to face as a man speaks to his friend (Exod. 20:11). Of course, verse 5 clarifies that this was a direct contact with the LORD that was overwhelming for Israel. They required a mediator.

- The Decalogue is a response to God's grace (v. 6). There are inevitable comparisons drawn between Deuteronomy and ancient Near Eastern treaties. Here is a striking one. Rather than describe how a superior nation had conquered a weaker one as ancient Near Eastern treaties would tend to do, here, we have the description of how the Incomparable God did not conquer Israel but treated her with kindness and grace. The law is preceded by God's gracious saving action.

The Decalogue (5:6-21)

Block is unusual in suggesting that 'there is no evidence within the Old Testament or the New Testament that the Decalogue was ever treated as more authoritative or weighty than any other parts of the Sinai revelation.'[4] Most recognize that there are unique features to the Ten Words:

- These words alone were spoken immediately by the voice of God to the people. The people then recoil and God speaks through Moses. Moses says that

---

4. Block, *Deuteronomy*, 169.

God 'added no more' after speaking the Ten Words to the people (Deut. 5:22).

- They were written by the finger of God himself (Deut. 4:13; 5:22; 9:10; 10:4).

- They are uniquely named as the 'Ten Words' (Deut. 4:13; 10:4; Exod. 34:28). (They are never actually referred to as the Ten *Commandments*.)

- They alone are preserved in the Ark (Deut. 10:2, 5; Exod. 25:21). The rest of the law, written by Moses, is placed by the side of the ark (Deut. 31:26).

- They were written by the finger of God himself (Deut. 4:13; 5:22; 9:10; 10:4).

- They're pure imperatives. The rest of the law works them out in hypothetical circumstances: 'If this, then that. ...'[5]

- Chapters 12–26 seem, in some sense, to be an unpacking of the Ten Words. The Decalogue seems to have a place in the centre of Old Testament law. The rest of the statutes flow from them, yet, at the same time, it is impossible to understand all that is meant by the Ten without reference to the rest of the law.

Apart from the commands to keep the Sabbath and honour parents, the Ten are negatively framed. They are placing boundaries within which Israel can operate with freedom. Tennis is a better game and more fun when there are white lines on the ground. No one complains that

---

5. Philip Ross, *The Finger of God* (Fearn, UK: Mentor, 2010), 90. (Thanks to Garry Williams for this reference.)

they're constricting; everyone can enjoy the game when they're in place.

No other gods (5:6-7)

There is a decision on where to include verse 6. Clearly, it is the first sentence of the LORD's speech, but it is unlike the rest of the section in not being a command.

There is value in reading verse 6 before each of the Ten Commandments – it is a reminder that God's grace precedes Israel's action. It makes the most sense to me to take verses 6 and 7 together as the First Word. God tells Israel two very important things before issuing a command:

- 'I am the LORD *your* God': There is a relationship here. There is a world of difference between the two sentences: (1) I am a dad and (2) I am your dad. You can be indifferent to the first but not the second. There is a crucial relationship already in place. God has revealed himself to Israel as Yahweh or the LORD.

- 'Who brought you out of the land of Egypt, out of the house of slavery': Redemption has been accomplished and the purpose is freedom from slavery – a point which is stressed more in Deuteronomy 5 (vv. 14–15) than Exodus 20.

'No other gods before me' stresses that the LORD must be first. It can be taken in two senses:

1. No other god *before* me – i.e. he has priority. Straight away, we're into the fact that these ten are making demands upon Israel's emotional life. This is not a law that can be prosecuted in the courtroom – it is an attitude of the heart. We see straight away that the Ten have a coherence to them. Why do

people lie? It's because they have broken the first commandment and love something more than God. It might be money, so someone lies on a tax form. It might be reputation, so someone lies to their boss.

2. No other god *besides* me – i.e. no syncretism or multiple gods. The literal Hebrew is strikingly vivid: 'No other gods upon my face'. You might imagine a man bringing home a mistress and having sex in front of his wife. The wife is outraged and says, 'No other women in my face!'

I'm not sure we have to choose between these two senses. The LORD is saying, No other gods ahead of me or alongside me. Jesus brings out the radical nature of this command:

> Whoever loves father or mother more than me is not worthy of me, and whoever loves son or daughter more than me is not worthy of me. (Matt. 10:37)

Wow, that is a challenging demand upon our emotional life!

You shall not make or bow down to an image (5:8-10)
If you take the traditional reformed division of the Ten Commandments, then this is the distinction:

- First Word – don't worship false gods
- Second Word – don't worship the true God falsely

So, the stress of the second command is that you cannot worship God on your terms or as you fancy. You worship him as he demands. As we saw in chapter 4, Deuteronomy stresses that God reveals himself in words. Supremely, he reveals himself in the Word – Jesus Christ, the exact image and likeness of God. We need the whole of Scripture to fill out our understanding of him. For example, if we *only* ever conceive of Jesus as 'Good Shepherd,' then we'll end up with a distorted mental image. We need to know him also as All-Powerful King (Rev. 1), and so on.

The words of verses 9-10 are harsh on our ears. It seems a little strong to say that making an idol of God is 'hating' him. Yet it is saying, 'I don't like you the way you are now, God – I think I can make a better version.' Perhaps think of a man asking a woman to marry him. She replies, 'Yes, if you lose three stone in weight, dye your hair a different colour, change your accent (I don't like it), retrain as a vet and give up your family (they're horrible).' The man protests, 'But those are the things that make me who I am. You're essentially saying you hate the person I am now and want lots of me to change.'

In that sense, replacing God with an idol of our making is hating him.

Whenever we read that God is jealous (v. 9), we have to remind ourselves that he is jealous for our good, not jealous of us or others. Perhaps zealous is more helpful as it loses some unhelpful connotations. But jealous does retain the sense that God loves us passionately; he is not indifferent to our neglect of him.

The iniquity being visited upon children is not automatic. Ezekiel 18:14-18 explicitly says that no one is judged for their parent's actions. The child of an unfaithful father can become a wonderful believer. However, parenting does have an impact! A parent who models the love of money is more likely to have a child who worships the same god. Even here though, we are to notice the imbalance between curse and blessing. Iniquity may fall on three or four generations, but steadfast love flows to thousands of generations.

You don't worship God when you dishonour his name (5:11)

To 'take the name of the LORD in vain' is to treat it as an empty or worthless thing. This has obvious implications for our speech. You break the command by trivializing the LORD's name, by making oaths in his name which you break and by presuming to prophesy in his name (Deut. 18:20).

Yet in the rest of the Old Testament this command is also broken by the behaviour of God's people:

- 'You shall not give any of your children to offer them to Molech, and so profane the name of your God: I am the LORD.' (Lev. 18:21).

- 'When they came to the nations, wherever they came, they profaned my holy name, in that people said of them, "These are the people of the LORD, and yet they had to go out of his land."' (Ezek. 36:20).

If you're known as a follower of the Lord (Jesus), then poor behaviour will mean that his name is misused.

Remember the Sabbath (5:12-15)

Only this and the fifth commandment are framed positively, although even here there is both a positive and negative element to the command. Positively, Israel was to keep the Sabbath as a day for the LORD. Negatively, they were not to do any work.

There are notably two differences between the formulation here and in Exodus 20:

1. There is an extra emphasis in Deuteronomy 5 on servants resting: 'that your male servant and female servant may rest as well as you' (v. 14). This is a

typical Deuteronomic emphasis on the benefits of life in the land being distributed to everyone. You, Israel, have been rescued by the kindness and mercy of the Lord, so show a similar kindness and mercy to others.

2. A different reason to celebrate is given. Rather than the justification in Exodus being God's work of creation climaxing in the Sabbath, here it is the work of redemption. Strikingly, the words for labour (v. 13) and slave (v. 15) have the same Hebrew root. The sense of the motive is as follows: 'For six days you shall *slave* and do all your work, but the Sabbath is a Sabbath to the LORD your God. ... You shall remember that you were a *slave* in the land of Egypt, and the LORD your God brought you out from there with a mighty hand and an outstretched arm.' You were slaves; you had to work continuously without any holiday or time off. So, now that the LORD has redeemed you, don't live as slaves. Don't demand that of other people either.

In simple terms, Exodus 20 emphasises that if you fail to take a day off you are denying that you are a creature dependent upon your creator and that you are made for more than this world. By contrast, Deuteronomy 5 stresses that if you fail to take a day off you are denying that God has redeemed you from slavery. You remain a slave.

Each preacher needs to reach their own conclusions on how to apply this rightly today (Rom. 14:5!). Personally it seems to me that the writer to the Hebrews is clear in chapters 3 and 4 that rest as a time (Sabbath) and a place (the promised land) was a pointer forward to the person who gives rest (Jesus) and the promised land (heaven). The first way to keep the fourth commandment is to stop slaving for salvation and rest in the redemption won by Jesus Christ. However, in broad terms (of course it varies somewhat for shift workers), a failure to take one day off a week appears to be a functional failure to trust God. It is a denial of our creaturely dependence upon God, and it is a denial that God has rescued us from slaving.

Honour your parents (5:16)

Many view this command as beginning the 'second table' of the commandments. If the first four are concerned with the worship of God, the next six are concerned with love of neighbour. If that is the case, it is striking that the 'neighbourly-focused' commands begin, again, with an attitude of heart: *Honour* your parents. Again, this is difficult to prosecute in the courtroom.[6] To honour is to treat as heavy or give weight to them. The opposite would be to trivialise parents or act as if they do not matter in your life. This command is reinforced with a promise: 'that your days may be long, and that it may go well with you in the land that the LORD your God is giving you'. It's a common thought in Deuteronomy (cf. 5:29; 6:3; 6:18). Obedience leads to blessing. 5:16 is similar to 4:40. The thought seems to be that parents were the primary means of passing on God's word to the next generation. The children had to be receptive to God's word through their parents, so that it would go well.

Why does *this* command get reinforced in this way? It may be that how you treat parents is a reflection of how

---

6. Although 21:18-21 is one obvious case where this has gone wrong!

you treat God. From a young age, they are the primary people of influence in your life and so, if you reject them, you will tend to reject all authority, even the Lord's. It is striking that in the New Testament lists of deplorable sins, dishonouring parents is there (Rom. 1:29-31; 2 Tim. 3:1-4). By contrast, the impact of the gospel will be that the hearts of children are turned back to their fathers (Mal. 4:6; Luke 1:17). There seems to be something fundamental about honour within the home to the whole structure of society. The Bible applies the titles of Father and Mother to kings, rulers, military chiefs, and prophets. In part, this is why the fifth commandment has been taken as applying to all relationships where there is a senior-junior structure.

Paul quotes this in Ephesians 6:1-3; possibly, given the emphasis upon God's predestining grace in that letter, the focus there is that those who have received the promise of an eternal inheritance should obey the command.

(In preaching a series on the Ten Words, this is in some ways the strangest because, for some people, it's an easy command to keep; yet for others, it is the hardest. In an era of increased family breakdown, the command to honour parents can be deeply painful for some to hear. Clearly, it looks different at varying ages and in divergent cultures. In the West, it can be that for eighteen years of childhood we honour by obeying, for twenty to thirty years as a young adult we honour parents by sharing our lives, and in later life, we honour parents by supporting them as they decline.)

No murder (5:17)

This is one of the more complicated 'Words' to explain. How we understand this commandment will deter-mine what we think about abortion, euthanasia, capital punishment, war, suicide, alcohol, tobacco, drugs, taking exercise, even dangerous sports and dieting.

A simple summary of 'You shall not murder' might best be summarized as 'Believers value life.'

Within Deuteronomy, amongst other things, you need to reckon with

- Unintentional, accidental killing or manslaughter (ch. 19);

- Principles of warfare (ch. 20); and

- Negligent failure to prevent death (by failing to provide safety features such as a parapet on the roof (22:8).

As with adultery, if preaching a sermon on this commandment, the preacher needs at some point to turn to Matthew 6 where Jesus explains that murderous acts begin with hate-filled hearts. Not to say lazily that hate is the same as murder – there is a difference! Yet they are on the same spectrum.

Apologetically speaking, it's worth noting that if you read the United Nations Universal Declaration of Human Rights, you'll see there is no rationale for human rights – no 'because ...'. It's simply stated as an axiom that all humans have a right to life. The Bible is clear that God demands an account for murder as all humans are made in his image (Gen. 9:5-6).

Hold fast to faithfulness (5:18)

Why is the commandment 'no adultery' as opposed to 'no sexual immorality' or 'no lust' (as Jesus applies it)? The later laws in Deuteronomy draw a distinction. Adultery meant the death penalty for the man and woman involved. Yet sex before marriage did not. The couple were to marry one another and the man was to pay a bride price (Deut. 22; cf.

Exod. 22:16). Earlier in Genesis, adultery was described as a 'great sin' (Gen. 20:9; 39:9).

Why is adultery different to other sexual sins? Presumably there is something in the fact that a covenant is broken. After the two examples in Genesis, the next time a 'great sin' is described in the Bible is three times in Exodus 32 in relation to the golden calf incident. The Bible draws a strong connection between idolatry and adultery. In addition, it seems that – given the biblical picture of Christ as a groom who is faithful to his bride, the church – an unfaithful husband suggests to a watching world that Christ is unfaithful. By contrast, the faithful spouse reminds us that Christ is faithful and he will hold us fast until we die (Eph. 5:32).

You shall not steal (5:19)

Stealing undermines trust and leads to the breakdown of society. The command assumes that God has given to humans the right, under him, to own property. God gave land to the Israelites and it is assumed in the New Testament that people own houses and land (Acts 12:12; 16:14-15; 21:8).

Amongst other things, the commandment precludes charging unfair interest (23:19); depriving people of their ability to work (24:5-6); slavery (24:7); failure to pay wages on time (24:15); a lack of generosity (24:19) yet also taking advantage of generosity (23:25); and accurate weights and measures (25:15).

In the New Testament, as well as the simple command not to steal, Paul makes frequent reference to hard work as the antithesis of theft (Eph. 4:28; 1 Thess. 4:11-12; 2 Thess. 3:10), as it provides for ourselves and others.

You shall not bear false witness (5:20)

This command is amplified in Deuteronomy 19:15-21. It's evident that this is primarily a court setting. There have to be multiple witnesses and scrutiny of witnesses (vv. 16-19) so that people take their responsibility seriously (v. 20).

Paul requires the same two to three witnesses when there is an accusation against an elder (1 Tim. 5). Slander is highlighted in the New Testament as a defiling sin that can cause great damage (Mark 7:22). This needs particular application in a social media age of easy and anonymous cruelty and rumour spreading. Gossip and exaggeration are also precluded.

No coveting (5:21)

Wright summarises this brilliantly:

> The inclusion of coveting shows that covenant loyalty in Israel went far deeper than external conformity to statute law. ... Deuteronomy is concerned to inculcate a social ethos in which motives and desires, intentions and attitudes, matter greatly. All the rhetoric, the didactic, hortatory style, the urgent appeals, glowing promises, and dire warnings are directed precisely to the heart and mind, the inner world of the will and purpose. There is nothing at all surprising, therefore, in the tenth commandment being posted to the same address.[7]

Some commentators link coveting with Levirate marriage in 25:5-10, which exposes the selfishness of the brother-in-law unwilling to marry. It's a fascinating case as there is no legal penalty but he is exposed to public humiliation. It seems that sometimes there is no need for a law; rather, it

---

7. Wright, *Deuteronomy*, 85.

is appropriate to obviously disapprove of selfish behaviour. The role of a community in shaping the behaviour of individuals is of enormous importance.

The appeal for a mediator (5:22-33)

Moses recalls what happened (5:22-23)

Verse 22 explains that the LORD spoke the Decalogue to 'all your assembly' at the mountain. Although 'the assembly' is a common term for the people of God standing in God's presence, the experience of Sinai is referred to as *'the day of assembly'* (9:10; 10:4; 18:16). It was a defining moment in who Israel was – the founding day of the nation.

The Israelites speak (5:24-27)

The people did three things:

1. They recognized that the LORD had spoken to them – that is, 'shown us his glory and greatness' (v. 24). It is not that they have seen God, but rather they have seen that God speaks. It seems to be the sound of the thundering voice that has them so terrified: 'If we hear the voice of our LORD any more, we shall die.'

2. So, recognizing that to hear God speak is to behold his glory and greatness in a way which they cannot withstand, they ask Moses to mediate (vv. 25-27a).

3. They commit themselves to hearing and obeying (v. 27b).

The LORD speaks (5:28-31)

This is a mixed response. On the one hand, the Lord agrees, 'They are right in all that they have spoken' (v. 28). Yet verse 29 contains a strong hint that their promised obedience will be short-lived. The obedience required focuses down on doing 'the whole commandment' (singular) in verse 31. Commentators disagree over what is meant by this. While it is possible here to take the 'whole commandment' in apposition to 'the statutes and the rules', Block thinks it refers purely to the first command of the Decalogue expounded in chapters 6–11.[8] I take it in a similar sense as most likely referring forward to the central commandment of 6:5.[9]

Moses concludes with exhortation (5:32-33)

Moses switches from narrative to exhortation, with the familiar encouragement that walking in God's ways leads to blessing.

From text to message
Getting the message clear: the theme

Moses reminds the Israelites of the people that they have been redeemed to be. The Decalogue is a summary of the sort of people that the Lord desires. The Lord is clear that this is a response to his salvation. These are not abstract and random rules – they are the personal gift of God who spoke face to face. They are rules designed to grant us freedom to live rightly.

Getting the message clear: the aim

Walk in all the way that the Lord your God has commanded you.

---

8. Block, *Deuteronomy*, 162.

9. Cf. 30:11 where 'the commandment' seems to refer to the immediately preceding 'turn to the Lord your God with all your heart and with all your soul.'

A way in

On a Formula One racing track there are safety barriers. I've never heard a driver complain about them; evidently, they value them and are glad that they are there. They provide the freedom to drive at 200 mph, which must be wonderfully exhilarating. Without them, it is far harder to stick to the track; drivers would be a lot more anxious about having an accident.

The safety barriers exist to give the drivers freedom to drive. The Decalogue or Ten Words does the same thing – they are God's protection or parameters around life which give us the freedom of living life to the full. They may be negatively framed, but they give us freedom to live.

Ideas for application

- **Instruction in the Decalogue equips us for modern life.** By contrast with my Christian sub-culture, the Puritans recognized that the Ten Commandments covered life comprehensively. When rightly understood and used, they would bring clear direction for the whole of life. This, rather than a spirit of legalism, explains their focus on catechetical instruction. Two fifths of the Shorter Catechism and one third of the Longer Catechism, for example, are devoted to a detailed exposition of the law. Far from being legalistic, the Puritans held that this alone provides a framework for the freedom of the Christian believer to live in the confidence that he does the will of God. Of course, the Puritans recognized that God's providence could be difficult to interpret and to experience. But they did not write books specifically on the subject of personal guidance. Having taught the comprehensive implications of the law, they did not need to.[10]

Details are good! Specific application is a blessing to God's people. Of course, we read the Ten Words through the lens of Christ. Jesus 'filters' the Decalogue, but also, in him, we have the perfect example of it being lived out, so we can see what it means more clearly. The Ten Words come to us from the lips of the risen Jesus who has fulfilled them perfectly. He has taken the curse for disobedience and so they come without curse, to us as Spirit-filled believers with power to keep it far beyond that of Israel.

- **Obedience is a response to God's grace.** We must keep stressing this. These laws cannot justify us, and they were never meant to justify Israel. We must also warn of the Christian tendency to view our relationship with God primarily through the lens of our obedience. Don't trust in your obedience. Trust in God's mercy. However, as believers saved by grace and united to Christ, of course we want to obey him.

  How we respond to God's law is not comparable to how we respond to traffic laws, for example. The LORD spoke face to face – personally and directly. Our response to the Decalogue is a response to his face. In every moral decision, we either spit or smile at the face of the Living God.

- **The Decalogue reveals the character of God to us.** He cares deeply.

---

10. Sinclair Ferguson, *Some Pastors and Teachers* (Edinburgh: Banner of Truth, 2017), 343.

- **The Decalogue confronts us with our sinful inadequacy.** When we hear the demands of a holy and glorious God, we should recognize that we need a mediator. We are so stubbornly sinful that we need God's requirements to be spelt out for us, otherwise we might think our lives are acceptable. If you hear the Decalogue and think, 'Yep, I can do that,' then you do not understand these words and you do not know the Lord.

- **The Decalogue is a description of the one perfect man.** Jesus is the living embodiment of these standards. So they should help Christians

  - understand more of his perfect character;

  - see how desperately we need him;

  - rejoice that we have his moral perfection imputed to us;

  - know how to thank the Lord, by keeping the commandments out of gratitude – for in doing so we are worshipping him.

John Frame expresses it very helpfully:

  - The first commandment teaches us to worship Jesus as the one and only Lord, Saviour, and mediator (Acts 4:12; 1 Tim. 2:5).

  - In the second commandment, Jesus is the one perfect image of God (Col. 1:15; Heb. 1:3). Our devotion to him precludes worship of any other image.

  - In the third commandment, Jesus is the name of God, that name to which every knee shall bow (Phil. 2:10-11; cf. Isa. 45:23).

- In the fourth commandment, Jesus is our Sabbath rest. In his presence, we cease our daily duties and hear his voice (Luke 10:38-42).

- In the fifth commandment, we honour Jesus who has brought us as his 'sons' (Heb. 2:10) to glory.

- In the sixth commandment, we honour him as the life (John 10:10; 14:6; Gal. 2:20; Col. 3:4), Lord of life (Acts 3:15), the one who gave his life that we might live (Mark 10:45).

- In the seventh commandment, we honour him as our bridegroom who gave himself to cleanse us, to make us his pure, spotless bride (Eph. 5:22-33). We love him as no other.

- In the eighth commandment, we honour Jesus as our inheritance (Eph. 1:11) and as the one who provides all the needs for his people in this world and beyond.

- In the ninth commandment, we honour him as God's truth (John 1:17; 14:6), in whom all the promises of God are Yes and Amen (2 Cor. 1:20).

- In the tenth commandment, we honour him as our complete sufficiency (2 Cor. 3:5; 12:9) to meet both our external needs and the renewed desires of our hearts.[11]

- **Humanity needs a law-giving God or there is no basis to agree upon common morals.**

As one example, in 2016 the *New Statesman* had an article on what humans should have as 'the Ten Com-

---

11. John Frame, 'Preaching Christ from the Decalogue,' n.p. Online: https://frame-poythress.org/preaching-christ-from-the-decalogue.

mandments for the Modern Age'. One philosopher, Julian Baggini, helpfully observed that all of the contributors basically agreed on the final five and disliked the first five, but without the first five, there is no reason to keep 'Do not kill,' etc. He commented, 'We want the protections of morality without having to defer to it; we want the fruits without the roots ... Something needs to do the work today that those first five commandments did for centuries.'[12] He offers no solution. The Bible is clear – there is a law-giving God.

Suggestions for preaching

If you're preaching an overview series on Deuteronomy, this could either be a single sermon on chapter 5 or perhaps combined with chapter 6. Naturally, there is also a series on the Decalogue that could be preached. That could be done in a more systematic fashion (which I think is the most common way) or could be done by taking the relevant passages of Deuteronomy which amplify on the Ten Words (see introduction to chapter 12).

How about an alliterative outline for chapter 5?

1. The design of God's law (5:1-6)

2. The details in God's law (5:7-21)

3. The danger of God's law (5:22-31)

Questions to help understand the passage

1. What are we told about the people that Moses is addressing (vv. 45-49)? What context is given before the law is actually delivered?

---

12. Julian Baggini wrote 'Thou shalt tolerate other gods', joining other writers in contributing to 'The Ten Commandments for the Modern Age' (*The New Statesman*, 12 January 2016).

2. What is stressed in verse 3? Why?

3. What is stressed in verse 4? Why?

4. What is Israel reminded of before any of the Ten Words are given (v. 6)? What has God done?

5. The Ten Commandments:

    i. What does 'no other gods before me' mean (v. 7)?

    ii. What is the difference between the commands of verse 7 and verse 8? What is the imbalance between what is promised to those who hate God and those who love him (vv. 9-10)?

    iii. What does taking the LORD's name in vain (v. 11) look like in 18:20?

    iv. What are the positive and negative elements of the fourth commandment (vv. 12-15)? Who is to benefit?

    v. What does the fifth commandment have attached to it that most others do not (v. 16)?

    vi. Read chapters 19 and 20. What jumps out as some of the principles of what it means to 'not murder' (v. 17)?

    vii. What explicitly is prohibited in the seventh commandment (v. 18)?

    viii. Read chapter 24. Again, what jumps out as some of the practical ways in which the eighth commandment (v. 19) is applied?

    ix. What is the primary setting envisaged of 'no false witness' (v. 20; cf. 19:15-21)?

    x. What is included in the list of things 'you shall not covet' (v. 21)?

1. What did the Israelites do when they heard God's voice (vv. 24-27)?

2. How does the LORD respond (vv. 28-31)? Do you think it is positive or negative?

Questions to help apply the passage

1. What is the impact of most of the Ten Words being framed negatively? What was the purpose of the first negative command in the Bible, 'Do not eat the fruit of that tree' (Gen. 2)?

2. The Ten Commandments:

    i. How does Jesus apply the First Word in Matthew 10:37? How is that a challenge to our inner emotional life?

    ii. While we're less likely these days in the secular West to make physical idols, how can we create mental images of God that are not true to how he reveals himself in the Bible?

    iii. What is the connection between taking God's name in vain and our behaviour (Lev. 18:21; Ezek. 36:17-20)?

    iv. If we never take time off from work and trust that God can provide, what are we claiming about ourselves and him?

    v. Is the command to 'honour' something which can be done in a formal way without our emotions being involved? What does it look like to honour your parents when you are under 20? Under 40? Over 40?

    vi. How does Jesus apply this in Matthew 6? Does this mean that hatred is equivalent to murder? What is the connection between them?

   vii. Why is adultery presented as, in some sense, worse than other sexual sins? What is marriage a picture of in the Bible and so what are we saying if we commit adultery?

  viii. What does the New Testament often hold up as the opposite of stealing (Eph. 4:28; 1 Thess. 4:11-12; 2 Thess. 3:10)?

    ix. What does lying do to our relationships?

    x. Where does coveting take place? So, could an Israelite have kept this law? How can we?

1. Overall, what do the Ten Words teach us about God?

2. More acutely, what do they teach us about Jesus?

3. What do they teach us about the Christian life?

4.

Love the Lord with All You've Got

(Deuteronomy 6)

Introduction

Chapter 6 contains the famous Shema of verse 4 and its implication in verse 5 that 'you shall love the LORD your God with all your heart and with all your soul and with all your might.' The call to love is essentially a call to loyalty. Jesus, when asked, expands this commandment out into two, but, here also in Deuteronomy, love for the LORD is seen in how you behave towards other people. The decision to love the LORD unconditionally will now become the dominant idea in the following chapters.

After the key command is issued, Moses delivers a succinct homily on the threats towards Israel's love for the LORD. It's a demanding chapter, but its central demand that love for the LORD is to be with the whole heart ensures that we cannot read Deuteronomy, or Old Testament law in general, as requiring merely formal legalism. Then, as now, Yahweh wanted his people's love – it is a love that is rooted in the heart and demonstrated in practical choices of daily life. It is a love that says, 'Lord, here is my diary and my wallet; here are my car keys and my house keys; here are my hopes and my dreams. They're all yours, Lord. I love you and you can see that in the choices I make to serve you.'

Listening to the text

We're in Moses's second speech which runs through to chapter 26. Chapters 5–11 are more like sermons, giving the overall direction of covenant life, while chapters 12–26 have the very specific laws.

Verses 1-3 can be taken together with 5:27-33. The end of chapter 5 has emphasised Moses's role as the covenant mediator and God's spokesman. From 6:1 onwards, we see him doing this in action. Some view 6:4 as an introduction to the law code, but the substance is continued from chapter 5 – especially the focus on loving Yahweh alone.

Structure

6:1-3	Moses's exhortation
6:4-9	Love the LORD with everything
6:10-19	Homily on three things that will challenge your love
6:20-25	Love him because he first loved you

Working through the text

Moses's exhortation (6:1-3)

Verse 1 begins with a conjunction, making it an explicit continuation of the preceding material. There is a question over how to take 'the commandment' (singular):

1. It could be in apposition, or equivalent, to the 'statutes and rules'. It seems at places in the book that the

singular term refers to the entire covenant text (e.g. 5:31).

2. It could refer to the central injunction of verse 5 as a summary of what has been said so far in chapter 5.

Although it is not completely clear, I prefer the latter here. Deuteronomy 12:1 introduces the detailed regulations with 'statutes and rules' and does not have 'the commandment'; this nudges us to view chapters 5–11 as the more general commandment of loyalty to the LORD, while chapters 12–26 are the statutes and rules. Also, the whole of chapter 6 is bracketed by reference to 'the commandment' (vv. 1, 25), again leading us to think of 6:5 as *the* commandment – the most basic demand of all (see also 30:11). Understood in this way, there is a central commandment – love the LORD with all you've got – and then there are numerous statutes and rules which show you how to love Yahweh in the details of life.

It is obvious in verse 2 that the way for Israel to show reverence to (fear) the LORD is through obedience. Moses again builds up the motivational clauses. They are to do the statutes and rules:

- That they may fear the LORD (v. 2)
- That their days may be long (v. 2)
- That it may go well with them (v. 3)
- That they may multiply greatly (v. 3)

The land flowing with 'milk and honey' is another motivating emphasis (11:9; 26:9, 15; 27:3; 31:20) and is suggestive of the choice food offered to guests. Clearly it is not literally true, but the land had relatively wonderful fertility compared to Egypt and its dependence upon the Nile flooding the plains to make the land good for use. (See comments on chapter 4, 'Is the promised land a gift of God or is life in the land conditional upon obedience?')

Love the LORD with everything (6:4-9)

The section is dominated by the profound statement of verse 4 and the wholehearted response of verse 5: *the* commandment. The fundamental commandment is loyalty to the LORD, but that is, of course, expressed in reality by walking in the LORD's ways and in obedience to the statutes and rules.[1]

Israel is commanded to 'hear' in verse 4 (also 5:1; 6:3; 9:1; 20:3; 27:9) – a listening that requires a response. (This is a response which they can only make if the LORD has circumcised their hearts; see 29:4. Here is the root problem for most of Moses's hearers: they could not hear and so the word of God never reached their hearts – they needed new hearts. See chapter 30).

All the commentaries will tell you that 'the LORD our God, the LORD is one' translates a mere four Hebrew words of two verbless clauses: 'Yahweh our-God, Yahweh one':

1. The emphasis may fall on the 'one-ness' of Yahweh: there is a singularity to him. He is consistent and unchanging. There is a unity of purpose, integrity and will within him. The fact that the word for 'one' ('*ehad*) is not used elsewhere in the Old Testament to mean 'alone' would point in this direction. When

---

1. See again 'Getting Our Bearings in Deuteronomy (p. 20). 'The commandment' (singular) can seem to refer to this one instruction or the entirety of Moses's instructions.

Jesus quotes this verse in Mark 12:29-33 he says, 'The Lord our God is one Lord.'

2. Yet the context pushes us to think primarily in terms of uniqueness. Block translates the verse 'Yahweh is our God, Yahweh alone.'[2] The uniqueness of Yahweh was asserted in the Decalogue and is in many ways the dominant issue of chapters 4–8. As such, verse 4 is a cry of allegiance issued by the true and faithful Israelite.

There is no one like the LORD and the response to this great truth is to love him (10:12; 11:1, 13, 22; 13:3; 19:9; 30:6, 16, 20). I found Block persuasive in arguing that the heart, soul and might should not be viewed as overlapping parts of the human person but here they should be viewed as concentric aspects of human life.

In the centre is the heart – the inner world of thoughts, emotions and will. Jesus brings this meaning out in the New Testament by adding 'mind' to the list of things involved in the greatest commandment. In English, we might use the idiom, 'It is my heartfelt intention,' meaning, I've thought long and hard about this and it's what I really desire to do.

Next is the 'soul', literally meaning 'up to the neck'. In other words this is the entire being – a person's words and actions.

Finally is 'might', which is strength or 'muchness'. This is all that you have. Perhaps 'resources' is a more helpful word for people to understand – it is your household and your possessions. However, 'resources' sounds a little drab.

---

2. Block, *Deuteronomy*, 182.

Perhaps it's helpful to envisage the woman of Mark 14 here – she breaks her perfume, costing a year's salary, over Jesus. It is an extravagant gesture involving her heart, her actions and her resources. What this little list of heart, soul and muchness reveals is that this is neither mere emotive love nor is it outward obedience. It is a love that is rooted in the heart and demonstrated in your choices. Love the Lord with your inner feelings, your mental capacity and your desires. Love him with your moral choices, your financial decisions and your time commitments.

These words are to be upon your heart. The NIV unfortunately goes for 'these commandments' but the word used here is the simple one for words or things (*davar*). Which words are they? In the flow of Deuteronomy, it makes most sense to read this as all of the words of the book: that would include commands but also words of exhortation and words of grace. Words of how the Lord had kept them in the past and made promises to them about the future. Fifty-one times in the book the heart is referenced. Chapter 30 is the key chapter with the greatest density, but loving Yahweh from the heart is central to chapter 6. Moses is not asking for mere legal obedience and knows nothing of works salvation. The Lord wants their hearts!

(The preacher needs to think hard in a series on Deuteronomy about how often to bring in the fact that the key problem for an Israelite was that they did not have the word of God in their heart. For the overwhelming majority, their issue was 29:4 – they did not have a heart to understand. They needed the Lord to circumcise their heart (30:6). It would be tedious to discuss this in every sermon, so some planning is required. As chapter 6 is a commandment in response to God's grace and his promises, I would personally be content to preach it as such to the Christian, in a sermon on chapter 6.)

Verses 7-9 emphasise how these words are to be kept central in all arenas of life:

- **Family (v. 7):** There is a word here to parents but, given that Moses is addressing the whole congregation, it is also a word to Sunday school teachers, those caring for students and all of us: we must be concerned for the next generation. Recite these words continually; impress them onto your children.

- **Personally (v. 8):** This is unlikely to be a command to be enacted literally, as firstborn sons were also to be as 'frontlets between your eyes' (Exod. 13:16). It's an idiom meaning they should be right at the front of your thinking, always on your mind. It's not a surprise, but I don't know anyone who truly delights in God and loves him in a Deuteronomy 6:5 fashion without spending time with God in his word. Jesus remains loyal when he is tempted by quoting from the word of God in Deuteronomy 6.

- **Society (v. 9):** By writing these words on the gates of houses they were ensuring that they were in the public domain. It's easy to dismiss this as a bit of 'the OT being OTT,' but there is a determination here to have one's life shaped by these words of God. How are we doing in a comparable fashion in the twenty-first century?

These words are to permeate every area of national, family and personal life.

Homily on three things that will challenge your love (6:10-19)

Here is advanced warning that loving the LORD whole-heartedly is difficult. Moses highlights three challenges that they'll face in the promised land:

- Do not forget (v. 12).
- Do not follow (v. 14).
- Do not put the LORD to the test (v. 16).

While the first two are clearly warnings of what jeopardises God's promise that they will dwell in the land, the third has a more positive thrust – here, Israel is told how they can secure the land.

Challenge 1: affluence (6:10-12)

Moses will have far more to say on this in chapter 8, but here is a wonderful list of things that Israel will inherit. The NIV obscures some of the obvious links. We would choose to say the list something like this:

- A building ('cities') you did not build
- A full house you did not fill ('provide', NIV)
- Dug pits ('cisterns') that you did not dig
- Plants ('vineyards and olive trees') that you did not plant

In other words, this promised land that they are about to inherit is a land of grace. It is utterly underserved and completely wonderful. The danger is that they will forget that it was the LORD who gave all these material riches to them.

Challenge 2: conformity (6:13-15)

Verse 13 puts Yahweh at the front of each clause: Israel owes everything to him. Yet resisting the flow of a culture is hard! I've met men who grew up in Apartheid South Africa and admit now to being horribly racist in the past. But everyone around them was. I've met a man who was in the Hitler Youth as a young boy. He admitted to having abhorrent opinions in the past. But everyone around him shared those views. It's hard not to chase after the gods of the peoples (v. 14) – be they Baal or whatever is dangled in front of our eyes by adverts and lifestyle magazines.

Verse 15 is a reminder that idolatry is the one sin above all others that invites the curses of the covenant. There is, of course, good jealousy and bad jealousy. Bad jealousy is insecure. It is the husband always asking his faithful spouse, 'Who are you seeing? Why are you talking to him?' Whereas good jealousy might perhaps be translated as being zealous. A man is appropriately zealous for his wife's honour and that of their marriage. Here, it is a sign that the LORD cares. He is not indifferent to his people's unfaithfulness.

Challenge 3: hardship (6:16)

A single event from Israel's history is singled out here – the complaining at Massah (Exod. 17:1-7). Israel's response to a shortage of water was to quarrel with Moses and grumble against the LORD, asking, 'Is God among us or not?' This is described as 'putting the LORD to the test' – essentially demanding that he prove himself to them.

The suggestion is that life in the promised land will be varied. Although Israel will inherit a wonderful land (v. 11), there will be times when they ask, 'Is God among us?' (It is possible that the testing is not for the same reason as at Massah, a lack of water, but rather that in a time of plenty Israel asks, Is God among us? Is it really from him that these blessings come?)

The opposite of testing God (6:17-19)

The opposite of testing God is spelt out in verses 17-19. Israel will enter the land by God's grace because he promised it to them. But the grace that keeps the people in the land is a grace that changes their lives. Only those who live good lives can live in the good land. Or, as Jesus might phrase it, 'Whoever abides in me and I in him, he it is that bears much fruit, for apart from me you can do nothing. If anyone does not abide in me, he is thrown away like a branch and withers' (John 15:5-6).

Eugene Merrill phrases it well:

> The pledge of redemption and conquest by Israel was a settled and non-negotiable matter (the unconditional side of the covenant), but their reality in the experience of individual Israelites or even a generation of them was contingent on covenant faithfulness (the conditional side). Failure to meet the conditions would result in judgment and even defeat and deportation, but it could never cancel out the eternal purposes of God.[3]

Love him because he first loved you (6:20-25)

Verses 20-23 could easily be deleted from the text with no loss of logical flow (v. 24 reads quite naturally after 17-19), but they are essential for capturing the logic of Deuteronomy. When your son asks why the family has to keep the law, the answer is not 'Do as you're told,' and or 'It's good for you.' Instead, the story of redemption is repeated.

In verse 20, the 'testimonies and the statutes and the rules' are three ways of describing the whole law or instruction of Moses. Essentially the son is asking, 'Dad,

---

3. Merrill, *Deuteronomy*, 173.

you know that we live differently to the people around us. We have different values and beliefs to them. Why is that? Why should I live differently to my mates, endure bullying at school and ridicule for believing what I do?'

The answer is: because we have been loved by the LORD. The four main clauses build up to the Israelites' response: 'We were slaves ... he brought us out ... he did signs and wonders ... he commanded us to do'.

Israel was freed by God in order to serve him. This is also a familiar description for a Christian:

- once we were slaves (v. 21);

- but we were rescued by a mighty victory (vv. 21-22);

- we are looking forward to the promised land (v. 23);

- so we respond to his grace by living for him in the power that he gives us (vv. 24-25).

The meaning of the law was found in the good news of what God had done by his grace for Israel. No Israelite would have kept the command to love the LORD with all his heart, soul and might unless he had a clear view of his rescue and his destination in the promised land. The Christian preacher will need to place this story of Deuteronomy 6:20-25 within the wider Bible frame:

When our children ask us in days to come, what is the meaning of the ordinances and customs that we observe, then we will say: 'We were slaves to sin, but the Lord Jesus rescued us from the kingdom of darkness and ushered us into his glorious kingdom of light, through his death and resurrection. He has brought us out in fulfilment of his promises and in accordance with his glorious plan of salvation, conceived before the foundation of the world. So the Lord commanded us to demonstrate our fear and love for him by keeping his commands for our good always and as an expression of our relationship with him. It will be a testimony to our righteousness, won by Christ, if we are careful to show that we love the Lord with all our hearts as he has commanded us. One day we will hear him say, "Well done, good and faithful servant" as we enter the promised land of glory.[4]

From text to message

Getting the message clear: the theme

God's uniqueness means that there is no other god. All that you have been given materially and spiritually comes from him and so the response is to love him.

Getting the message clear: the aim

Love the Lord with your emotions, your thoughts and actions, and your possessions and abilities. Give him every part of you.

A way in

We recently went on a tour of the D-Day Normandy landing sites and museums. Apart from the extraordinary planning that went on ahead of the invasion and the bravery of the men involved, the thing that jumped out from reading letters and commentary was *loyalty*. Men in the 1940s were not really focused on expressions of love or getting in touch with their feelings, but they loved one another. It was obvious in their loyalty to one another, their determination to never leave a man behind, and their refusal to abandon their mission because they knew others were relying on them. Their love was seen in complete loyalty to the cause and their fellow soldiers. It was a

---

4. Adapted from Block (Block, *Deuteronomy*, 202).

love that sacrificed everything, even their lives. Here, in Deuteronomy 6, Yahweh is calling for a love that is seen in loyalty to him.

Ideas for application

- Some conceive of love for the Lord in emotional terms; others in very practical terms. The command of 6:5 demands not merely emotive love nor outward compliance. It's both. It's worth asking a Christian which way they tend to lean and therefore what probably needs adjusting. This is a love rooted in the heart but demonstrated in daily choices.

- It's worth asking how we expect 'these words' (the words of the whole book; v. 6) to be on our heart. If this is the way that love for the Lord will grow, then how are we ensuring that it happens? Are we concerned personally and also for the next generation?

- Are we aware of what the great challenges are to our love for the Lord? Are we aware of the pull of trusting in affluence, conformity to the gods of our culture, and a grumbling testing of the Lord?

- Are we telling one another the story of salvation and reminding one another of God's good promises? If we fail to do that, the cost of obeying God's commands may seem a bit arbitrary. Yet if we remember what the Lord has done and has promised, then loving him is the obvious response.

Suggestions for preaching

Chapter 6 is a very natural unit to take as one sermon. If you are doing a short series, it is possible to cover chapters 5 and 6 together. Chapter 5 could be a longish introduction and then the bulk of the sermon could be on chapter 6 as, in some sense, the unpacking of the first commandment.

A simple structure could be along these lines:

Love the LORD with all you've got

- Love the LORD with everything (6:4-9)
- Love the LORD with loyalty (6:10-19)
- Love him because he first loved you (6:20-25)

Questions to help understand the passage

1. What seems to be the main point of contact between chapters 5 and 6? (What is emphasised in the first four commands of the Decalogue? How is this similar in chapter 6, for example vv. 5, 13-15?)

2. So, what do you think 'the commandment' (singular) is in verses 1 and 25 (given the emphatic nature of v. 5)?

3. What does the LORD desire for Israel in verses 1-3?

4. Having read chapter 5 (especially 5:6-10), what do you think it means that 'the LORD is one' (cf. 6:14-15)?

5. What does it mean to love the LORD with heart, soul, and might (v. 5)?

6. How was Israel to take responsibility for having 'these words' on their hearts (vv. 6-9)?

7. What is the danger that Israel is warned of in verses 10-12?

8. What is the danger that Israel is warned of in verses 13-15?

9. What is the danger that Israel is warned of in verse 16? What happened at Massah (cf. Exod. 17:1-7)?

10. What is the antidote to this testing (vv. 17-19)? What was required for the people to hold onto the promise of God?

11. What is the question being asked in verse 20? What is the answer that is given?

12. What, ultimately, was the purpose of the Lord's redeeming Israel from slavery and taking them into the promised land (v. 24)?

Questions to help apply the passage

Verses 4-9

1. Practically, what encouragement is there for us in knowing that Yahweh (the Lord) is unique? What does that mean for our security, his promises, the future of the world?

2. Love is meant to be from the heart – what does that tell you about what it involves?

3. Love is commanded – what does that tell you about what it involves?

4. Talk about what each of these three words means – heart, soul, might. Why does Jesus add 'mind' in Mark 12:32-33?

5. None of us are going to claim to do this perfectly, but which arena do we think we need to address most – your heart/emotions; your soul/thoughts and actions; or your might/resources?

6. What is required for anyone to have the word of God on their heart (Deut. 30:6; John 3:3-6)?

7. What are you doing to ensure that these words are on your heart (v. 6)?

Verses 10-19

8. Have you known times when life is going well and you have the resources you need? Have you known the temptation to forget the Lord? How is thanksgiving a great antidote (vv. 10-12)?

9. Are you conscious of the pressure to conform with the gods of the surrounding culture? If not, does that mean you've already begun to serve these other gods (vv. 13-15)?

10. Which of the gods of the twenty-first century world has the greatest appeal for you?

11. Verse 16: What circumstances cause you most to grumble, test the LORD and ask, 'Is God really there? Is he on my side?'

12. Look up Matthew 4:1-11. What was dangled in front of Jesus when he was tested? How did he resist? (What did he quote?)

Verses 20-25

13. Have you been asked, 'Why should I live differently to the world around me? What's the point in doing that?'

14. How is Moses's answer in verses 21-24 similar to the answer a Christian would give? Can you rephrase it entirely into Christian language?

15. To avoid confusion, in what sense is obedience in response to God's promises, righteousness for us (v. 25; cf. John 15:5-6 and James 2:20-26)?

5.
Chosen for Holiness
(Deuteronomy 7)

Introduction

If you are preaching an overview series of Deuteronomy (again, that's quite a sensible idea when preaching it for the first time), then it is entirely possible to preach chapters 7–11 in one sermon. The uniting theme is 11:16 where it says, 'Take care lest your heart be deceived.'

Three times across these chapters we read a phrase like 'Do not say in your heart' (7:17; 8:17; 9:4) and Olson provides the pleasing headings of 'Beware the Gods of Militarism, Materialism and Moralism.'[1] These were all challenges to Israel's wholehearted love of the Lord which has just been commanded in chapter 6. However, it is a rich section and each chapter 'preaches well' and so chapters 7–11 can also be preached very effectively as several sermons.

Chapter 7 is clearly a tricky and, at first read, an offensive text. It is important to remember that Moses is not primarily declaring legislation but preaching for effect. The

---

1. Olson, *Deuteronomy and the Death of Moses*, 52.

main point of the chapter is 'Do not compromise.' Don't compromise morally, spiritually or doctrinally. Do not compromise with other religions. There must be a radical distinctiveness about God's people.

Listening to the text

We're still in the section of chapters 5–11, dealing with the fundamental covenant stipulation – love the LORD with all your heart. There is, biblically speaking, little new here: the law on destroying Canaanite religion has already been given in Exodus 23:20-33. The LORD also gave them the reason there: 'They shall not dwell in your land, lest they make you sin against me; for if you serve their gods, it will surely be a snare to you' (Exod. 23:33). Block helpfully observes that while the law is given in a mere 150 words in Exodus, this is a sermon preached with rhetorical effect in Deuteronomy, hence needing longer (350 words).[2] The focus is not on the act of 'devoting to destruction' but on Israel's unique status and the need to preserve it. Divine grace which requires holy living is at the heart of the chapter.

We must remember that Israel was the hope of the world (4:5-8). They were meant to be distinctive and attractive to the watching world around them. So there is

- a short-term aim: the destruction of the dangerous Canaanites …

    in order to fulfil …

- a longer-term aim: blessing for the world through God's chosen people.

---

2. Block, *Deuteronomy*, 206-8.

Structure

7:1-5   Devote to destruction so that your sons don't bow
          down to other gods

          7:6-11   God chose you to be holy

          7:12-16 God will bless your obedience

          7:17-21 God is in your midst

7:22-26 Devote to destruction so you're not ensnared by
         other gods

Working through the text

Do not compromise (7:1-5)

It is clearly Yahweh's work that they are entering the
land, as the seven nations – listed to give the sense of how
overwhelming they must have felt – are 'more numerous
and mightier than you. Verses 1-2c are a long, multi-part
'*when*' clause concluding with '*then* you must devote them
to complete destruction'. The Hebrew word *herem* can be
explained as 'an absolute and irrevocable renouncing of
things or persons, a refusal to take any gain or profit from
them'.[3]

The following verses, 2d-5, explain what this does
not mean. They are not to destroy through assimilation
(v. 4); nor is it possible that the polytheism of altars to
Baal and Asherah poles can coexist with Yahweh, who is
unique (v. 5). Notice that the stress of verse 5 falls upon
the destruction of altars, pillars and images, rather than
the peoples.

What this looks like in practice is a little harder to say.
Clearly, Israel could capture cities whole as the spoils of

---

3. Wright, *Deuteronomy*, 109.

war because God has told them that they would (6:10-11). Later in Deuteronomy, a distinction is drawn between cities at a distance and Canaanite cities, and a preference is expressed for peace through negotiation for the former (20:10-20).

When we read the following accounts, only in four places is this *herem* – devotion to destruction – actually carried out (the cities of Jericho in Josh. 6:24; Ai in Josh. 8:28; Hazor in Josh. 11:13-14; Laish in Judges 18:27). Although not entirely clear, the Jebusites appear to be absorbed into the tribe of Judah after the capture of Jerusalem (2 Sam. 5:6-10). McConville captures the reality well: 'The concept of complete annihilation of the nations is always a kind of ideal, symbolising the need for radical loyalty.'[4]

It's worth stressing that this is not genocide, as it is not an assault on the basis of race or ethnicity. Rather, it is the wiping out of an utterly wicked group of idolaters. Chapter 12:31 describes the Canaanites in these terms: 'Every abominable thing that the Lord hates they have done for their gods, for they even burn their sons and their daughters in the fire to their gods.'

When we see the conquest of Canaan as God's judgment upon an utterly wicked people, it moves it out of the (mislabelled) category of genocide and into the category of God's judicial sentence falling upon the wicked.

We find ourselves longing that Moses's audience had listened more carefully when we read later in the Bible that 'Judah did what was evil in the sight of the Lord ... they also built for themselves high places and pillars and Asherim on every high hill. ... They did according to all

---

4. McConville, *Deuteronomy*, 161.

the abominations of the nations that the LORD drove out before the people of Israel' (1 Kings 14:22-24).

The key point is that Israel was the only hope for the world and so had to remain holy and distinctive without compromise in order to tell the world about the true and unique God.

The truth of God's revelation was at stake.

The LORD chose you (7:6-11)

The logic is: God chose you,

> not because you were numerous
>> but because he loves you and promised.
>>> *Therefore* know (v. 9), and do (v. 11).

Israel needs to know of God's love for them if they are going to keep 'the commandment and the statutes and the rules' (the last time these three appear in combination, after 5:31 and 6:1).

Israel's status as a chosen people is certainly no basis for pride as the choice found its origin in God rather than in them. Rather, her status as chosen brings added responsibility to be worthy of her calling.

We recognise the language of 'treasured possession' from Exodus 19:5. It is also used of Israel in Deuteronomy 14:2 and 26:18 but then rarely otherwise (Ps. 135:4) until the LORD promises through Malachi that he will have a new treasured possession of those who fear him (Mal. 3:17). Preachers need to bring home the delight of this as it's central to the motivation for godly living here.

There is similarity and difference in Israel's status and that of the Christian:

- There is similarity in that election brings responsibility. Just as, here in Deuteronomy 7, 'The LORD chose Israel ... therefore be careful to do the commandment', so the Christian knows that 'he [the Father] chose us in him [Christ] before the foundation of the world, that we should be holy and blameless before him' (Eph. 1:4).

- Yet there is a level of threat here and conditionality which is far greater than the warnings of the New Testament. As we read through Deuteronomy, it becomes obvious that if Yahweh is going to keep 'the oath that he swore to your fathers' then something radical and not-yet-explained will need to happen. Israel in Moab was a people *not characterized* by regeneration, so the law aggravated nationalistic and legalistic pride. Israel needed the promise of a new heart which will come in chapter 30.

- Overall, there is continuity between the covenants, but the new covenant is wildly greater. The preacher must not flatten salvation history! It would have been far more uncomfortable being an Israelite under Mosaic law than it is to be a Christian under Christ. Moses is far less clear on grace, at this stage of history, as he proclaimed a covenant of types and shadows.

The LORD provides for you (7:12-16)

These verses assume that verse 11 has been kept: 'because you listen ... and do' (v. 12). All of the blessings of verses 13-16 depend upon Israel's obedience. To phrase the question bluntly: Can Israel lose its privileged status? For a time, yes, although never ultimately. As Wright observes: 'Obedience to the law was not the means of gaining the covenant, but the means of maintaining and enjoying it.'[5] Correcting a wrong understanding of election is important in the whole of chapters 7–11. While acknowledging the differences of the new covenant, Christians, like Israel, must avoid a wrong concept of election which presumes upon God's grace as an excuse for immorality.

As well as insisting upon obedience as response to their election, verses 12-15 encourage Israel that Yahweh is the source of all the blessings that they desire. It is foolishness to turn to other gods, because it is the LORD who has the power to give them blessing in the land. Yet even though it would be folly, verse 16 is a reminder that the system of fertility worship had a seductive pull. Even today, it is easy to be drawn to what is seen and felt, rather than to trust by faith in the true God who provides.

So do not fear but destroy false worship (7:17-26)

Verse 17 is the first of the three 'If you say in your heart' statements in chapters 7–9. The issue is that they are afraid (v. 18) and dread the other nations (v. 21) because they are larger and stronger (v. 1). The antidote is to 'remember what the LORD your God did to Pharaoh and to all Egypt'. As Craigie phrases it: 'There was a danger that they might let their minds reflect on the strength of their enemy rather than upon the strength of their God.'[6] In particular, they should remember:

- God's power (vv. 18-20). He conquered mighty Egypt and so he can certainly handle these relatively small nations. He has shown that he can achieve this.

---

5. Wright, *Deuteronomy*, 117.

6. Craigie, *The Book of Deuteronomy*, 181.

- God's presence (vv. 21-22). He is in your midst.
- God's promise (vv. 22-24). See the repeated emphasis that 'he will'. They needed to remember that the key to victory lay with God not with them.

Verses 25-26 return to the central concern of the chapter. Here, the focus is very obviously upon the carved images that are an abomination. In these concluding verses, it is the images (and not the Canaanite people) which are to be devoted to destruction, which reveals that it is not just fear of opponents in view but also the allure of idols.

The strength of language reveals that it was clearly a very real temptation that Israel would succumb to her fear and coveting. They must not be ensnared by an abomination (the first of twelve references in Deuteronomy). The sorry story of Achan in Joshua 7 reveals how serious it was to avoid compromise on this issue.

From text to message

Getting the message clear: the theme

Israel had been chosen by God to be his treasured possession, holy to the LORD. This should deliver them from fear and compromise when they enter the promised land and are scared that they are unable to resist the Canaanites.

Getting the message clear: the aim

Do not compromise with the culture around you out of fear, but live distinctively as a people holy to the Lord.

A way in

With hindsight we might ask: How was it that the majority of German Protestant churches in the 1930s compromised with the Nazi regime? Compromise seemed like a good idea at the time. It meant that the churches did not have to fear what would happen to them. They could still get on with teaching the Bible and happily meet together on Sunday. However, it was a disastrous compromise that discredited those churches for years.

Ideas for application

- Moses is warning against other gods that challenge Yahweh. Even for Israel, it was not *primarily* Baal and Ashtaroth that were the temptation, but rather the fear of political powers (ch. 7), the self-sufficiency that wealth provides (ch. 8) and self-righteousness (chs. 9–10). Those three remain today.

- In particular, here in chapter 7, there is a strong warning about the contagious power of the physical world. Being drawn away from the Lord to what we can see and hold tangibly is a timeless temptation. This chapter warns that it is seductive and an abomination, especially when you are scared about what happens when you stand up to the culture that surrounds you.

- Don't be afraid of the political or cultural powers around you. Remember who your God is! In some countries, this is a daily struggle as you are told to place allegiance to the state ahead of Jesus. In other places, the squeeze is on and the temptation is more to go quiet on parts of the Bible that will be unpopular with the surrounding world. Yahweh had done the harder thing in rescuing Israel from Egypt, and now he would do the easier thing in conquering the Canaanites. In a similar way, the Lord has done the harder thing in moving us from death to life, and he will do the easier thing of helping us to resist sin. We can trust in his power and his presence with us.

- At the same time, we have a role to play in resisting sin. We may recoil from the violent language of Deuteronomy 7, but it's worth remembering that Jesus demanded similar aggression against pervasive threats to our love for God. In Matthew 6, he states that if a hand causes you to sin, then you should cut it off, and if an eye causes you to sin, then gouge it out. In other words, sometimes drastic steps are required to prevent you becoming compromised and drifting away from the love of God. This is a really helpful passage to preach in order to strengthen people's resolve in their battle with sin.

- The holiness of God's people matters (1 Pet. 2:9-12)! It is an important accent in the book of Deuteronomy (7:6; 14:2, 21; 26:19; 28:19) and is perhaps stressed here more than many places in the Old Testament.

Although it is not the application of the text, it is unwise to preach this chapter without an eye on apologetics. This is not genocide, as destruction was not on the grounds of race or ethnicity but idolatry. It is worth remembering that the LORD promised Israel that the same judgments would fall upon them if they became idolatrous like the Canaanites (Deut. 28–29). There are numerous helpful books to read. Chris Wright's *The God I Don't Understand* is very useful as he is very familiar with Deuteronomy as well as the apologetics issues. In simple terms this command was:

1. *limited* (Only four cities are recorded as being destroyed.)

2. *judicial* (The Canaanites were abhorrent. Israel could not tolerate child sacrifice any more than the Allies could tolerate Auschwitz.)

3. *unique* (Christians do not live in one physical land this side of heaven.)

All the way back in Genesis 15, God had told Abraham that the Canaanites would be destroyed but not at that point because their sin was 'not yet complete.' In other words, a group had to reach utterly abhorrent levels of wickedness for the LORD to act in such a comprehensive act of justice in history. No other Old Testament war is described in these terms. The command to carry out *herem* is uniquely applied to the conquest of Canaan and the removal of all threats to Israel's distinctiveness.

Suggestions for preaching

As indicated above, you could preach chapters 7–11 as one sermon:

- Don't say in your heart, 'I can't resist the pull of the culture' (7:17)
- Don't say in your heart, 'I achieved success' (8:17)
- Don't say in your heart, 'I am superior to you' (9:4)
- ⇨ But you need a circumcised heart (10:16)

For chapter 7, a simple structure could be along these lines:

Chosen for holiness

- Don't serve other gods as the LORD has chosen you (7:1-16)
- Don't fear other nations as the LORD is with you (7:17-24)

- You're a treasured possession chosen for holiness
  (cf. 1 Peter 2:9-10)

Questions to help understand the passage

1. What is stressed about the nations in the land
   (vv. 1-2)?

2. What is Israel to do and how is that explained
   (vv. 3-5)?

3. Who is responsible for the defeat of the Canaanites
   (v. 2)?

4. How is Israel described (v. 6)?

5. Why was she chosen (negatively and positively)
   (vv. 7-8)?

6. What do they need to know and what will that
   enable them to do (vv. 10-11)?

7. Who is the source of all the material blessings Israel
   will desire in the land? Is it Baal and Ashtoreth
   (vv. 12-16)?

8. What might the Israelites say in their heart (or
   mumble under their breath) when they encounter
   the nations in Canaan (v. 17)? What causes this
   mumbling (v. 18)?

9. What should deliver them from this fear (vv. 18-24)?

10. So what should be done with the idols and why
    (vv. 25-26)?

Questions to help apply the passage

1. What is it in your life that does most damage to
   your wholehearted love for Jesus? What are you
   doing about it?

2. What sins are you putting to death right now?

3. Do you think you ever take the sort of radical steps that Jesus insists upon (Matt. 5:29-30)?

4. Where are you most vulnerable to compromising theologically?

5. Where are you most vulnerable to compromising morally?

6. What does it mean for you to be a part of God's treasured possession?

6.

Don't Take Pride in
Your Success
(Deuteronomy 8)

Introduction

We're still in a section (chs. 7–9) on the dangers to wholehearted obedience to the LORD. Chapter 8 contains the second of the three warnings: 'Do not say in your heart' (7:17; 8:17; 9:4). This is within the larger section of chapters 5–11 addressing the fundamental covenant stipulations ahead of the detailed chapters 12–26.

I hope it's an encouragement to preachers to say that, if it is read well to a church family, chapter 8 addresses such timeless concerns that it barely needs any further comment! Moses has given us a great sermon! McConville calls it 'perhaps the greatest statement of human dependence on God for everything.'[1]

Listening to the text

The key language of the text is 'remembering' or 'not forgetting' (vv. 2, 11, 14, 18, 19). In particular, it is forgetting God and taking pride in the affluence that your labours

---

1. McConville, *Deuteronomy*, 162.

have achieved, rather than acknowledging that he is the one who provides. Each of the three warnings: 'Do not say in your heart' in chapters 7–9 is followed by a call to 'remember' or 'not forget' the LORD's actions. Herein lies the key to obedience. By contrast, the temptation to forget the LORD and their dependence upon him will be a constant one for every generation of God's people. Remembering is not *just* a moral failure – it is also presented as a relational one. Forgetting all that the LORD had done was offensive to the God who had rescued and sustained them.

It is one of the chapters in the book with a dense concentration of 'heart' (vv. 2, 5, 14, 17).[2] The question lurking in the chapter is over whether Israel has learned the lesson of God's miraculous provision in the wilderness: that they are dependent upon him. The movement towards a negative conclusion to the chapter indicates that they have not learned this lesson. (This becomes explicit in 29:4.)

Notice the typical Deuteronomy reference to 'today' in verses 1, 11 and 19. As throughout the book, 'today' is the day of decision. Each day is one when we must resolve not to murmur in our hearts but to trust the Lord.

Structure

Intro: You need to do the commandment (v. 1)

Remember God's provision in the wilderness (vv. 2-6)

For he's bringing you to a land of abundance (vv. 7-10)

Take care lest you forget (v. 11)

Lest you forget him in the land of abundance (vv. 12-13)

Remember God's provision in the wilderness (vv. 14-17)

---

2. The heart has four references in chapters 4, 8, 28, 29 and *eight* references in the crucial chapter 30.

Conclusion: If you remember you'll live but if you forget, you'll perish (vv. 18-20)

Working through the text

You need to do the commandment (8:1)

In verse 1 Moses returns to speaking about 'the whole commandment' (singular; see comment on 6:4 – the fundamental commandment is loyalty to the LORD). The rest of the chapter is clear that in order to 'do' this commandment they will need to remember and avoid forgetting (keep the commandment(s); vv. 1, 2, 6, 11). Although they cannot be collapsed into each other, there is a sense in which to remember the LORD means to depend upon him, which means to obey him, which means to love him. Craigie expresses it well: 'The act of remembering prompts obedience to the covenant law, for it brings to the forefront of the mind, the reality and faithfulness of God; forgetfulness is tantamount to disobedience, for the self and human concerns have pushed to the background of the mind the reality and claims of God.'[3]

Remember God's provision in the wilderness (8:2-6)

Moses is not denying that Israel's wandering in the wilderness was a punishment for her rebellion (1:34-40) but here focuses upon the positive function of their wandering: God humbled them (not so much here as punishment but for education) to test them. There are two aspects to this test:

1. A test of obedience (v. 2)
2. To teach them (v. 3)

---

3. Craigie, *The Book of Deuteronomy*, 185.

Avoid getting tied in knots over the limits of divine knowledge, prompted by the text saying God was 'testing you to know what was in your heart' (v. 2). There is no need to deny omniscience by saying he lacked knowledge or by crushing the language of the text with systematic considerations. While God is unchanging, he does relate to us in real time. He has conversations with humans in time and space.[4] Deuteronomy 8 is saying much the same as 1 Peter 1:6-7: '[F]or a little while, if necessary, you have been grieved by various trials, so that the tested genuineness of your faith – more precious than gold that perishes though it is tested by fire – may be found to result in praise and glory and honour at the revelation of Jesus Christ.'

Verse 3 reveals God's great provision was so that 'he might make you know that man does not live by bread alone, but man lives by every word that comes from the mouth of the LORD.' This is obviously not meaning 'food is irrelevant and you just need the Bible', but rather that they were dependent upon God. Natural means and their own resources were not enough to get Israel through the wilderness. They required God to supernaturally provide for them. The wilderness removed normal human resources but instead God provided a divine internet order every morning! More than that, their clothing did not wear out and they couldn't even get a blister (v. 4). The LORD was

---

4. I'm grateful to James Robson for drawing my attention to Bruce Ware's helpful comment on immutability: 'Scripture does not lead us to think of God as unchangeable in every respect (absolute immutability). Importantly, God is changeable *in relationship* with his creation. … In this relational mutability, God does not change in his essential nature, purpose, will, knowledge or wisdom; but he does interact with his people in the experiences of their lives as these unfold in time' (Bruce Ware, *God's Lesser Glory* (Leicester: Apollos, 2001), 73-74).

disciplining them (v. 5) – again, not in the sense of punitive discipline but remedial. He was educating them. He was training Israel to learn that they could rely on him and indeed, they had no choice but to rely upon him.

Verse 6 reveals that the purpose of this divine tuition was that they keep the commandments of the God who provides for them. To depend upon the LORD means to remember him, which means to obey him, which means to love him.

These words in 8:2-6 will provide the background for the even more solemn charge of 29:1-5.

For he's bringing you to a land of abundance (8:7-13)

Verses 7-11 are one long temporal sentence: 'When the LORD brings you in ... be careful.' The description of the land is rhetorical in its abundance and is obviously a contrast to the barren wilderness. As opposed to the scarcity of the wandering years, now they 'will eat bread without scarcity' and 'lack nothing' (v. 9). Essential goods are there but also treats such as honey. The appropriate response to their satisfaction should be that they bless the LORD 'for the good land he has given you' (v. 10).[5]

In verse 11, to forget the LORD involves two things:

1. neglecting to remember all that God has provided for them, whether miraculous in the wilderness, or now in the land of plenty (remember vv. 2, 16)

2. failure to keep his commandments, rules and statutes.

---

5. 'Good land' appears in 1:25, 35; 3:25; 4:21, 22; 6:18; 8:7, 10; 9:6 and 11:17.

These two are intimately connected: if you recall who God is and how he has treated you, you will want to obey him.

Obedience is further explained in verses 12-14. Here, the focus is not simply on the land's natural resources (as it was in verses 12-13) but also upon how Israel uses the resources. By focusing on what they had achieved with the God-given resources the temptation was that they would become proud.

Remember God's provision in the wilderness (8:14-17)

The pride described in verse 14 comes from forgetting what God had done in the past (vv. 14-16) and also ignoring the fact that he provides you with the *strength* to achieve anything in the present (vv. 17-18). This is important in application – it's not just that God gives us opportunities; he gives us the strength to make use of them. He could have withdrawn your strength at any point resulting in your having nothing!

Note again in verse 16 that the wilderness experience was meant to teach them dependence upon him: '[T]hat he might humble you and test you'. This passage is different from 6:10-11 where they were going to inherit wealth. Here, the Israelites are tempted to think that they are entrepreneurs who have generated wealth by themselves.

Conclusion (8:18-20)

Barker observes that there is a movement from positive to negative through the chapter.[6] Whereas verse 1 has a positive motivation, by the time we get to verses 18-20 there is a negative threat. While verses 7-10 end in praise, verses 12-18 end in forgetfulness and pride. The exhortation to

---

6. Barker, *The Triumph of Grace*, 76.

obey appears four times in the first half of the chapter but is absent in the second half, perhaps suggesting that this exhortation will be ignored.

Wright comments: 'Following chapter 7 with commands to ruthlessly exterminate the nations, this threat [of v. 20] is particularly chilling.'[7] We must remember that Deuteronomy presupposes the fallen human condition. We inherently have hearts unable to respond rightly to God. McConville helpfully summarises the logic of obedience in chapter 8: 'Yahweh gives, therefore Israel must obey (as in 7:11) and on the other hand Israel must obey in order to continue to possess (7:12). The appeal to the promise to the patriarchs in 8:1 holds this balance.'[8]

(The preacher must make a decision on how frequently to remind their hearers that Deuteronomy has two melodies playing throughout. The resolution only comes in chapter 30. Yet it would be very tedious if we preached each sermon as a call to choose to love and obey the Lord but undermined that appeal each week by saying, 'Of course Israel didn't but Jesus did – phew.' Preachers need to teach both that Christians hear these texts with different hearts to the Israelites AND that we are still called to love and obey the Lord.)

From text to message

Getting the message clear: the theme

There's a real danger that when life goes well and we have successfully created affluence, we may forget that God gave us all that we have and become proud.

---

7. Wright, *Deuteronomy*, 128.

8. McConville, *Deuteronomy*, 168.

Getting the message clear: the aim

Don't say in your heart, 'Look at what *I* have achieved,' but instead, respond with faithful obedience.

A way in

Can you name the most popular song played at funerals for each of the last four decades? I'm sure that you can with a little thought. Yes, it's 'My Way', most popularly performed by Frank Sinatra. It's a rousing song celebrating one man's achievement.

> *Yes, there were times, I'm sure you knew*
> *When I bit off more than I could chew*
> *But through it all, when there was doubt*
> *I ate it up and spit it out,*
> *I faced it all and I stood tall*
> *And did it my way …*

And Deuteronomy 8 warns us, 'Don't say that!'

Ideas for application

- Human resources are not enough! That is the point of the central declaration of 8:3. We are utterly reliant upon his provision.

- It's a timeless temptation to believe that 'my power and the might of my hand have gained me this wealth [or success]'. We have to remember the Lord!

  o You might say in your heart, 'Look at the wealth I've created.'

    But the Lord gave you the raw materials.

  o You might say, 'No one gave me wealth – it's my brain and talent that have earned it.'

    But the Lord gave you an agile mind and creative abilities.

○ You might say in your heart, 'Maybe, but I worked harder than other people to make use of them.'

But the Lord gave you the power to work hard.

○ Dare I suggest to some readers: You might say in your heart, 'I've grown a church due to my preaching, leading and hard work.'

But the Lord arranged all of the circumstances of your church; he gave you a receptive congregation, good models you learned from and the health to keep going.

- Deuteronomy 8 is a helpful passage when people are struggling with the problem of fitting together God's provision and my labours. When Jesus tells us not to be anxious and that God is a Father who will provide what we need (Matt. 6), he does not envisage us lounging on our sofas all day long awaiting a divine paycheck to arrive. God gives us the gifts with which to create wealth. Our role is to use them and give thanks, recognizing that he gives us the might of our hands in order to earn money.

- As with each of these sermons in chapters 7, 8 and 9 we need to ask the question, 'What are you saying in your heart?' This is not referring to a transitory thought but rather a pattern of rebellious thinking that is deep-seated. What are the thoughts that commonly roll around in your head? Are they thoughts like 'Look at what I've achieved' or rather 'Look what the Lord has given me and enabled me to do?'

- Jesus was also tested in the wilderness so that God might know what was in his heart (8:2). Jesus did not rely upon his own strength or wisdom. He relied upon his Father's provision. He was, of course, the true and obedient Son whereas Israel was not. The Christian does not fear as Israel feared, because Christ has secured our place in the promised land of heaven. Yet we must not presume upon election, like Israel did. We must heed the warning 'Do not forget'.

- Christians hear this chapter with born-again hearts. The basic question remains the same for Christians as it was for Israel: Will you take pride in your achievements or will you give thanks to God and recognize your dependence upon him? However, we do not fear as Israel did (vv. 18-20), as we know Jesus 'perished for us'. Christians have new hearts and so have a power to resist this sin that Israel did not. However, the temptation to rely upon self and the resources we have in this world remains huge.

Suggestions for preaching

- Remember God's provision in the barren past (8:2-11)
- Don't forget it's God's provision in the wealthy future (8:11-18)
- ⇨ Depend upon the Lord

Questions to help understand the passage

1. The LORD gives Israel a history lesson. What is the big danger in the chapter (vv. 2, 11, 14, 18, 19)?

2. What are the two reasons we are told that the LORD led Israel for forty years in the wilderness (vv. 2-3)?

3. How did Israel survive in the wilderness (vv. 3-4, 14-16)?

4. What were they meant to learn (vv. 5-6)?

5. What is about to happen (vv. 7-10)?

6. What is the danger (vv. 11-14)? In particular, what might they say (v. 17)? (How does this relate to 7:17 and 9:4?)

7. What must they remember (v. 18)?

Questions to help apply the passage

1. Do you think our culture tends to celebrate independent entrepreneurs or does it recognize that success comes from the opportunities we have been given?

2. Do you recognise that God has given you all that you have? When are we tempted to think, 'Yes, but that success was down to me'?

3. Have times of hardship taught you lasting lessons of dependence upon the Lord?

4. How can giving thanks and 'blessing the Lord'(v. 10) be a great antidote to pride in your accumulation?

5. What is the parallel for the Christian to not forgetting the Lord's activity in 8:14-16?

6. What can you do to maintain your dependence upon the Lord in times when you have plenty and life appears to be under your control?

7. What can we learn from Jesus quoting Deuteronomy 8 as a response to the temptation of not relying upon God (Matt. 4:4)?

7.

How Will You Enter
the Promised Land?

(Deuteronomy 9:1–10:11)

Introduction

This is a rich and cleverly constructed section which continues to give us little confidence that Israel will actually obey the LORD. Since the call of 6:5 to 'Love the LORD your God with all your heart', Moses has warned the people of the challenges to wholehearted love. After compromise (ch. 7) and pride in material wealth (ch. 8), Moses here warns against self-righteousness with the third 'Do not say in your heart …' (7:17; 8:17; 9:4).

Moses tells them not to say, 'It is because of my righteousness that the LORD has brought me in to possess this land' (9:4) and underlines the point by saying that their possession of the land is 'not because of your righteousness' (9:5, 6). The question which they have in common with us is: 'On what basis will you enter the promised land?'

Much of the chapter retells the story of Israel's rebellion with the golden calf at Mount Sinai (Horeb). It is the second account of Israel's failure told at length in Deuteronomy, after the account of rebellion at Kadesh Barnea in chapter 1. Our expectations of Israel's success continue to be managed downwards! They are a helpless, weak and sinful people. Their only hope is the grace of God, and in particular here they need one to intercede between them and the LORD – just like we do. Compared to the Exodus account, Moses here seems to stress the importance of his intercession and God's graciousness even more highly. We are being prepared for the fact that Israel will not love the LORD wholeheartedly; they need a mediator.

Listening to the text

Block views 9:1 as the third major section of the second address (4:45–26:19) due to the 'Hear, O Israel'. Yet in subject matter we are still looking at the challenges to Israel's wholehearted love.

The section is held together by repeated references to possessing the land or dispossessing other nations: (vv. 1, 3, twice in 4, twice in 5, 6, 23; 10:11). How will Israel possess the land? It is not due to them; it is because of God's grace grounded in his promises.

Structure

9:1-6   Don't falsely claim that you'll possess the land because you are righteous

9:7-24   A review of your history will show that you are stubbornly rebellious

9:25–10:11   The only way the covenant is preserved is through your mediator

Working through the text

The Lord gives you the land to possess (9:1-6)

The section begins with a reminder of the challenge ahead (vv. 1-2): the nations are 'greater and mightier than you' and include the dreaded Anakim.

Yet Israel is not to fear (v. 3) but rather 'Know [cf. 9:6] …
that he who goes over before you as a consuming fire is the
LORD your God. He will destroy them and subdue them
before you.' He will destroy the nations and therefore Israel
will drive them out, 'as the LORD has promised you.' (The
preacher is wise to keep bearing in mind the offence this
invasion causes to the modern mind and perhaps remind
the congregation that this destruction of the Canaanites
was limited, judicial and unique; cf. ch. 7.)

Consequently, it would be madness to say in your heart
'after *the LORD your God has thrust them out* before you',
that it is because of my righteousness (vv. 4-6). It is not
merit that gets Israel in but it is the work of God. He drives
the nations out (three times in vv. 3, 4, 5).

The imagined Israelite speaker assumes himself to be
morally virtuous, but this is quickly revealed to be smug
self-righteousness with three brief arguments:

1. The Canaanites were utterly wicked (v. 4b). That
   does not mean that you are upright (v. 5a), merely
   that there are people more deplorable than you. (We
   might say, Oh, so you're not a serial killer? Erm, well
   done, but that doesn't make you a righteous person.)

2. The reason you will possess the land is that the LORD
   is keeping his promises to the patriarchs (v. 5b).

3. To clarify further, you are not righteous; in fact,
   you're incredibly stubborn (v. 6). (Compare 10:16 –
   and notes – where 'stubborn' is paralleled with having
   an uncircumcised heart. Here is the real problem.)
   They must 'know', not in the sense of cognitively
   comprehend, but rather have a deep-seated trust in
   God's work and his provision for them.

Mr Israelite says, 'I have got into the promised land because I am a more righteous person than those Canaanites. I'm morally better.' Don't say that!

Israel is stubbornly rebellious (9:7-24)

Remember your rebellion (9:7)

The section is framed by references to Israel being rebellious (v. 7 and v. 24). Although Horeb will be the focus, the habitual nature of this rebellion is stressed in verse 7 ('from the day you came out of the land of Egypt until you came to this place') and also in verses 22-24 ('You have been rebellious against the LORD from the day that I knew you').

We get a double imperative in verse 7: 'remember' and 'do not forget' how Israel provoked the LORD, which perhaps reveals how strong the tendency towards self-righteousness is.

Recalling the events of Sinai (9:8-11)

This pattern of rebellion was evident 'even at Horeb'. At the first church in the wilderness (Acts 7:38), at the place where the LORD revealed his terrifying glory – the place where the law was given. Even after that generation had witnessed the plagues and the parting of the Red Sea, after the LORD's rescue of them out of slavery – even there and even then, they rebelled.

The LORD's response (9:12-14)

1. He distances himself from Israel. No longer 'my people', they are rather 'your people whom you have brought out from Egypt' (v. 12).

2. The LORD's assessment is that they are a 'stubborn' people (v. 13)

3. He tells Moses to 'let me alone' to give full vent to his fury (v. 14)

4. He expresses his intention to start again with Moses (v. 14)

In preaching this, it is important to bring out the LORD's frustration with Israel. He is portrayed as wanting to be left alone to destroy Israel. Despite his remarkable kindness in rescuing them, they have been wilfully and stubbornly rebellious. The LORD is slow to anger but here he says 'enough'.

Moses's reaction (9:15-17)

Moses notes that the mountain was burning with fire (cf. vv. 9, 10, 21; 10:4), a reminder of God's nature as a consuming fire – one who is not to be trifled with. Moses notes the speed with which they have turned away (v. 16). He first smashes the tablets to indicate that the covenant is broken (v. 17) and then he prays.

Moses intercedes for Israel (9:18-24)

The chronology differs here from the Exodus account where the LORD relents in response to Moses and then Moses smashes the covenant when he sees the calf and Israel's dancing. McConville notes vividly that, in Deuteronomy, 'unlike Exodus, the covenant lies in pieces before any such relenting.'[1] In verse 18, Moses appears almost magically before the LORD without ascending the mountain again. The impact is to emphasise the importance of Moses's intercession. We are not told the content yet, but rather

---

1. McConville, *Deuteronomy*, 184.

that Moses feared 'the anger and hot displeasure that the
LORD bore against you'. This text stresses the divine wrath
and Moses's sacrificing for their sake (v. 18: no food or
water for forty days because of the sin of the people) more
than Exodus. It also has a more personal note to it: 'The
LORD listened to <u>me</u>' rather than merely he 'relented' in
Exodus.

There is a strange frequency of reference to 'forty days
and forty nights' (vv. 9, 11, 18, 25; 10:10).[2] The latter three
refer to Moses's intercession, perhaps showing that this
intercession is as important or perhaps that it is more
important than even the giving of the law in verse 9 and
verse 11. The law has not solved the problem of sin but
Moses's mediation can do so for a while.

In verse 20, we are given this additional note that Moses
intercedes for Aaron, which again spotlights the key work
of Moses. Similarly, in verse 21, whereas Exodus records
that the Israelites were made to drink the ground-up
golden calf as punishment (Exod. 32:20), that is absent
here so that the emphasis falls on the effectiveness of
Moses's intercession as atoning for their sin.

Verses 22-24 show that this is a habitual pattern of
rebellion. Verse 23 has the threefold 'you rebelled ... did
not believe ... or obey his voice'.

Moses's prayer and the LORD's response to it (9:25–10:11)

The actual content of Moses's prayer has been held back
until now for effect. It would have chronologically fitted

---

2. Is Moses representing Israel in some way here (given that they would
spend forty years in the wilderness)?

in at verse 18, but its later placement alongside the LORD's response in 10:1-11 stresses the importance of the prayer of Moses in restoring the covenant.

Moses's plea (9:25-29)

Moses refuses to accept the LORD's destruction of Israel. The content begins in verse 26 with Moses's insisting with the LORD that Israel is '*your* people and *your* heritage, whom *you* have redeemed'. This sentiment is then repeated in verse 29, bracketing the two main grounds for the appeal:

1. Remember your servants (v. 27). This is most naturally taken as the same thought as verse 5: remembering the promises to the patriarchs. Would your promises trump the stubbornness (cf. vv. 6, 13) of your people? I watched my son in a cricket match recently when, after a colossal and unassailable first innings total, the captain promised every player at least two overs. One lad bowled an absolute howler which cost 30 runs. In any normal game, he would never have bowled again, but the captain still gave him a second over *because he had promised.*

2. Consider your reputation (vv. 28-29). 'LORD, if Israel dies here, the Egyptians will laugh at you and think you too weak to save your people.'

It's striking how centred upon the LORD this appeal is: there is no repentance from the people nor is there any expressed intention to obey going forward. Moses uses three words to describe the Israelites in verse 27 as he asks God to overlook their 'stubbornness', 'wickedness' and 'sin'.

Israel is utterly undeserving and completely reliant upon their mediator appealing to the LORD for mercy.

The LORD's response (10:1-11)

When Moses destroys the stone tablets they are mentioned seven times in 9:9-17, and here as they are replaced in 10:1-5 they are mentioned another seven times. Restoration is complete. That is expressed further by this language:

- 'tablets … like the first' (10:1)
- 'I will write … the words that were on the first tablets' (10:2)
- 'tablets of stone like the first' (10:3)
- 'in the same writing as before' (10:4)

What are verses 6-9 doing here when they seem to interrupt a sensible conclusion in verses 10-11? They highlight that Moses's prayer for Aaron (9:20) was also answered so that Aaron lived until the final year in the wilderness. They remind us that the Levites were the custodians of the covenant tablets. Yet perhaps most importantly, they pick up again the theme of journeying to the land. With the covenant restored, Israel can move forward again.

They do also introduce a certain narrative tension. Although we know that the LORD listened (9:19) and that the covenant tablets have been remade, it is only in verse 10 that we are told explicitly that the LORD listened to the prayer of 9:25-29. Certainly, verses 10-11 are a full conclusion to the unit, bringing together the themes of 'forty days and forty nights' and 'the LORD listened' and did not 'destroy', with a final comment that the journey to 'possess' the land can continue.

From text to message

Getting the message clear: the theme

Israel will take possession of the promised land because of God's grace. They do not deserve it because of their righteousness; they can only rely on his promises. Their past behaviour reveals that they are stubbornly rebellious as a people. Even at Horeb they broke the covenant, but God's grace, through his mediator, triumphed to renew it.

Getting the message clear: the aim
Don't think you'll enter the promised land because you're better than others, but rather rely upon your mediator.

A way in
How would you feel if someone said to you, 'I deserve to stay in the UK because I'm a moral person but you don't. You should be deported because you're immoral.' If the government resolved that it would kick out the bottom 20 per cent of undesirables from the country and deport them to Mars courtesy of Elon Musk, would you be confident of remaining? On what grounds?

Ideas for application
- Israel made it to the promised land of Canaan by undeserved grace, and the only way to enter the promised land of heaven is by God's undeserved grace. Do not say it is because of your righteousness. Appeal to God's promise in the gospel.

- Don't say, 'I'm a better person than you'! We love to compare ourselves to others and find all manner of criteria to feel superior: 'I'm a better recycler than you'; 'I contribute more to the economy than you'; 'I'm more woke than you'; 'I'm better educated than you'; etc. This becomes very easy when we compare ourselves to wicked people. Just because you're not abhorrently wicked, it does not mean that you are actually morally good. We love to compare righteousness horizontally with others and can always find someone worse than us. God requires us to compare our righteousness vertically with him. Then we're in trouble.

- One timeless problem that this illustrates is racism. The Israelites thought themselves morally superior to the Canaanites in a way which cultures still think today.

- Moses models, in shadow, the work of Jesus. Moses stood in the breach (cf. Ps 106:23). He pleads for mercy and suffers for the sake of a stubbornly rebellious people. He is offered the kingdom of the world (as replacement for Israel) but declines. He argues passionately for the reputation of the LORD. He is the one who saves the people when they deserve to be destroyed by God's wrath. Yet, in his work, Jesus does not ask his Father to overlook or 'not regard' our sin – better than that, he actually pays for it.

Suggestions for preaching

How will you enter the 'promised land'?

- Not because you're good (righteous) ... (9:1-6)

- ... because you're really stubborn (9:7-24)

- So, trust in one who pleads for you (9:25–10:11)

Questions to help understand the passage

1. What is the issue that Moses is addressing in verses 1-6?

   - What are we told about the challenge of possessing the land (vv. 1-2)?

- Yet why should Israel be confident (v. 3)?
- Why will the LORD drive out the nations from before Israel (vv. 4-5)?
- What is not the reason (v. 6)?

2. What is the theme of the section bracketed by verse 7 and verse 24? How is Israel described?

3. What double command does Israel get in verse 7? Why? What does it do (to remember and not forget how they had provoked the LORD)?

4. What did Israel do at Horeb (Mount Sinai) (vv. 8-11)?

5. What was the LORD's response (vv. 12-14)? How are the LORD's 'feelings' described?

6. What did Moses do (vv. 15-21)?

7. What conclusion does Moses draw in verses 22-24?

8. Why do you think the content of Moses's prayer is not written in the main story but placed after it and after the conclusion of verses 22-24?

9. Given that Moses can summarise Israel as 'rebellious against the LORD from the day that I knew you' (v. 24), what hope can they have (v. 25)?

10. What are the grounds for Moses's appeal in verses 26-28?

11. What is the point of recording the account of new tablets being cut in 10:1-5? What has Moses's prayer achieved?

Questions to help apply the passage

1. What is the parallel today of Israel entering into the promised land of Canaan? So what is the parallel mistake to 9:4 that people might claim?

2. Why do people enjoy comparing themselves to wicked people? (By reading about them in the press, or by tut-tutting about the poor behaviour of others?)

3. Where do you draw the line between good people and bad people?

4. How does reading of the LORD's frustration with Israel's sin make you think about your sin?

5. Moses appeals to the LORD on the basis of his promises and his reputation. How might that affect the way you pray to the Lord?

6. In what ways does Moses foreshadow for us the work of Jesus? In what ways is Jesus a better mediator than we see here?

7. On what basis do you think you'll enter the promised land of heaven?

8.

What Does the Lord Require of You?

(Deuteronomy 10:12–11:32)

Introduction

There is very little that is new in this section, as it summarises all that has come before. It is Moses the preacher driving home his main point, that Israel must choose to love the LORD *today*. There are lots of interesting elements in this section: it is the most dense treatment in Deuteronomy of the value and place of the land and it is another fascinating section on whether Israel will choose to obey or not.

Yet, in preaching this, we must not lose sight of the main purpose: it is calling for a decision 'today' to love and obey the LORD. All of Moses's preaching in Deuteronomy is aimed at that response.

Within that, the subject that has preoccupied us since chapter 6 continues here – namely, how it is that Israel will occupy the land of Canaan. The LORD requires wholehearted love, but the underlying impression of chapters 7–10 is that they will fail. They will have other obsessions occupying their hearts and so will rebel against the LORD. That pessimism lurks again in this passage.

Before we get to the detailed laws given in chapters 12–26, Moses wants to be clear that the law will not solve the problem of the human heart.

If you are preaching an overview series of Deuteronomy, it is unlikely you will preach this as a sermon but rather, it will be contained in one sermon on chapters 7–11 (see notes on chapter 7). If you are preaching a longer series in the book and intend to take a pause at chapter 11 before returning later to pick it up at chapter 12, then I imagine that, in preaching a sermon on 10:12–11:32, you would want to also take the congregation to chapter 30 and especially verse 6 to see how the tension between God's promises and Israel's stubbornness will be resolved by the LORD.

In terms of applying this section, it is set up easily by the opening question: 'What does the LORD require of you?' As a Christian believer, what does God now want me to do? It's an eminently practical question!

Listening to the text

'And now' (10:12) marks a new section in the book, introducing this speech in the same language as 4:1. It is a unified speech up to 11:32.

The themes overlap and get repeated, but it is clearly a passage calling for Israel to choose to follow the LORD.

There are some notable densities of key words in the section:

- 'Today' (10:13; 11:2, 8, 13, 26, 27, 28, 32). This has the impact of reminding Israel that they are at the moment of decision (with the typical Deuteronomy emphasis that every day is the moment of decision).

- 'Heart' (10:12, 15, 16; 11:13, 16, 18). While spread across two chapters, this is one unit and so, apart from chapter 30, this is one of the densest sections of the fifty-one occurrences of 'heart' within the book. It highlights what precisely the LORD requires – not mere legal conformity but also wholehearted affection. It also reveals the great need – the heart must be 'circumcised' if Israel is to cease being stubborn.

Structure

10:12–11:1	A summary call to loyalty
11:2-7	Love the LORD and consider the past
11:8-12	Love the LORD and enjoy the land
11:13-25	Love the LORD and take care of your heart
11:26-32	Make your choice today

Working through the text

A summary call to loyalty (10:12–11:1)

All mention of the failure at Horeb now fades away and this restatement of the Shema emphasises that the golden calf has been dealt with by Israel's mediator. The command to circumcise the heart (v. 16) is clearly important in the flow of the whole book and, given its contrast to stubbornness, it is evidently a response to the problem of the previous section (9:6, 13, 27).

Consequently, Barker places verse 16 at the centre of a chiasm:[1]

10:12-13 Basic command

    10:14-15 Introductory reason for command of verse 16

        10:16 Command: circumcise the heart

    10:17-19 Supplementary reason for verse 16

10:20-22 Summary, basic command and reason

---

1. Barker, *The Triumph of Grace*, 103.

There is good logic to this and it does helpfully highlight verse 16. However, it is also possible to understand the section as three overlapping answers to the question of verse 12, followed by a brief conclusion. All three answers give some content to what is required and then a reason grounded in God's nature.

Question: What does the LORD *your God require of you? (10:12a)*

First Answer (10:12b-15)

There is little that is new here as the LORD commands Israel to 'fear' (5:29), 'walk' (5:33), 'love' (6:5), 'serve' (6:13) with 'heart' and 'soul' (6:5) and 'keep the commandments' (4:2). Once again, it is striking that the LORD requires both internal emotions and external actions, not mere moralism. It was never meant to be a religion of external conformity; Jesus attacked the Pharisees for reading Deuteronomy that way! Without love, these actions are merely legalistic duties. Without action, the expressions of love are vacuous.

The reason for the command lies in God's character, described in a pair of contrasts: 'He owns everything but he cares for *you*' (vv. 14-15). In view of God's gracious choice, the call to utter devotion is completely reasonable.

Second Answer (10:16-19)

The call to 'circumcise … the foreskin of your heart' must be viewed as fundamental to the LORD's requirement for his people. It is a response to the LORD's love of verse 15, hence the word 'therefore' in verse 16. Barker summarises numerous commentators by saying, 'The generally adopted meaning of a circumcised heart is a heart which is submissive, responsive to God and humble.'[2] The meaning is clarified by the parallel command in 16b: 'be no longer stubborn.' This stubbornness was the major failure of Israel described in the previous section (9:6, 13, 27). So, it appears that a circumcised heart is crucial to avoiding stubborn rebellion. Israel will not love the LORD and keep his commands unless their hearts are circumcised. The question looms: 'Can *they* do this?'

Again, the motivation for the repentance lies in a pair of contrasting truths about God: 'He has no rivals and he cares for the powerless.' Although a familiar Bible truth, it is not evident in history that one without rivals cares for the little people. There will be a great deal of detail in chapters 12–26 about what it means to love the sojourner; here we are reminded that the command to do so is grounded in the character of God, who loves sojourners, and Israel's own experience. You cannot pull the law away from who God is and the salvation he has granted. Although much of what the LORD requires has been described, there are actually only two imperatives in the section: 'Circumcise your hearts and stop being stubborn' (v. 16) and 'Love the sojourner' (v. 19). It really does matter how we treat the 'nobodies'!

Third answer (10:20-22)

Four more imperatives are followed by more reasons grounded in God's character and work. The reuse in verse 22 of the phrase 'and now' from verse 12 rounds off the section. In verse 12 the emphasis falls on what is required of Israel, and in verse 22 it is upon how the LORD has kept his promise of Genesis 12. If Israel has any chance of doing what is required, they must keep looking to God's promise.

---

2. Barker, *The Triumph of Grace*, 105.

Conclusion (11:1)

This verse seems to be a summary answer to the question that had been asked in verse 12. What is required? Love the Lord your God and keep his commandments. Block makes the helpful point that there is nothing here about sacrifices or other forms of worship. The emphasis clearly lands upon devotion and moral obedience.[3]

Love the Lord and consider the past (11:2-7)

The language of 'today' comes to the fore in chapter 11, forcing the choice upon Israel. This choice is reinforced further by the rhetorical impact of Moses's declaring:

- 'I am not speaking to your children who have not known or seen it' (v. 2)

- 'For your eyes have seen all the great work of the Lord' (v. 7)

This latter statement is not literally true, as 1:34-40 reveals that the generation addressed in Deuteronomy were *not* those who had seen what is described, but Moses is stressing rhetorically, 'I'm speaking to YOU. *You lot* standing in front of me. Don't say this is a matter for the last generation or the next one. YOU need to make a decision today.'

Let me say again: don't get lost in the details. The application is very clear: 'Choose to obey the Lord.'

Israel is to consider multiple truths about the Lord: his discipline, greatness, mighty hand and outstretched arm, his signs and deeds. We are told 'He did' these things to four groups (vv. 3, 4, 5, 6), but essentially two events are highlighted here:

---

3. Block, *Deuteronomy*, 276.

1. God's deliverance from external enemies (vv. 2-5, recalling Exodus 14)

2. God's deliverance from internal enemies (v. 6, recalling the rebellion of Num. 16 against Moses's leadership)

Knowing these truths about the Lord they shall keep the whole commandment (v. 8) (singular – stressing both that *the* commandment is for fundamental loyalty and also the unity of the law, cf. 6:1).

Love the Lord and enjoy the land (11:8-12)

Verses 8 and 9 have a typical Deuteronomy comment on how Israel will possess the land. It is by *both* the need for obedience (v. 8) and God's prior promise to grant it.

It is worth noting that the emphasis in verse 8 on the necessity of obedience 'that you may be strong, and *go in and take* possession of the land that you are going over to possess' prevents the simplistic formulation that people sometimes use: 'Israel entered the land due to God's grace but could only stay by obedience.' That formulation cannot be sustained by reading the text properly. 11:22-23 is similar: 'If you will be careful to do … then the Lord will drive out all these nations before you.' Again, obedience is required *for entry*.

In 11:8-9, they enter by obedience AND due to God's promise. Wright phrases it nicely: 'They were two sides of the same truth, combining, as Deuteronomy characteristically does in so many other ways, the priority of divine grace and the necessity of human obedient response.'[4]

---

4. Wright, *Deuteronomy*, 154.

In 11:8-17, we have one of the most significant passages on Israel's relationship to the land in the book. Here in verses 9-12, Moses describes the land in utopian and beautiful language. So, the land 'drinks water by the rain from heaven.' Most striking is that it is 'a land that the Lord your God cares for. The eyes of the Lord your God are always upon it.' It is wonderfully tender and intimate language.

Love the Lord and take care of your heart (11:13-25)

Verses 13-17 seem to repeat the idea (seen in chapter 6 and 8) that, after an initial burst of enthusiastic commandment keeping and the subsequent enjoyment of God's blessing, Israel may find that affluence deceives their hearts and they turn to worship the fertility gods of the culture around them. That would be madness given the Lord's care and control of the land (v. 12), and they would suffer for it.

The antidote (in similar language to chapter 6) is to lay up the words of Moses in their hearts (vv. 18-21). If they do this, then the Lord will allow them to enter in and take possession of the land. Yet again it will also be 'as he promised you'.

Make your choice today (11:26-32)

The climax to this passage and the whole of the argument since chapter 5 comes in 11:26-32. Moses draws attention to this with 'See!' in verse 26 (1:8, 21; 4:5; 30:15; 32:39). We are introduced to a one-off ceremony that Israel is to carry out when they enter the land. More details are given in 27:11–28:68, which helps to form the outer frame to these verses, around chapters 12–26. In a highly visual act, the nation is told to choose between blessing or curse. Mayes suggests that Gerizim was covered with vegetation but Ebal was dry and barren, which certainly makes sense of the visual ceremony.[5]

From text to message

Getting the message clear: the theme

The section draws together the main themes of chapters 4–10 (and indeed repeats the language) in order to press Israel to choose to obey the commandments ahead of the detailed stipulations of chapters 12–26. The failures at Horeb disappear and it is a forward-looking text.

Getting the message clear: the aim

What does the LORD require of you? It is to choose each day to love him from the heart and demonstrate that love in obedience.

A way in

What does the Lord require of me? You could ask that in a crass, calculating way: 'Okay, I'm a Christian, forgiven in Jesus, so ... how little commitment can I get away with? What's the minimum required time, money, effort required by God, now that I'm in? How worldly is it acceptable to be?' But most believers will ask with integrity, 'What *do* you want me to do for you, Lord?' Here is a text that answers that question precisely. Typically for Deuteronomy, he wants you to decide each day to love him and to reveal that love in action.

5. A. D. H. Mayes, *Deuteronomy* (NCB; Grand Rapids: Eerdmans, 1981), 218.

Ideas for application

- The LORD wants internal emotions and external actions. Both matter. You might think of a marriage where the husband obeys all the requests of his wife to cook and do the gardening. She meets all the requests of the husband for ironing and planning holidays. They keep one another's rules, but ... it is a loveless and joyless marriage; they barely speak to one another. OR in another marriage there are grand gestures of flowers and extravagant gifts. There is great passion in the marriage. Yet he never lifts a finger to help at home and she's having an affair; neither is demonstrating much practical love. We would say that neither of these is a healthy marriage: there should be affection and action. The LORD wants nothing less. (Please note, these are comments made in the context of a series in Deuteronomy when love has already been defined primarily as loyalty. See notes on chapter 6.)

- The same imbalance can happen in churches. Some may be very strong on biblical teaching and moral obedience but cannot cope with emotional expressions of faith. It is viewed as dangerous and a slippery slope to ignoring God's word. Others may have *nothing but* emotionalism – individuals may appear to be in raptures on a Sunday but are bullying staff and are utterly worldly during the week. Neither is healthy. The LORD does not want begrudging compliance nor excitable worldliness. He requires love and obedience.

- The Lord desires moral obedience! What does the Lord require of you? There is nothing in this passage about how to conduct worship or how to offer sacrifices. It becomes evident in Israel's later life how easy it was to substitute the form of religion in place of obedience to what God had commanded.

- If you fix your eyes upon the Lord, then you will obey him. McConville comments on these verses: 'The commandments are not detachable from the question of who he [the Lord] is, which is why the preaching in Deuteronomy can run seamlessly from the exhortation to obey the commandments to the warning not to run after other gods.'[6]

- If you're in a long sermon series, here would be an appropriate place to pause and ask, How could Israel circumcise their hearts when they were so stubborn? How can we love the Lord in this sort of way with a radical obedience to what he commands? We need more than the law external to us! We need the Lord to circumcise our hearts if we are to live for him. The tension between God's promises of blessing and Israel's inability to change their stubborn hearts is only resolved in 30:6: God has to change the heart!

Suggestions for preaching

When preaching this passage as a sermon, I did not have the whole passage read, nor did I cover every section. Some may feel uncomfortable with that but I was chiefly concerned with bringing the main point of the text to the congregation, demonstrating that and then driving it home. I might gently suggest that if you are resolutely committed to preaching every word of Deuteronomy, you

---

6. McConville, *Deuteronomy*, 208.

will need a congregation with extraordinary patience as you preach chapters 12–26!

What does the LORD require of you?

- A heart that produces action (10:12–11:1)
- A heart that chooses him (11:18-32)
- A heart that he gives (10:16 and 30:6)

Questions to help understand the passage

1. What does the LORD require of Israel (v.12)?

2. What are the two truths highlighted about the LORD in verses 14-15?

3. What should Israel do then (v. 16)? How do these two things relate to one another?

4. Why should Israel love the sojourner/foreigner (vv. 17-19)?

5. Why should Israel fear and serve the LORD according to verses 20-22? Why in verse 21? Why in verse 22?

6. What is Israel to consider in verse 25? What in verses 26-27?

7. How good is the land going to be (vv. 8-12)? What is required of Israel (vv. 13-17)? What is the danger? What is the antidote (vv. 18-21)?

8. What is Israel commanded to do when they enter the land (vv. 26-32)? Why?

Questions to help apply the passage

1. Moses asks a great question in verse 12 – how would you put that in your own words?

2. What is the impact of describing what the LORD requires in five different imperatives (vv. 12-13)?

3. How should a Christian apply 10:16 (cf. 30:6 and 1 Pet. 1:22-25)?

4. What would a Christian consider, rather than the LORD's deeds of salvation from Egypt and judgment of Numbers 16?

5. How can you get these words of the Lord into your heart (11:18)?

9.
Don't Worship like That
(Deuteronomy 12)

Introduction to chapters 12–26

If you haven't guessed it, I have to warn you that it is harder to preach chapters 12–26 than chapters 1–11, as we're no longer 're-preaching' Moses's sermons but, instead, it's statutes and laws. Yet this is what obedience looks like! All of the rhetoric of chapters 1–11 is designed so that Israel does chapters 12–26.

It is a sensible approach to preach through Deuteronomy in two series – one on chapters 1–11 and then a second on chapters 12–34. If that is the approach taken, then you will need to make it obvious to people how chapters 12–26 fit into the book. Crucially, we must not abstract law from the story of salvation. As you read through this section it is obvious that there are constant motivating factors: 'Live this way because God is like this' or 'Act that way because the Lord has treated you in that way.' Torah is not presented as a burdensome imposition but as a good gift to a people that the Lord has graciously redeemed.

May I similarly suggest to preachers that these chapters are also a good gift and not a burden to us! There are challenges here, but also they teach familiar biblical truth in different language and in a different way and so can bring home God's word with a freshness if handled well. However, let me briefly mention three obvious difficulties.

First, we will be conscious of the considerable revelatory gap between the original audience and us. There will be disagreement amongst readers but, personally, I would understand the laws in chapter 12–26 as a gracious gift to a people already redeemed – that is, this is obedience that is meant to flow from faith. Yet we live this side of the work of Jesus Christ! He is the Lord's final and clearest revelation and we must allow him to filter or interpret all the laws of Deuteronomy.

So, although I would insist on a basic continuity between the covenants, it is a significant mistake to flatten progressive revelation. In simple terms, it would have been far more uncomfortable being a believing Israelite under the Mosaic law than it is to be a Christian under Christ. Moses in Deuteronomy is far less clear on grace than the New Testament writers are. The covenant in Deuteronomy is one of types and shadows; we now live in the sunlight.

Second, there is also a large cultural gap – Israel was wearing clothing, celebrating festivals and capturing cities in a way that we are not. Yet, the Lord is the same and we learn much of what pleases him here. Again, familiar truths expressed in an unfamiliar genre can hit us afresh.

Third, how do we structure a sermon series here? Although there is a discernible movement through chapters 12–26 which seems to expound the Decalogue, it is by no means clear cut and sections seem to blur between, say, adultery and lying (see below). Alongside that, the laws on 'not lying' and 'not stealing' look very similar, as do the motivations for living this way. So, although I would highly commend a sermon series on the Decalogue where you illustrate from chapters 12–26 (see notes on chapter 5), I would not work through each verse in these chapters in ten sermons.

Introduction to chapter 12

Chapter 12 focuses on Israel's distinctive worship. It contains similar ideas to chapter 7 in that Israel must not be like the other nations; they must demonstrate exclusive loyalty to the LORD. It therefore expands out the first two commandments. Although there is attention upon worship at the place the LORD chooses, this place is not named because the focus is not really *where* but *who*. One place is set apart for the worship of the one true God, not many places for many 'godlets'.

There are plenty of details here on what food you can eat and where, but don't get bogged down in the detail! The main theme is obvious: Israel is to worship the LORD alone.

As suggested below, it is quite possible to take the section 12:1–14:21 as one sermon.

Listening to the text

Structure of chapters 12–26

The whole section is framed by the blessings and curses from Gerizim and Ebal in 11:26-30 and 27:1-26. Chapter 12 also shares conceptual links with 25:17–26:15 where they are told to 'blot out' the memory of Amalek and there is the injunction to go to the place the LORD has made his name dwell (26:2).

More broadly, here is a reminder of where the chapters fit into the book:

4:44 'This is the law'

5:1 'Moses summoned all Israel and said'

    12:1 'These are the statutes and rules that you shall be careful to do'

    26:16 'This day the Lord your God commands you to do these statutes and rules'[1]

29:1 'These are the words of the covenant that the Lord commanded'

29:2 'Moses summoned all Israel and said'

Deuteronomy claims to be an exposition of the torah. This is made explicit in 1:5 which 'describes Moses's speaking as "expounding" the law'.[2] This word has the meaning of 'explain' or 'prove' and is restated in Deuteronomy 27:8.

This 'explaining' of the torah begins with repeating the Decalogue in order (Deut. 5), which was spoken to all of Israel (5:22). Then Moses expounds the Ten Words in consecutive chapters, according to general agreement among commentators. I'm sympathetic to Block, who suggests that the description of chapters 12–26 as an exposition of the Decalogue is 'forced',[3] but there is *something* of that structure here:[4]

---

1. 'Statutes and rules' is found in 4:1, 5, 8, 14, 45; 5:1, 31; 6:1, 20; 7:11; 8:11; 11:1, 32; 12:1; 26:16, 17 and 30:16. The phrase is strikingly absent between chapters 12–16 as these statutes and rules are described in detail.

2. Paul A. Barker, 'Moses the Preacher: Deuteronomy 1–4,' pp. 32-52 in *Serving God's Words: Windows on Preaching and Ministry* (ed. P. A. Barker, R. J. Condie and A. S. Malone; Leicester: IVP, 2011), 33.

3. Block, *Deuteronomy*, 301.

4. Thanks to Ryan Muir for this table.

Word	Currid[5]	Kaufman[6]	Merrill[7]	Walton[8]
1st	6:1–11:32	12	12:1-31	6–11
2nd	12:1-31	12	12:32–13:18	12
3rd	12:32–14:21	13:1–14:27	14:1-21	13:1–14:21
4th	14:22–16:17	14:28–16:17	14:22–16:17	14:22–16:17
5th	16:18–18:22	16:18–18:22	16:18–18:22	16:18–18:22
6th	19:1–22:12	19:1–22:8	19:1–22:8	19–21
7th	22:13–23:14	22:9–23:19	22:9–23:18	22:1–23:14
8th	23:15–24:7	23:20–24:7	23:19–24:7	23:15–24:7
9th	24:8-16	24:8–25:4	24:8–25:4	24:8-16
10th	24:17–26:19	25:5-16	25:5-19	24:17–26:15

It is possible to divide chapters 12–26 in two. We get the phrase 'When the LORD your God cuts off the nations' twice, at 12:29 and 19:1. There also seems to be a shift in form from 19:1 to a more formal tone with less exhortation or reasons given for acting in a certain way.

Structure of chapter 12

The clear theme of chapter 12 is that Israel must worship the LORD exclusively. It is to live distinctively from all other nations. The chapter is framed by the command 'You shall not worship the LORD your God in that way [like the nations]' (vv. 4, 31).

---

5. John D. Currid, *Deuteronomy* (EPSC; Darlington: Evangelical Press, 2006), 21-24.

6. Stephen A. Kaufman, 'The Structure of the Deuteronomic Law,' *MAARAV* Vol. 1/2 (1978–79), 113-114.

7. Merrill, *Deuteronomy*, 218-331.

8. John Walton, 'Deuteronomy: An Exposition of the Law,' *Grace Theological Journal* 8:2 (Fall 1987), 213-25.

Nelson observes the following chiastic structure:[9]

> v. 1 These are the statutes and rules you shall be careful to keep
>
>> vv. 2-7 Don't worship the LORD your God like the nations
>>
>>> vv. 8-12 When you enter the land
>>>
>>>> vv. 13-19 (2nd sing. takes over in v. 13.) Only make offerings at the place; non-sacral killing allowed
>>>
>>> vv. 20-28 When you enter the land
>>
>> vv. 29-31 Don't worship the LORD your God like the nations
>
> v. 32 Everything I command you shall be careful to keep

While this helpfully highlights the theme of 'Don't worship like the nations', it is perhaps simpler to divide the text:

- Worship at the place the LORD has chosen (vv. 2-14)

- There's a difference between meat for sacrifices and meat for dinner (vv. 15-28)

There are some key words which are repeated frequently:

- the 'place'
  - the 'wrong place' (vv. 2, 3)
  - the place that 'God will choose' (vv. 5, 11, 14, 18, 21, 26)
  - not 'any place that you see' (v. 13)

- 'You shall not' (vv. 4, 8, 25, 31)

9. Richard Nelson, *Deuteronomy* (Louisville, KY: Westminster John Knox Press, 2004), 150.

- 'do what is right in the sight of the LORD' (vv. 25, 28)
- 'rejoice before the LORD' (vv. 7, 12, 18)

There are many negatives here which drive the rhetoric:

- 'not as the nations' (v. 4)
- 'not in every place' (v. 13)
- 'not in your towns' (v. 17)
- 'not eating sacrifices to the LORD' (v. 23)
- 'not as the nations' (v. 31)

However, this is to ensure that they enjoy the LORD rightly. Any sermons on this chapter must capture the tone of 'rejoicing before the LORD' (vv. 7, 12, 18) alongside the serious instruction to destroy idols.

Working through the text

Introduction (12:1)

The language of 11:31-32 is repeated here to tie these two sections together. These are not statutes and rules to tear out of their context of what the LORD has done for Israel. Although the land is not yet in Israel's possession, Moses can say the LORD 'has given' it. This is presented as a certainty.

Worship the LORD in the way he desires (12:2-14)

Although the text repeatedly mentions 'the place', it is never named and the focus is upon the contrast between acceptable and unacceptable worship. It must not be like the pagans nor as you desire. This section falls somewhat into two:

Don't worship like the pagans (12:2-7)

There is no ambiguity in verses 2-3! Israel is to 'destroy ... tear down ... dash ... burn ... chop ... destroy' anything which could be a threat to them. The variety of places named –'high mountains ... hills ... every green tree ... altars ... pillars' – shows how pervasive these places of idolatry had become. Israel was entering a culture where they were surrounded by false gods at every turn.

The purpose of this destruction is to 'destroy their name out of that place' in order to establish the LORD's name (v. 3). There is a conscious rejecting of the Canaanite gods.

Verse 6 is not an exhaustive list. The point is, whatever your worship consists of, give it to the LORD.

Happily, in verse 7, eating is commanded, as is rejoicing 'in all that you undertake'. Eating is an act of fellowship and communion and so it's natural to do it in the LORD's presence. It is also a recognition that all the blessings of the land have come from the LORD's hand, not local fertility gods.

Don't worship as you see fit (12:8-14)

While verses 2-7 are clearly focused upon the future, verses 8-14 address a present problem amongst Israel: everyone is 'doing whatever is right in his own eyes' v. 8) They are prepared to burn offerings 'at any place that you see' (v. 13). Clearly a free-for-all had already crept into Israel's worship as they were ignoring the requirements previously set down (Lev. 17:1-9).

The section (from v. 2) is rounded off in verses 13-14; Israelite worship is only to be carried out at the place chosen by the LORD.

12:15-28

I don't suppose many will preach on these verses.

They anticipate a time when Israel is spread throughout the promised land and not all gathered at one central sanctuary. A distinction is drawn between animals that are to be sacrificed and those which are just for a meal. Any food type specifically offered to God by way of tithe or vow offering had to be brought to the sanctuary (vv. 17-18 and v. 26).

If they were killing an animal to eat, then the blood could be poured on the ground (vv. 16, 23). But if an animal was killed as a sacrifice, then blood had to be offered on the altar at the sanctuary (v. 27). 'The idea seems to be that blood, as the very essence of life, must be returned to the earth from which the Creator at the beginning had brought it forth.'[10]

This concession reveals that the LORD is not a killjoy. If you crave meat, then eat meat 'whenever you desire' (vv. 20, 21).

Concluding injunction (12:29-31)

Israel is told again: don't worship like them. It is striking that the temptation to follow the false gods will still exist after the Canaanites have been destroyed (v. 30). The temptation to worship as we desire and on our terms, rather than on God's terms, is a recurrent one!

The section concludes with the shocking revelation that idolatrous worship can lead to horrific behaviour (v. 31). When a modern audience is horrified by the command that Israel should dispossess the Canaanites of their land, it is worth being clear how wicked they were. No one today would live next door to neighbours who carried out child sacrifice and say, 'Live and let live.'

---

10. Merrill, *Deuteronomy*, 226.

From text to message

Getting the message clear: the theme

Israel's worship must be distinctive and not like the Canaanites. Their loyalty is to be exclusive and so one place is established to worship the LORD, unlike the many places of the pagans.

Getting the message clear: the aim

Worship the Lord exclusively and do so in the way he desires.

A way in

If I were to stand here today and confess I'm having extra-marital affairs with multiple women, would that be okay?

No! I imagine you'd be outraged because, when married, you should reserve exclusive devotion for your spouse. You would rightly insist that I cut off all those relationships and love my wife alone.

That's what the Lord is asking here in Deuteronomy 12. We may at first think the emphasis upon exclusive devotion to him is a little strong, but it is no more than we expect of a marriage.

In the wedding ceremony the question is put: 'Will you take X to be your wife? Will you love her, comfort her, honour and protect her, and, *forsaking all others*, be faithful to her as long as you both shall live?' 'I WILL.'

That's what the LORD is commanding here – that his people love him, forsaking all others.

Ideas for application

- We must worship the Lord in the way he requires, not in the way we desire. This applies to

1. the unbeliever. For example, I read an interview with the actress Dawn French – *The Vicar of Dibley*. Asked if she was a believer, she answered, 'I think like a lot of people I've got my own little version of religion going on.' That's very common but not acceptable to the Lord.

2. the believer. Sometimes you'll hear Christians say, 'I don't like the worship at that church,' by which they may mean the music or sermon. Okay, fine. But the significant question is, Does God like it? You can't just worship as you please. We might think, *'I would love to worship the Lord at a time and in a way that is convenient to me.'* But he has established the manner in which we are to worship him.

- The New Testament is clear that 'the place' is no longer a physical location but it is a person. The tabernacle/temple gives way to Jesus (John 2 and 4). Wright helpfully comments: 'The valuing of a place because of Yahweh's choice and presence rather than because of its location, sows the seeds for the N[ew] T[estament]'s transference of the significance of the place of worship.'[11] Ultimately, every knee will bow the knee and acknowledge that there is only one name in which salvation can be found (Phil. 2:9-11). We must worship him alone.

- Deuteronomy 12 also provides certain principles for our worship. Clearly, it is concerned with when Israel gathers together and Christians know that worship is the whole of our lives. Yet it is worth observing that Israel's worship was to be:

---

11. Wright, *Deuteronomy*, 163.

1. responsive. Their loyalty is a response to what
   the LORD has done. He has given them the land
   (v. 1), blessed them (v. 7) and will give them an
   inheritance. The Christian lives a life of loyal service of the Lord in view of his mercy towards us,
   his blessing and our hope of inheritance.

2. joyful (vv. 7, 12, 18). Joy is not incidental to the life
   of a believer; it is essential. To be lukewarm as a
   Christian is to violate the first commandment, as
   it reveals that emotionally we value other things
   before the Lord and expect them to bring us
   delight. The Lord does not ask us merely to 'grin
   and bear it' in the Christian life – he wants our
   emotional life to be centred upon him.

3. costly. All Israel was obliged to travel to the central
   place three times a year – that's a lot of time lost
   in travel and expense too. Taking all your servants
   with you (v. 12) means that they are not working
   either. Tithing 10 per cent of produce is expensive,
   especially if there are free-will spontaneous acts
   of generosity as well. Israel then had to know that
   the LORD had blessed them with these animals,
   these crops; we have to know now that the Lord
   has blessed us with all we have. Worship that
   pleases the Lord will cost us, but how offensive to
   try and worship him on the cheap.

4. social. 'You and your households … your male
   servants and your female servants' – all are
   involved (vv. 7, 12). This is for everyone. You can't
   claim to love God but exclude those God loves.
   Christian life is to be lived together. 'No worship

that claims to love God but excludes those whom
God loves can be acceptable to God.'[12]

Suggestions for preaching

Some thoughts on chapters 12–26

- It is possible in an overview series of Deuteronomy to
  preach one sermon in a representative section of these
  chapters. I know of at least a couple of preachers who
  have done that to show how one might apply this section.

- The first occasion that I ever preached through Deuteronomy, I did an overview in ten sermons and our
  small groups covered chapters 12–26 in a few studies
  midweek (with the other studies being in chapters
  1–3 to help orientate, followed by studies in chapter
  4 and chapter 30 because they are so important for
  reading the book rightly).

- My preference now would be to preach Deuteronomy
  in two sermon series: the first on chapters 1–11 and
  a second on chapters 12–34, within which I would
  take chapters 12–26 in five sermons:

    ○ 12:1–14:21   Worshipping him rightly
                    (first to third commandments)

    ○ 14:22–16:17   Enjoying his rest
                    (fourth commandment)

    ○ 16:18–18:22   Valuing his leaders
                    (fifth commandment)

    ○ 19:1–23:18   Obeying his morals
                    (sixth and seventh
                    commandments)

---

12. Wright, *Deuteronomy*, 166.

○ 23:19–25:16 Following his generosity
(eight, ninth, tenth commandments)

- This is my suggestion, were you to preach a sermon just on this chapter:

'You shall have no other gods before me'

○ Don't worship like them (vv. 2-7, 29-32)

○ Don't worship as you see fit (vv. 8-14)

○ Do worship the LORD alone
- responsively
- joyfully
- in a costly manner
- socially

Questions to help understand the passage

1. What is the issue that tops and tails the chapter (vv. 4, 31)?

2. What is Israel to do (vv. 2-3)? How many verbs are there here? How many different places were gods kept? So, what is God asking them to do?

3. What are they positively to do (vv. 5-7)?

4. What existing problem was there (vv. 8, 13)?

5. What again did the LORD tell them to do (vv. 11-12)?

6. Who was to be involved (vv. 7, 12)?

7. However, if the meat is not to be used in a sacrifice, what is God's command (vv. 15, 20-21)?

8. What is the mood that God commands (vv. 7, 12, 18)?

9. How dangerous are the false gods (vv. 29-31)?

Questions to help apply the passage

1. Is exclusive love a good thing? If you commit to loving a spouse and forsaking all others, what does that mean? How do our 'nos' strengthen our 'yeses'?

2. Israel was to destroy the name of false gods in order to establish the name of the LORD. How do we do that as Christians (e.g. 2 Cor. 10:15)?

3. Is there still one place where all believers are to gather (John 2:19-21; 4:21-26; Heb. 10:24-25)?

4. What principles can we draw about the right way to worship the one true God?

   - vv. 4, 31
   - vv. 7, 12
   - vv. 7, 12, 18

10.
The Truth Matters
(Deuteronomy 13:1–14:21)

Introduction

If you have this read aloud in church, most people will probably react with shock! On the one hand, we feel a long way from a culture which was prepared to stone people to death (v. 9). Yet I wonder if this verse is also alien to us because we simply do not have such a high regard for God's truth as we should.

I imagine many will be tempted to avoid chapter 13, and you will know the people to whom you are preaching. Yet it is a striking passage on how important it is to listen to what is taught and check that it accords with what God has revealed. If we are unwilling to teach Deuteronomy 13, I wonder if we are willing to teach Galatians 1:8-9 or 2 Peter 2?

As suggested in the previous chapter, there is an argument for taking 12:1–14:21 together in one sermon with the theme 'Worship him rightly', as these chapters seem to cover the ground of the first three commands of the Decalogue.

Were you to preach chapter 13 on its own, most commentators view this as an amplification of the third command. It is linked thematically with 14:1-21 by the need for Israel to be exclusively loyal to the LORD and to maintain their distinctiveness as a holy people.

Listening to the text

Block considers chapters 12–14 as one chiasm and there is plausibility to this, although it perhaps downplays the call for radical loyalty of chapter 12.

> Eating in the presence of Yahweh (12:5-14)
>> Eating in your towns (12:15-27)
>>> Remaining true to Yahweh (12:28–13:18)
>> Eating in your towns (14:1-21)
> Eating in the presence of Yahweh (14:22-29)

It is natural to quickly notice the unusual things that we do not like ('put to death') and take for granted the truths which are familiar ('the LORD redeemed you' in v. 5 and 'brought you out of slavery' in v. 10). While that is unsurprising, it will lead to imbalance and so we must observe the motive clauses throughout the chapter too.

Working through the text

13:1-18

The end of chapter 12 – and especially the general warning of 29–31 – leads fairly naturally into the specific warnings of chapter 13. However, while in chapter 12 the focus is on loyalty in worship, here in chapter 13 the warning is against following other gods.

Although the word order varies slightly, verses 2, 6 and 13 contain the same wicked suggestion: 'Let us go and serve other gods ... which you have not known'. The chapter breaks clearly into three paragraphs addressing different sources for the heresy.

1. The prophet or dreamer (13:1-5)

It is striking here that the sign or wonder from the false prophet actually comes to pass. It's not a cheap trick – there really is a supernatural miracle that happens. BUT a miracle does not authenticate someone who is advocating disobeying God's clearly revealed word. Other religions report miracles having taken place, and they may well have done. But just because a miracle is genuine, that does not authenticate truth. It is sadly very easy for us to recognise this behaviour – the prophet who claims special access to knowledge and an intimacy with God. They may be impressive, but if they encourage you away from the True and Living God, don't listen!

Verse 3 begins with a simple instruction and is far less dramatic than what is to come in verse 5. Yet, as Wright observes, in the contemporary church 'we have failed the test of verse 3'.[1] Perhaps we are too ready to indulge the false prophet or dreamer.

Verses 3-4 also reveal that God has a purpose in allowing these deceptive signs and wonders to encourage heretical teachers. Once again, it is a test of Israel's wholehearted love. Verses 3-4 set up a contrast between the speculative teaching of the prophet or dreamer and the revealed voice of God through Moses. There is an expectation in verse 4 that those walking after the LORD, keeping close to him and his voice, will see through miraculous deception. The pattern of life described in verse 4 produces a healthy immune system against the virus of heresy.

---

1. Wright, *Deuteronomy*, 178.

In verse 5, the action required is dramatic. The reason given is that he has taught 'rebellion'. It is not a small thing to chase after other gods. Rebelling against the god 'who brought you out of slavery' is both madness (as he is obviously powerful) and gross ingratitude (because he did it for you).

They are to 'purge the evil from your midst'. This is a command that comes numerous times (17:7, 12; 19:13, 19; 21:9, 21; 22:21-22; 24:7; 26:13-14) and always comes with the death penalty.[2] Again, perhaps living with a deadly coronavirus transformed our view of what is acceptable. In order to purge the virus, we have accepted the crippling of our economy and quarantines of fourteen days. Israel is commanded to purge evil from their midst in order to maintain their relationship with the LORD of life.

2. The close friend or family (13:6-11)

This is far harder. Purging evil is emotionally devastating when it is a family member. The temptation will be to side with them rather than the LORD.

The list of close relations given in verse 6 slows us down to consider them one by one and builds to 'the wife *you embrace*' or your 'friend *who is as your own soul*'.

However, they tempt in the same way as the false dreamer or prophet.

Verse 8 seems to recognise the strong inclination we will have to compromise and so we get five negatives: You shall not 'yield ... listen ... pity ... spare ... conceal'. But you shall kill him. We find verse 9 horrible. Yet presumably it is a test of loyalty. Although it would be emotionally

---

2. Although 19:9 is not explicit so perhaps uncertain.

traumatic, the reason is given in verse 10. One person is stoned to death to save the whole community from being drawn away from the LORD who saves. Sin which is not purged will end in devastation for the whole community.[3]

3. The city that rebels (13:12-18)

The concept that 'worthless fellows have gone out among you' (v. 13) sounds quite familiar to New Testament ears.[4] This takes a little more investigating to track down the suspects, compared to a public speaker or family member (v. 14), yet it is clear that this city has become completely 'Canaanised' and so they are treated like a pagan city of Canaan: the whole place is 'devoted to destruction'. This occurs once during Israel's history, to Gibeah in Judges 19–20 (where worthless fellows[5] cause the problem), but ultimately, it is the fate of the whole nation at the hands of the Babylonians in 587 B.C.

Live like a holy people (14:1-21)

Although we're no longer dealing with warnings against being led after other gods, the issue in 14:1-21 remains the distinctiveness of Israel; they are not to live like the other

---

3. Consequently, there is a vast difference between this and honour killings which sometimes appear in the news. There, a family feels shame because of the behaviour of (most commonly) a daughter and so kills her to remove shame from the family – ultimately that is a selfish desire. Here, the stoning to death is to protect the community by preventing their drift into idolatry. It is an altruistic desire and a desire for the honour of the LORD.

4. 'From among your own selves will arise men speaking twisted things, to draw away the disciples after them' (Acts 20:30); 'They went out from us, but they were not of us' (1 John 2:19).

5. The same term in Judges 19:22 as here.

nations. The section is framed by the unusual phrase for Deuteronomy, 'You are a people holy to the LORD your God' (vv. 2, 21). It appears in this precise form in 7:26,[6] which suggests further that, although we are talking about various foods, the issue is distinctiveness, just as it is there.

While verses 2 and 21 frame the section, the main part of the text alternates between foods that Israel can eat and those they cannot, with the division into

- creatures on the land (vv. 4-8);
- creatures in the sea (vv. 9-10);
- creatures in the sky (vv. 11-20).

The natural question to ask is, Why are some of these foods an abomination (v. 3)? In context the answer seems to be that to eat them would be a denial of Israel's distinctiveness. There is something rather relentless about food prepared daily which was to remind God's people that they were different from the nations around them.

The New Testament is clear that the time for these food laws has come to an end. Jesus declared all foods clean (Mark 7:29) and Peter's vision reinforced this point (Acts 10:10-16). Of course, this is not to suggest that Christians are to be any less exclusive in their loyalty to Jesus, but that this distinctiveness is to be seen in other ways.

From text to message

Getting the message clear: the theme

The LORD chose Israel to be holy to him – that means listening exclusively to him and not false prophets (ch.

---

6. The word 'holy' only appears a surprising twelve times in the whole book (5:12; 7:6; 12:26; 14:2, 21; 23:14; 26:15; 26:19; 28:9; 32:51; 33:2, 3).

13) as well as living with daily food reminders of their distinctiveness (ch. 14).

Getting the message clear: the aim

Do not remotely entertain false teaching which leads you away from the Lord who alone can redeem you.

A way in

A few years ago, it was unthinkable to people in the UK that crowds at sporting fixtures would be banned, that people would wear face masks to go into shops or that they would stay at two metres' distance from one another, even avoiding hugs with good friends. Yet our behaviour changed when we knew that we needed to avoid passing on the deadly Covid-19 virus. What once seemed bizarre became normal.

Many of the things we read in chapter 13 seem bizarre or outrageous to us, but when we understand that they are designed to protect God's people from a far greater virus, they make more sense.

Ideas for application

- False prophets and dreamers still exist and we still need to be warned against them.

  We should not be surprised by heretics or those in other religions who are able to perform signs and wonders. We're told to expect them! (See Matt. 24:24 and 2 Thess. 2:9-10.)

  Although we may recoil from the severity of the punishments in Deuteronomy 13, the New Testament does not. Indeed, Galatians 1:8-9 suggests a fate worse than being stoned to death: the false teacher is

to be *'eternally* condemned'. Similarly, a passage such
as 2 Peter 2 describes at great length the deceptions
and judgment of false teachers. There will always be
those who claim to speak for God, but do not, even
though they may be able to perform supernatural
miracles. Crucially, the question to ask is, Do they
lead people to Jesus or not? One significant test in
the New Testament is described in 1 John 4:1-6. The
way to tell truth apart from error is to know that false
prophets will say what the world wants to hear (v. 5)
and will not listen to the teaching of the apostles
(v. 6). They will always provide for the passions of
those with itching ears (2 Tim. 4:3-4).

- We still need to 'purge the evil' from our midst,
  although that looks very different.

    In the New Testament, this is to be done through
    excommunication as a feature of church discipline.
    Indeed, Paul commands the Corinthians to 'purge
    the evil person from among you' (1 Cor. 5:1-13; cf.
    1 Tim. 1:19-20). Yet in the New Testament, discipline is
    for the sake of rehabilitation, not primarily retribution
    or deterrence. The purpose is both to protect the flock
    and bring the false teacher to repentance; that should
    always be our hope (2 Tim. 2:25-26).

- The tone with which we teach on a passage such as
  this is very important. Although the command for
  absolute loyalty to the Lord is in no sense diminished,
  it is essential that anyone listening to a sermon on
  chapter 13 knows that Christians follow Jesus, who
  was willing to die for his enemies. He remains the
  only way to be saved, which is why we're so desperate

to protect the gospel message from corruption. Yet he was put to death for the sins of others; he was not pitied or spared; he was devoted to destruction (13:5, 8, 15). So it is that Christ's followers must be willing to die for the sake of their enemies, not kill them.

- Loyalty to Jesus comes ahead of loyalty to anyone else.

  As Jesus expresses it: 'Whoever loves father or mother more than me is not worthy of me, and whoever loves son or daughter more than me is not worthy of me' (Matt. 10:37). He takes priority in our hearts (and again here, the issue of whom we love reveals that these are not designed to be mere rules for external conformity).

- There are few pastors who have not had the experience of seeing a keen Christian drift and adopt more liberal positions because of a dear relative who is not saved or a child who declares themselves trans or a close friend who is sexually immoral. The temptation to adjust the truth of what God has said to accommodate their rebellion is very strong. Yet ultimately, we are not loving them by helping them turn away from the one and only Saviour. Moses warns the people ahead of time that this temptation will come. Pastors today are wise to do the same.

Suggestions for preaching

If we take the larger section you could use this outline:

Worship him rightly (12:1–14:21; first to third commandments)

- Don't worship like that (ch. 12)
- Do purge the evil from among you (ch. 13)
- ⇨ Loyalty to the Lord matters!

If you preached chapter 12 separately, then an outline might be:

No idols! (13:1–14:21; second and third commandments)

- Purge the evil from among you (ch. 13) ...
- ... for you are a people holy to the Lord (ch. 14)

Questions to help understand the passage

1. What are the three potential sources of false teaching that leads away from the LORD in chapter 13? What is the wicked thing that they all say (13:2, 6, 13)?

2. Why might the false prophet appear to be from God (13:1-2)?

3. But what is the obvious indication that they are not (13:2)?

4. What is meant to be the believers' first response (13:3)?

5. Why does God permit this (13:3-4)?

6. Why does this matter so much (13:5, 10)?

7. What are we meant to feel from the long list and intimate descriptions of 13:6?

8. Why do you think that there is such a long list of 'do nots' in verse 8? What does this reveal about the strength of the temptation?

9. The city which is an abomination is to be devoted to destruction in the same way as Canaanite cities. What does this reveal that they had become?

10. Look at 14:2 and 21. What is the purpose of this section? How do all the various food laws help remind Israel that they are holy or distinctive to the LORD?

Questions to help apply the passage

1. What should our response be to signs and wonders or miraculous prophecies?

2. How are Christians meant to purge the evil from their midst? (See, for example, Matt. 18:15-17; Rom. 16:17; 1 Cor. 5:1-13; 2 Thess. 3:14; Titus 3:9-11.)

3. Have you ever seen this happen? If never, is that a good thing or a bad thing, do you think?

4. What sort of loyalty does Jesus call for (e.g. Matt. 10:37)?

11.

Have an Open Hand, Not a Begrudging Heart

(Deuteronomy 14:22–16:17)

Introduction

This section is one of the simplest to delineate in chapters 12–26. Its subject matter is clearly to encourage generosity within Israel. It also has a density of references to the 'year' which fall almost exclusively within 14:22–16:17, emphasising the topics of 'releasing' and 'celebrating' at fixed points in the calendar. Nearly all commentators recognise this as expanding on the fourth commandment, and 15:15 effectively quotes from 5:15 to connect these chapters to the need to keep the Sabbath.

Rejoice and share the LORD's tithe together (14:22-29)

Release loans in the seventh year (15:1-18)

Rejoice and share the LORD's goodness together (16:1-17)

At the heart of the simple chiasm are the instructions on how to treat those who have fallen into debt. It is typical of Deuteronomy that a concern for the poor is sandwiched between two passages which consider how to worship before the LORD. A concern for the poor and marginalised within Israel is an indispensable part of worshipping the LORD. Indeed, when you get to 26:12-15 it seems as if care for the poor and vulnerable is *the* key test of whether one had kept the law or not.

It remains a long section to preach and so it makes sense to focus on chapter 15. The preacher will notice that less than half of chapter 15 contains legal detail. The bulk of Moses's preaching here is exhortation. That not only makes it easier for us to preach than some sections, but perhaps Moses's example should make us consider the balance between explanation and exhortation in our own sermons?

In a culture increasingly marked by expressive individualism, the relentless concern for the good of the community in Deuteronomy is a challenge to us. Some may wriggle uncomfortably at the general push that the whole book has to resist material accumulation for individuals at the expense of the community, which finds a focus here in chapter 15. However, it's not as if the New Testament expects anything less (cf. Acts 4:34; 1 John 3:20-21). We should still open our hands in generosity to others in the church who are in need.

Listening to the text

As in 14:1-21, there is a concern with eating in 14:22-29, but verse 22 also introduces a time marker: 'You shall tithe all the yield of your seed that comes from the field year by year.'

This concern with periodicity is a feature of the whole of 14:22–16:17. While references to 'years' occur twenty-nine times in the entire book, thirteen of them are in our current passage (with only two other references in the entirety of chapters 12–26). These regular events in time are an amplification of what it meant to keep the Sabbath.

In both 14:22-29 and 16:1-17, there is a focus upon laws of sacrifice and feasting at the place that the LORD has chosen. They effectively frame chapter 15 to demonstrate that formal times of worship and practical living go hand in hand. Moses knew the truth of Romans 12:1!

Some other words and themes which are obvious:

- Once again, there is a danger in the heart (15:7, 9, 10).

- More obvious is the attention given to having an open hand (14:25, 29; 15:2, 3, 7, 8, 10, 11). Rather than clutching possessions tightly, Israel is to hold them loosely and give up their tithe (14:23-29), pledges (15:1-11), debt slaves (15:12-18) and firstborn animals (15:19-23).

- There is a great deal of emphasis upon God's blessing (14:24, 29; 15:4, 6, 10, 14, 18). Israel needs to know that generosity is made possible, both practically and emotionally, by the LORD's blessing of them. The picture is somewhat of a virtuous cycle:

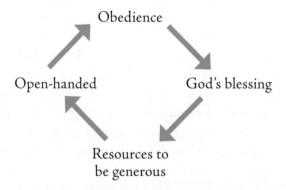

If Israel obeys, then the LORD will bless the work of their hands (14:29), which enables them to be open handed to those who need it, in obedience.

Working through the text
14:22-29

Here again is the call to celebrate God's goodness in his presence. Israel is told to 'rejoice before the LORD your God' six times in the book (12:7, 12, 18; 14:26; 16:11; 27:7).[1] The picture is of the LORD as the host, inviting people to his house to enjoy how richly he has blessed them.

In fact, there are two reasons given for celebrating this tithe:

- to learn to fear the LORD (v. 23; cf. 4:10 and 17:19)
- to rejoice before him

The LORD does not want this journey to be a burden and so makes it as easy as possible to bring the tithe in the form of money, 'in your *hand*' (vv. 24-26). Do note his generosity! Israel is to spend the money 'for whatever they desire'.

This section is similar in content to chapter 12 until we come to verse 27, which suggests (especially as we enter into chapter 15) that the main concern in this short section is to include the whole nation in God's blessing. The Levites were those without any land and so this was the only way for them to share in God's blessing. Along with the familiar landless trio of widow, fatherless and sojourner in verse 29, the concern is that no one is deprived of God's blessing, which was displayed in bounteous crops and herds. The tithe here is not strictly speaking welfare but ensures that no one in the community is prevented from celebrating God's goodness.

---

1. Looking at 14:23; 15:20 and 16:16, these verses do not command the people to rejoice but have the same sense to them. The remaining uses of 'before the LORD your God' in the book are 17:12; 18:7; 19:17; 24:4, 13; 26:4, 5, 10, 13; 29:10, 15 and 31:11 and often have the sense of standing before the LORD as judge.

McConville is worth quoting at length:

> The special provision in 14:28-29 is remarkable – one of the best expressions of Deuteronomy's aim to create a society in which no one would be permanently disadvantaged, or consigned to a second-class status. Deuteronomy is otherwise realistic about the likely persistence of poverty (15:11) as even Jesus was (Mark 14:7). Yet the ideal is a constant project for Christian people. And it is not just 'charity', but the conferring of worth, dignity and belonging.[2]

I expect that most Christian churches see a similar phenomenon at work in wealthier members subsidising poorer ones – for church weekends away, annual dinners or church meals – to ensure that no one is excluded from giving thanks for what the Lord has done. Moses would approve.

15:1-11

The unit of 15:1-18 is held together by the idea of debt and the seventh year (vv. 1, 2, 12). There are two clear sections:

- verses 1-11 deal with the release of debt (vv. 1, 2, 9)
- verses 12-18 deal with how to release those who had sold themselves into debt slavery

Verses 1-11 have a particular concern with an Israelite's duty to his brother (vv. 2, 3, 7, 9, 11). (Although 'brother' does appear also in verse 12 where, interestingly, it is revealed to be an inclusive term which could be either a man or a woman.)

It's worth observing that although Deuteronomy has a particular concern for the 'widow, fatherless, and

---

2. McConville, *Deuteronomy*, 254.

sojourner',[3] chapter 15 has a slightly different concern. Moses has in view people who, in other circumstances, could support themselves; however, they are ensnared by debt. 'The goal of these laws ... is not the long term charity provided to the widow, fatherless and alien ... Rather these laws seek to break the cycle of debt and enslavement and re-integrate these poor into the economy as independent, productive members.'[4] Here is an early form of enhanced debt counselling service or 'Israelites Against Poverty' designed to pull Israelites back onto their feet.

Verses 1-3 deal with the legal terms. I leave you to decide whether you think the release is a deferral for one year (like a mortgage holiday) or cancellation entirely.[5] It does not greatly affect the thrust for a contemporary congregation. Do note though that this is a requirement for Israel: verse 3 is clear that, while you may choose to be kind to a foreigner, that is not an obligation in the way that it is to release the debt of a brother.

Verses 4-11 are motivations to act in this way. Within this, verses 4-6 set up an ideal standard and then verses 7-11 deal with real life. The most obvious contrast is between verse 4 and verse 11. Verses 4-6 are part of the virtuous circle outlined above. Israel has to trust that obedience will lead to blessing. Given their failure thus

---

3. The three are bracketed together eleven times. They were to be beneficiaries of declarations concerning justice (10:18; 27:19), in receipt of tithing (14:29; 26:12-13) and of gleaning (24:17).

4. Nelson, *Deuteronomy*, 192.

5. You can follow the argument in the commentaries. It's finely balanced, but verse 9 tips me into thinking that it is the whole loan in view, not merely giving one year free of interest or enabling someone to use their land for the year.

far to 'strictly obey the voice of the LORD', it is no surprise
that this ideal picture is immediately followed by a more
realistic one in verses 7-11. The LORD knows what his
people are like!

Verse 7 sets up the scenario and gives a clear reminder
that they are dwelling in 'land that the LORD your God
is giving you'. They have received their wealth from the
open-handed God.

A close connection is drawn between a hard heart and a
shut hand. Allow me to point out again that Deuteronomy
is not interested in *mere* outward compliance with the law;
the LORD desires the heart to be right. The call is for Israel
to have soft hearts and open hands.

Moses is a good preacher and so anticipates the objections of his audience in verse 9. 'Take care lest … in your
heart' (cf. 7:17; 8:17; 9:4). If the Sabbath year is coming
and you know that your loan will never fully be repaid,
there is a natural tendency to 'look grudgingly on your
poor brother and give him nothing'. Moses bluntly states
that this refusal to help is sin (v. 9) and you must repent
of it and give freely.

Is this shrewd money management? On the face of it,
no. Yet once again, obedience in this will bring blessing
(v. 10). Obedience is always the shrewd choice, even if
we wait until eternity for the reward. Don't begrudge or
resent the opportunity to help someone gain their financial
independence.

Verse 11 acts as a summary: 'Open wide your hand.'
Israelites were to be more concerned with helping those in
the community who have fallen into debt than with their
own accumulation of wealth. Let money fall from your
hand to where it can aid a brother in need.

15:12-18

These verses discuss Israelites who have sold themselves into slavery. Although there is a further reference to the seventh year, this is not the Sabbath year but rather the seventh year of service.

When their term of service is done, the master is to send them on their way in an open-handed fashion (v. 13), not leaving them empty-handed.

Verses 14 and 15 give two motivations to obey based in God's generosity to masters:

- The LORD God has blessed you – you should be similarly generous.

- The LORD redeemed you from slavery and brought you out of Egypt with riches, so you should send your slave on their way generously too.

After the exception for those who want to stay, there is a further encouragement to the masters. Again, Moses anticipates the natural response of his audience in verse 18, but they are not to think it too hard when this slave goes free as the master has benefitted from a brilliant financial arrangement. The section again concludes with the promise of blessing (cf. v. 10).

15:19-23

Upon a first read, this is an abrupt change of subject, but the return to eating in the presence of God is the balance to 14:22-29 and therefore highlights the importance of 15:1-18 as central to the whole section. Here again, Moses is concerned with the vertical aspects of Israel's activities. Only the meat of an unblemished animal is worthy of being sacrificed before the LORD. Indeed, the firstborn *must* be dedicated and consumed before him.

16:1-17

This section describes the three annual festivals when Israel was to gather at the place that the LORD had chosen (vv. 2, 6, 7, 11, 15, 16). Typical for Deuteronomy's concern with exhortation, there are fewer details here than in Exodus 12 and Leviticus 23 when the festivals are introduced. The section is concerned with many of the same themes as chapter 12: their worship is to be:

- responsive (vv. 1, 5, 10, 15) to the God who has recused them and blessed them materially;
- joyful (vv. 11, 14, 15);
- costly (the pilgrimages must have been a significant endeavour); and
- social (vv. 11, 14).

Passover or Unleavened Bread (16:1-8)

These two festivals are combined. The primary reason for the Passover is verse 3: 'That all the days of your life you may remember the day when you came out of the land of Egypt'.

Weeks (or Pentecost in Greek texts) (16:9-12)

The chief function of this was to offer 'a freewill offering from your hand' in proportion to how the LORD had blessed each family. The list of those to take with you seems even longer than in 12:12. Table fellowship really matters.

Booths (16:13-15)

After all the crops were brought in, Israel could celebrate a 'harvest festival'. Verse 15 has a delightful stress on the work of your hands being 'altogether joyful'. Or, as the NIV has it, 'your joy will be complete' – a phrase that finds a deeper meaning on the lips of Jesus (John 15:11).

Summary (16:16-17)

The people[6] are not to appear before the LORD 'empty-handed' (the same term as in 15:13). The LORD delights in the generosity of his people, both to the economically vulnerable and also to him, their God.

It strikes me that perhaps in the Western church some of us have unwisely jettisoned an annual calendar. Christmas remains, but for many Easter is a great four-day holiday rather than any time with the Lord. It seems to me that many churches from my own tribe largely ignore Pentecost (perhaps wary of associations with churches which have lost biblical authority). Yet Pentecost should be a celebration that all are welcome to be included in the people of God, just as in Acts 2 the gospel was for people of all languages.

The LORD gave an annual calendar to Israel to help them remember his goodness and be altogether joyful.

From text to message

Getting the message clear: the theme

Laws concerning treatment of the poor show that having a greater concern for the poorest and most vulnerable in Israel was more important than growing one's own wealth. Israel was to pass on the LORD's generosity rather than keep it for themselves as individuals.

Getting the message clear: the aim

Be open handed in generosity towards the economically vulnerable within the church.

---

6. This is the only place where males are specified. Presumably, this was the minimum acceptable requirement for obedience (given v. 11 and v. 14).

A way in

I was with a family the other day when a mum gave two pounds to her five-year-old and said he could go into the sweet shop and buy a paper bag's worth of sweets. He proudly did so and exited the shop delighted. Mum gave the further instruction, 'Now Daniel, share them with you brother.' At this point, it was striking to see Daniel tighten his fist around the bag and declare, 'I don't want to.' Probably not an atypical response for a small boy and you can imagine how the conversation continued: 'But Daniel, I gave you the money for the sweets and I'm asking you to share with your brother. If you don't share then there'll be no sweets next week. ...'

It took some cajoling to get Daniel to release his grip around the sweets.

But, I wonder, are we any better with the resources that the Lord has given us?

Ideas for application

- The New Testament sees these verses fulfilled in two different communities:

    o the church (Acts 2:4-47 and especially Acts 4:34)

    o ultimately in glory

- The poor will always be with you (Mark 14:7). However, this does not mean we can adopt a callous disregard to the poor. 'As the context shows, Jesus's intention was not to give the disciples an excuse to neglect the poor. Quite the reverse! He acknowledged that the obligation to remember the poor is ongoing and indisputable. But in this very special situation, he commended the woman's act of extravagant devotion, as she anointed him.'[7]

- You cannot ignore the financial plight of other Christians in your church. In his commentary on 1 John, Colin Kruse suggests that Deuteronomy 15 is the backdrop to what John writes:[8] 'If anyone has the world's goods and sees his brother in need, yet closes his heart against him, how does God's love abide in him?' (1 John 3:17). Different churches will establish different ways of helping those in financial need. It can all be informal in smaller churches, while larger churches may find it better to adopt some form of 'Deacons' Fund' which wise people administer. Of course, it's not enough to simply hand out money; this takes involvement in people's lives. Sometimes, the time spent helping people out of debt is possibly more costly than then money required.

- More broadly, chapter 15 encourages a general attitude of sitting lightly to possessions as 'ours'. The church should be a mutually supporting body where people insure others on their cars and are open handed with clothes and meals, where interest-free loans are arranged to get church members out of a debt spiral.

- Table fellowship really matters. No one is to be excluded (16:11) and that remains the case today – along ethnic lines, as well as social ones (Gal. 2:12).

---

7. Brian Rosner, 'Should We Remember the Poor?' *The Briefing* 341 (Feb. 2007). Thanks to James Robson for pointing this out.

8. Colin G. Kruse, *The Letters of John* (PNTC; Leicester: Apollos, 2000), 138.

- Generosity is empowered by God's blessing. That was true in a material sense but surely must also be so for those who have every spiritual blessing. The Christian knows that our whole lives are based upon his kindness to us. If we're hard-hearted, we need to remember that Jesus's heart was broken that we might live. If we're tight-fisted, we must remember that Jesus opened his fists and had nails driven through them for us. If we think that others are undeserving, then we must remember that Jesus has cancelled our debt of sin even though we are undeserving. We have *every* reason to be open handed and soft hearted.

- Echoes for the nations? Although Israel was not obligated to foreigners in the same way as to a brother Israelite, I wonder if we should still advocate for a similar approach to the most vulnerable in national policy, even though we are not personally required to act. I know some will avoid this topic, but, personally, I might gently and tentatively suggest that, when we know that this is the kind of behaviour that pleases God, Christians would surely want to encourage this in a secular society. Nationally, a concern for the most vulnerable is natural for followers of this Lord and has resulted in wonderful schemes such as 'Christians Against Poverty'. Internationally, chapter 15 may have something to say to crippling international debt that seems to doom some poorer nations to perpetual dependence.

Suggestions for preaching

In a 'three-pointer', after an introduction to the theme, I would briefly explain the frame for chapter 15, that Israel is to celebrate the LORD's goodness and not appear empty handed (16:16) before the LORD who has given them everything (14:29; 16:17).

The bulk of the time would be in chapter 15 explaining what was required, our possible objections and the motivations for opening our hands. I'd ensure there was a good amount of time to place this within a New Testament frame.

Have an open hand not a begrudging heart

- Rejoice that the LORD has blessed the work of your hands (14:22-29; 16:1-17)

- Open your hands so that there are no poor among you (15:1-11)

- Open your hands so that there are no poor in Christ (Acts 4:34 and ultimately Rev. 21)

Questions to help understand the passage

1. Read 14:22-29. What has God done for Israel? What was Israel to do by way of response? Where? What is the mood of this little passage?

2. How were Israelites meant to treat their brothers and sisters (15:1-11)?

3. What are the motivations for cancelling the debts of a fellow Israelite in verses 4-11?

4. What is the danger that may lurk in their hearts (v. 9) and how can they overcome this temptation (vv. 10-11)?

5. Again, what is the motivation for releasing a brother or sister from their contract (vv. 14-15)?

6. What is emphasised about the three festivals outlined in 16:1-17?

Questions to help apply the passage

1. How do you ensure that the poorest Christians in your church are wisely looked after?

2. Are there any who are excluded from meals or church social events purely because they cannot afford it?

3. How do you celebrate God's generosity towards you 'before his face'?

12.

What Do We Do Without Moses?

(Deuteronomy 16:18–18:22)

Introduction

This again is a well-defined section within chapters 12–26, focused on leadership structures in Israel. The death of Moses was introduced at the beginning of the book (1:37; 3:23-29) as was the need for good leadership to be appointed (1:9-18). This issue of how Israel will continue without Moses is always there in the background in Deuteronomy and at points like these chapters, and especially chapters 31–34, comes very much to the forefront. The thrust of this section is that, if you want there to be justice, choose leaders who love God's word and listen to God's people.

The unit is held together by subject matter and generally is seen as an explication of the fifth commandment to honour parents. However, Olson helpfully captures an important difference: 'The primary thrust of the commandment concerning parents is that authorities are to be honoured. The primary thrust of the *statutes and ordinances* that explicate the parents commandment is that authorities are to be worthy of the honour they receive. Leadership brings responsibilities.'[1]

Israel is told here that they are not to expect too much or too little from their leaders. If there is to be justice in the land, then the people must be active in appointing judges and even the king (albeit one the LORD chooses). However, the LORD himself appoints priests and above all the prophets. For when Moses has gone, it is the voice of God speaking through his prophets that must rule. Don't allow any human too much power.

There is a great deal of practical wisdom here for how we should run our churches – again, not expecting too much or too little from our leaders. It is also a passage which makes us cherish, more than ever, the leader we have in Christ.

Listening to the text

Structure

There are five expressions of leadership:

16:18–17:7	Local courts
17:8-13	The central sanctuary court
17:14-20	The king
18:1-8	Priests and Levites
18:9-22	The prophet

Nelson is typical of several commentators in referring to this section as 'Constitutional proposals'.[2] There is obvious sense to that and the section does commend a separation of powers to prevent any one person or group from aggregating

---

1. Olson, *Deuteronomy and the Death of Moses*, 78.

2. Nelson, *Deuteronomy*, 210.

too much power to themselves. However, 16:18-20 seems to function as an introduction to the section with its repeated call for 'Justice and only justice.'

Working through the text

Appoint judges to help you bring justice (16:18–17:7)

16:18-20

The 'You' of verse 18 and throughout the section is singular, referring to the entire people of Israel. The people are responsible for choosing the judges and again in verses 19-20 it is the people (singular) who are addressed.

There are three things to avoid:

- Do not pervert justice (literally 'turn' or 'bend') (cf. 24:17; 27:19)
- Do not show partiality (literally 'regard faces') (cf. 1:17; 10:17)
- Do not accept a bribe

This last prohibition is given at greater length. A bribe 'blinds the eyes of the wise and subverts the cause of the righteous'. Presumably, this was therefore the greatest danger for Israel? It was precisely this crime that the sons of Samuel were guilty of (1 Sam. 8:3), but then of course Samuel should not have appointed them as judges.

For us, we need to remember that not all bribes are obvious financial ones; there are more subtle sins of collusion where we allow ourselves to be blinded to an obvious fault in a leader because he benefits us personally.

The conclusion is the rhetorically powerful 'Justice, and only justice, you shall follow'. Moses is not drawing up a constitution but rather he is exhorting them so that they are clear on what matters. Justice matters to the LORD: 'The Rock, his work is perfect, for all his ways are justice' (32:4).

16:21–17:1

It seems strange that this threefold prohibition 'interrupts' the command to appoint judges and then a case study of local courts. Yet it seems that these three examples of evil behaviour are precisely the sort of abomination that the local courts are meant to deal with.

Asherah poles and pillars were typical of the Canaanite fertility cult, while a blemished offering is an abomination (cf. 15:20-21). An abomination? Yes, because the Israelite had broken the fundamental call to love the LORD wholeheartedly. It is striking that Malachi later attacks the quality of the priest's sacrifices (Mal. 1:6–2:9). God had told them that it was an abomination; they should have known!

17:2-7

Here, we see the local courts functioning. We should notice that the crime that is given as an example of the courts in action is idolatry, for there is nothing worse in Israel. The language is striking: it is 'evil' (vv. 2, 5, 7), 'transgressing his covenant' (v. 2), and 'an abomination' (v. 4).

This case is blatant (presumably the sort of syncretism described in 16:21) and therefore not 'too difficult' (v. 8) to be dealt with at the local level.

The process followed is a thorough one and we must be clear who is addressed. Moses does not say 'they' referring to the local judges but 'you'. Throughout the passage, the 'yous' are singular as the whole community is responsible for the process:

- If the people hear rumour of a transgression, it is not to be ignored (v. 4).

- There must be a diligent investigation, not merely hearsay or gossip (v. 4).

- The case must be heard in public (v. 5).

- There must be multiple witnesses (v. 6).

- The witness must be involved in carrying out the sentence (v. 7) – no doubt to prevent frivolous cases.

The purpose of this whole process is to 'purge the evil from your midst'. The sentence seems harsh to us, but we must remember that sin being purged was essential to national security (see chapter 13). Western governments still take that threat very seriously (e.g. break the Official Secrets Act in the UK and you'll go to prison for fourteen years).

Do precisely what the judge tells you (17:8-13)

Some cases are simply too difficult to resolve (v. 8). Whereas once they could be brought to Moses (1:17), when in the land they will need to go to the central court. This is described as being at 'the place that the LORD your God will choose'. In other words, they are to go to where the sanctuary/tabernacle/temple is. Consequently, they will bring the case to the Levitical priests and the senior judge (you can make up your own mind whether you think he is a separate official or one of the Levitical priests appointed as 'judge' for the year).

The process here is very different. There is no investigation and no right of appeal. Rather, the people bring the case and then the judge and Levites 'declare to you from *that place that the* Lord *will choose*' (v. 9). The people then must do precisely what they are told and there is no latitude to act more severely or leniently. Failure to follow the precise instructions of the central court is presumption and anyone so guilty must die. All of this suggests that the judge and Levites have had a word from God about the case, or possibly used the Urim and Thummim (Deut. 33:8) to determine the outcome.

The fact that disobedience to the priest or judge is evil that needs purging – akin to idolatry (v. 7) – all points to this presumptuous disobedience ignoring what God has said.

Notice again the role of the people. While they must listen to the judge, their task is to (1) present the case and (2) implement its decision. Justice cannot be left to someone else – the whole community must be involved if you want 'justice, only justice'.

Limit the powers of the king (17:14-20)

Israel would have been struck, hearing this, by how limited the king was. He has a highly restricted role. Although Israel will request a king 'like all the nations that are around me', the Lord says he is 'one from among your brothers' – a levelling title. The king does not appoint any of the other leaders in the section 16:18–18:22. He functions more like a CEO. Wright observes that this is not the exalted picture of the Psalms: 'The way of the king in Deuteronomy is not a reflection of the deity but a model of the true Israelite.'[3] Was it a mistake for Israel to ask for a king at all? Well, in the flow of 1 Samuel it does seem to

---

3. Wright, *Deuteronomy*, 208.

be a rejection of the Lord's provision for them. Yet 'if the request for a king had been intrinsically incompatible with theocracy, it would doubtless have received a resounding rejection in the language of chapter 7.'[4]

Three times we are told that the king 'must not acquire ... for himself':

- **Horses** which were the key military hardware of the day, granting power. (It was especially bad if you trade with Egypt to get them – a 'moral reversal of the exodus.'[5])

- **Wives** who had influence (through marriage alliances, cf. 1 Kings 11:1-4). Although possibly it was as simple as distraction by involvement (31:3).

- **Wealth** (it's *excessive* wealth *for himself* that's precluded).

There is one thing that is non-negotiable in the king's job description (vv. 18-20): he must invest significant time in studying God's torah. Naturally, he would have had many other tasks to do, but this one cannot be ignored. It carries numerous benefits: it brings the fear of the Lord,[6] humility and a long reign with a dynasty. The commandment of verse 20 is best understood as Deuteronomy's fundamental call for loyalty to the Lord (cf. 6:5).

Provide appropriately for the priests (18:1-8)

This section is again addressing the people, not actually the priests. It is not a description of the Levites' role (primarily

---

4. Wright, *Deuteronomy*, 208.

5. McConville, *Deuteronomy*, 294.

6. Block observes: 'For the first time in the book, the Torah is portrayed as a medium by which the fear of the Lord is instilled in the heart (mind)' (*Deuteronomy*, 420).

to minister at the sanctuary and to preserve and teach the law) but rather the people's responsibility to them. The focus is on providing an 'inheritance' for them (four times in vv. 1-2) as, although the LORD is their inheritance, they still need food to eat.[7] They are to be generously provided for (vv. 3-4; cf. 1 Tim. 5:17-18). This is a group *not* chosen by the people, but by God (v. 5). Nevertheless, the people are to provide for them. They are not to take their spiritual leaders for granted.

Verses 6-8 deal with the particular issue of a Levite who leaves one of the forty-eight Levitical cities (established so that everyone in the land can receive priestly care; Num. 35:1-8) and works at the sanctuary. He is still to receive 'equal pay for an equal job' while on his chosen secondment.

Listen to God's chosen prophet, not other voices (18:9-22)

Here the question of what to do when Moses is gone becomes acute. Where will the people turn to receive a word from God? It is hard to fit this section into 'constitutional proposals'. There is no legal tone to the language. In fact, its place at the end of the leadership discussion and its emphasis upon God's appointment of the prophet stress that this is the most important of all the roles.

Not this abominable way! (18:9-14)

Verse 9 is clear – Israel does not need to try and manipulate God like the pagans do. Nine types of behaviour are prohibited. At the top of the list is the utterly despicable

---

7. The provisions in the law which gave Levi no land seem wisely designed to prevent the clergy from amassing wealth and power alongside their spiritual role. A lesson sadly forgotten in church history.

practice of child sacrifice (12:31), something seen vividly in 2 Kings 3:27 when the king of Moab sacrifices his son in a desperate attempt to turn the tide of battle. Yet all of these prohibited practices are similar in trying to manipulate gods onto your side or extract information begrudgingly from them.

This abominable (v. 9 and twice in v. 12) behaviour is not allowed and it's also unnecessary. The LORD is already their God and speaks clearly.

But the LORD will raise up a prophet (18:15-19)

Verse 15 acts by way of contrast to the preceding. It is the one that the LORD raises up from among your brothers: 'It is *to him* you shall listen.' Here are some notable features of this prophet:

- He comes from God's initiative. The prophet is not chosen like a judge or even requested like a king. There is more emphasis here on God's choice than in the case of the Levites. Moses quotes the LORD's own words directly in verses 17-20, underlining the importance of this role.

- 'Like Moses'. In what way? Certainly as a mediator, as verse 16 explains; this new prophet will act like Moses did at Horeb when the people beg Moses to stand between them and God. This new prophet will bring them God's words, just as Moses did.

- He carries God's authority – 'My words in his mouth …' (v. 18) – so that everyone is obliged to listen: 'I myself will require it of him' (v. 19). Just as in 17:10, this is not an optional word; all Israel must submit to it.

It seems unlikely given Israel's history that the reference to 'the prophet' singular means only one other person in history, as the LORD has numerous faithful prophets that speak to Israel with his authority. That said, by the time of the New Testament, there does seem to be an expectation of one 'Prophet-like-Moses' figure (John 1:21-22; 6:14; Acts 3:22-24)[8] so we must not ignore the Messianic expectation here in Deuteronomy. In preaching this section, it is not enough to have the prophet as one of five expressions of leadership; his role is distinctive and climactic.

False prophets (18:20-22)

Given the enormous authority of the prophet, there will always be the temptation for some to pretend to speak for God (vv. 20-22). If they are proven false, they must die. Of course, the test that Moses sets in verses 21-22 could take a long time to disprove them, but McConville's suggestion that this false prophet is claiming a word of judgment (hence 'You need not fear him') has much to commend it. 'Here the danger is not that the people ... should go over to other gods but that they might needlessly fear.'[9] If it is a dramatic word of judgment against an individual, then the threat possibly would be shorter term.

Overall, 18:9-22 stresses that Israel does not need to resort to manipulating God to reveal what is important, nor must they make do with vague suggestions from God. The LORD has given them the torah and, alongside that, he will raise up prophets that speak with his authority.

---

8. Thanks to Stephen Boon for this correction.

9. McConville, *Deuteronomy*, 303.

From text to message

Getting the message clear: the theme

The subject is the leadership structures that Israel is to implement in the land when Moses has gone. There is an emphasis upon the people being proactive – they must choose the judges and they must ensure that there is no partiality, bribery or perversion of justice. They cannot just leave it to leaders. They cannot presume that their leaders will act morally – temptation affects everyone. Yet they must also recognize the authority of leaders, provide for the Levites, obey *absolutely* judgments that come from God and listen to God's prophet.

Getting the message clear: the aim

How can we ensure that there is 'justice, only justice'? The people must be involved and the leaders must love God's word.

A way in[10]

Pete the Pastor has been told that one of the Elders at his church has been giving a few of the single women at church a lift home after meetings. One of them felt very uncomfortable. The Elder is a complete stalwart of the church and a big giver. What should Pete do?

Colin the Curate is keen to take a week's study leave to study the Bible and pray. He asks but is told that everyone is too busy for him to spend extra time reading the Bible. What should he do?

---

10. Adapted from a terrific sermon on this passage that I heard Kirk Patston give at SMBC Preaching Conference in Sydney (https://www.smbc.edu.au/store/smbc-media/between-rescue-and-home).

Helen the Homegroup Co-leader is a little troubled by one member of their group who relentlessly talks about how 'the church leadership' is wrong to talk about God's wrath. What should she do?

Ideas for application

- If Christians want to see justice in church then they need to appoint good leaders and be involved. It will not happen on its own. It's no good ignoring things because 'It's none of my business and I don't want to get involved.' Moses's examples are primarily ones of idolatry and heresy; so again it is not merely left to the pastors to address these issues.

- If you want effective church ministers, then ensure that they're supported financially. Failure to pay a pastor appropriately is disobedience (1 Cor. 9:3-11).

- When we have a clear word from the LORD in Scripture, obedience is not negotiable. We should not turn aside to the right or the left when God has spoken – that would be presumptuous and incur his displeasure!

- Christian leaders are vulnerable to the temptations of power, influence and wealth too. It is possible for a minister to lord it over a church of 1,000 or a church of 50. The size is indifferent. It's important to have a suitable 'separation of powers' within a church, rather than one man 'acquiring for himself' all influence. Christian leaders can also be prone to partiality; treating 'valuable' members of the church differently to those who are a 'drain' on resources.

- Many of us instinctively will say, 'Aha, Jesus fulfils these roles as prophet, priest and king.' Indeed, but perhaps slow down and suggest at least three ways in which he does so:

1. Jesus was the Israelite who was the victim of 16:19-20. He was opposed by priests who used false witnesses to convict him. He was betrayed for a bribe of thirty pieces of silver. He suffered under the unjust leadership of Pilate who showed partiality in convicting an innocent man. He was mocked by a king in Herod, who had no interest in the law of the Lord. His death was the greatest perversion of justice ever seen.

2. He is of course, truly the prophet, priest and king – the one who fulfils all of those offices perfectly and ultimately. He not only studied the law of the Lord, he knew it perfectly. We do not weigh his words like any other prophet; we know that he spoke the very words of God. We undoubtedly owe him the first fruits of our labour. Justice will only come ultimately when he reigns (see Ps. 72).

3. The risen Jesus appointed some to serve him as apostles and still today as pastors and teachers. The people *must* listen to them. The leaders *must* love God's word and listen to the concerns of the people.

Suggestions for preaching

This is a very practical passage with much that we can learn about the type of leadership we desire in church, the need for thorough investigations of accusations, submission to the authority of God's word and our hope in the one who fulfils all of the roles described and will ensure that there is justice.

How can we ensure that there is 'justice, only justice'?

- What would you do in these scenarios (such as in 'A way in')?

- The people must be involved (16:18-20)
  Although the passage has five expressions of leadership, the role of the people in choosing some of these leaders and bringing injustice before them is essential.

- Leadership must be spread (16:21–18:22)
  A look at each of the five with a practical application from each to church life.

- We need the Son who reigns with justice (cf. Ps. 72)
  Jesus is so much greater than these. We need him for there to be justice.

  ⇨ So, what should we do in those scenarios?

Questions to help understand the passage

1. Who is addressed in 16:18-20? So, who is responsible for ensuring there is no perversion of justice or bribery?

2. We read about the establishment of local courts in 16:18–17:7. Given the examples that Moses gives, what issues would they be handling? How do the three prohibitions of 16:21–17:1 fit in?

3. What is the process to be followed in the local courts?

4. What cases go to the central court (17:8-13)? What are the two responsibilities of the people in this scenario? How much latitude do they have?!?

5. What expressly is the king not to do (17:14-20)? What is the one thing he *is* to do?

6. Who is being spoken about and who is being addressed in 18:1-8? What are the people to do?

7. Why do verses 9-14 appear immediately before the appointment of a prophet in verse 15?

8. What is different about the prophet's appointment?

Questions to help apply the passage

1. Use the questions in 'A way in' to help apply some of the principles.

2. What can we learn from the positive and negative commands given regarding the king?

3. What can we learn from how the Levites were to be treated?

4. What can we learn about how we should take *the* prophet's words?

5. How did Jesus get on in front of judges, priests and the king? How does he fulfil these roles wonderfully better than anyone else?

13.
Matters of Life and Death
(Deuteronomy 19:1–22:8)

Introduction

The first verse of chapter 19 seems to function as the introduction to 'part 2' of the laws in chapters 12–26. 'When the LORD your God cuts off the nations …' only appears here and 12:29. There is certainly a shift of style, to a less exhortatory and more casuistic one, from here until chapter 26. Dare I mention that this makes chapters 19–26 the most difficult section of the book to preach? Some may want to preach one representative sermon from the whole section. I am suggesting taking it in two sections:

19:1–23:18   (the Sixth and Seventh Words of the Decalogue)

23:19–25:16 (the Eighth, Ninth and Tenth Words of the Decalogue)

However, in a longer series, it is quite possible to slow down and spend a sermon on each of the Ten.

Most commentators[1] take 19:1–22:8 to be an explication of the Sixth Word: 'You shall not murder'. As such, it is the

---

1. With the notable exception of Block, *Deuteronomy*, 448.

longest section in chapters 12–26. The Hebrew word for
murder or kill has a range which can include manslaughter
and (as the ESV footnote at 5:17 helpfully points out) 'death
through carelessness or negligence'. After Deuteronomy
5:17 it occurs next in our current text, at 19:3, 4 and 6.

There are clearly some parts of the section which we
struggle to fit under the Sixth Word. Perhaps most obvious is
19:14, which seems a bizarre interruption until you consider
the option that Moses does not limit murder to killing with a
sword. Removing someone's means of economic production
(i.e. stealing their land) comes under the same rubric. There
is a concern for systemic and economic damage which can
'kill' a family by removing their source of income.

However, there are some laws which simply seem to have
jumped from the 'wrong' place. For example, the regulations
concerning transvestitism in 22:5 make more sense with
22:9–23:18 where there is a concern for maintaining proper
boundaries in sexual relations. While we may have preferred
Moses to order his material more precisely, the somewhat
overlapping nature of the regulations reminds us that life is not
always clear cut and if we obsess about 'which command does
this law derive from', we are perhaps missing the point. Life is
messy but it is all to be lived under God's law. Perhaps Olson
goes a little far in describing these as 'transitional units',[2] but
the ambiguity over the boundaries of each section in chapters
19–26 reminds us that the law is meant to be kept as a whole.

The section has a concern with both preserving innocent
life and punishing when required. Olson expresses it well:
'The overarching theme of these diverse laws is the conflict
between two forces: the priority of live-giving compassion

---

2. Olson, *Deuteronomy and the Death of Moses*, 91.

versus the necessary but ambiguous limits of reality and death … The scales tip decidedly in favour of mercy, compassion and humaneness in these matters.'[3]

Listening to the text

- Apart from the word for murder/kill (19:3, 4, 6), there are multiple references to death or dying in this section (19:5, 6, 11, 12; 20:5, 6, 7; 21:21-22).

- Olson makes the intriguing observation that there are also multiple references to wood/ tree as a source of death (19:5; 20:20; 21:22-23) and life (20:19; 22:6).[4]

Structure

Although there are lots of subunits, the chapter divisions do reflect the major sections by topic:

- Chapter 19 covers judicial process to protect innocent life.

- Chapter 20 has laws concerning annual warfare.

- Chapter 21 talks about mitigating misconduct to keep the God-given land holy.

- Chapter 22:1-8 relates to respecting the value of all life.

Working through the text

Establish guilt rightly (19:1-21)

Cities of refuge (19:1-13)

Broadly, we have a law in verses 1-3, explanation in verses 4-10, and the obvious exception in verses 11-13. The basic

---

3. 19:1-10, 15; 20:10-15, 19–20; 21:10-14, 15–17; 22:1-4, 6–8 (Olson, *Deuteronomy and the Death of Moses*, 90).

4. Olson, *Deuteronomy and the Death of Moses*, 89.

aim behind this law is given twice: the innocent should not be punished and the guilty must not go unpunished:

- 'lest innocent blood be shed in your land that the LORD your God is giving you for an inheritance, and so the guilt of bloodshed be upon you' (v. 10).

- 'Your eye shall not pity him, but you shall purge the guilt of innocent blood from Israel, so that it may be well with you' (v. 13).

Don't deprive another family of their inheritance (19:14)

As above, the presence of a seemingly intrusive law amongst the regulations governing matters of life and death is presumably intended to show 'the life and death significance of land boundaries in an agricultural society'.[5] In the list of those to be cursed in chapter 27, moving a landmark comes immediately after dishonouring parents (v. 16) so this is evidently a serious matter. 'Justice outside the town walls – in the fields – is as vital as justice inside the gates.'[6]

Actions to deter perjury (19:15-21)

Here are regulations that could easily flow from the Ninth Word of 'Do not lie', yet they also fit in this chapter as they are concerned with the protection of innocent life.

The dispute is to be taken to the judges of 17:8-9. They are to decide the matter – there is to be no room here for personal vengeance as it is the work of the central court to decide the verdict.

Verse 21 is a well-known verse for which the Bible is criticized for encouraging violence. Yet in the context

---

5. McConville, *Deuteronomy*, 309.

6. Block, *Deuteronomy*, 456.

here, it is simply saying that the punishment should fit the crime. If you accuse a man of stealing when you didn't see him commit a crime, then you deserve the sentence that he would have served. It is not an encouragement to violence but rather, as verse 20 shows, it was meant to be a deterrent.

When Jesus addresses this issue in Matthew 5:38-39, it seems that he is criticizing the Pharisees for taking a verse about how the central courts handled such matters and using it to justify personal revenge. It was never meant to be that. Jesus encourages an attitude of personal self-sacrifice rather than vengeance.

Wage war justly (20:1-20)

We move from individual violence to corporate violence. The chapter has three sections introduced with 'When' (20:1, 10, 19):

- The priests should encourage fearful troops (vv. 1-9).
- Pursue peace where possible (vv. 10-18).
- Demonstrate ecological restraint (vv. 19-20).

The priests should encourage fearful troops (20:1-9)

The chapter considers rules for 'when you go out to war'. This is not, therefore, referring to the one-off conquest of Canaan but the seasonal campaigns that kings ventured out on.

The odds appear to be stacked against Israel (v. 1) and so it is natural that they would fear (v. 1, v. 3 – where four different terms are used – and v. 8). Crucially, they need reminding that the LORD who conquered the might of Egypt is with them and he can certainly cope with local warlords. This is not a battle they can lose! Moses gives the priests a script to read out before battle (as the same key truth of the LORD fighting for them applies to every battle).

Indeed, as the odds are so obviously with Israel and her LORD, troops are free to leave. The three exemptions of new house, new vineyard and new wife appear together also in 28:30, where it is viewed as utterly futile to have these things but never be able to appreciate them: 'aspects of normal life in the land take precedence over the requirements of the army.'[7]

There is then a fourth exemption granted for those who are still fearful (v. 8) because the LORD can defeat enemies with any number.

Pursue peace where possible (20:10-18)

There is a massive difference between cities that are far from you (vv. 10-15) and those that are Canaanite (vv. 16-18).

Verses 10-15 propose very different action from that of chapter 7, when Canaanite cities are to be devoted to destruction (*herem*):

- If a city surrenders, there is to be no violence (vv. 10-11).

- If one of these cities makes war, then the males are to be killed to weaken the city (vv. 12-14), but everyone else shall survive.

- Yet Canaanite cities are to be utterly destroyed (vv. 16-18). This is not only due to their complete wickedness but also because they pose a long-term threat to the faithfulness of Israel and her distinctiveness. This is the emphasis of verse 18 (see also notes on chapter 7). This violence was essential

---

7. Craigie, *The Book of Deuteronomy*, 274.

to ensure Israel was not contaminated but survived as God's light to a desperate world.

Demonstrate ecological restraint (20:19-20)

These verses seem to have a twofold reasoning. First, trees have not made war against Israel (v. 19); second, they provide food and so it is an act of self-harm to destroy them. Although there are difficult calculations to be taken in modern warfare about the best way to preserve the greatest number of human lives, it is perhaps an indication that total war – where any civilians, animals and crops are fair game in the pursuit of a quick victory – cannot always be justified.

Handle life's mess fairly (21:1-23)

There are five sections to the chapter, handling situations of distress or wrongdoing. The first and last concern the defilement of the land, the middle three all concern issues of inheritance. Yet all broadly continue a concern with separating life and death and mitigating the worst impact of these scenarios.

The people must deal with the crime of an individual (21:1-9)

This is a fascinating law. If there is an unsolved crime in the land, then it cannot be ignored. There is a guilt upon the whole people (v. 8) showing that crimes in the land have a corporate element to them: they are an offence against the LORD who has given the land (v. 1).

It is serious enough that the elders and judges must come and decide which city is most proximate to the murder (v. 2). The elders of this city must take responsibility (vv. 3-8).

The strange ritual of verses 3-4 does not appear to be a sacrifice as there is no altar or priest involved. It is perhaps best understood as a re-enactment of the murder with the aim of removing the defilement of the land. The fact it takes place in a remote place may remind us of the scapegoat in Leviticus 16.

The purpose is clearly explained in verse 8: *'their* blood guilt be atoned for.' The word for 'atone' features in Deuteronomy only here (twice) and in the Song of Moses (32:43). Christian readers will have Hebrews 10:4 in their ears.

There is a corporate responsibility here of the whole people for the crime of one individual.

As Block puts it: 'When a person violates the righteous standards of God, unless the community responds to the crime, the guilt of the individual rests on the heads of all.'[8]

The humiliated must be shown compassion (21:10-14)

Although we may want more from the regulations protecting captive women, this is a benevolent ruling when compared to what often takes place in war zones today. It is the power of the conquering soldier that is limited and the rights of the vulnerable captive that are protected. She is given the rights of a wife, is protected from rape or slavery, is given time to mourn and she is free to leave if his ardour towards her cools. In verse 11, the word for desire does not necessarily have negative connotations. It is used of God's desire for captive Israel in 7:7 and 10:15.

The inheritance of the firstborn must be protected (21:15-17)

Bigamy is never actually prohibited in the Old Testament law but it's clearly not what God desires (Gen. 2:18-25),

---

8. Block, *Deuteronomy*, 492.

and throughout Genesis examples of its practice are shown to cause enormous problems or disaster. Certainly, in Deuteronomy, the king (as a model Israelite) is only to have one wife (17:17). The rightful inheritance of the land matters more than a man's affections.

The rebellious son must be punished (21:18-21)

These verses continue the theme of a family's inheritance being threatened – this time by a rebellious son. Potentially, this could be the loved son of verse 16. This is not an infant, but a young man who has grown to be a glutton and a drunkard: his behaviour has become a public issue seen by others in the community. In striking terms, the young man is 'stubborn and rebellious' (vv. 18 and 20). This has to be addressed. How would Israel learn to stop being stubborn (9:6, 13; 10:16; 31:27) and rebellious (1:26, 43; 9:7, 23, 24; 31:27) if they tolerate that sort of behaviour in the midst of families and communities? There is again a motive of deterrent in verse 21: Israel shall 'see and fear'.

We may find such a law abhorrent, but there is no account in the whole Old Testament of this being carried out. At points the deterrent may have worked in civilizing the behaviour of young men.

It is certainly striking that the parents are not involved in the punishment, preventing a cruel father carrying out an unjustified attack or indeed good parents being deeply distressed by the whole scenario. It is the whole community that must be involved in redressing delinquent behaviour: 'all the men of the city shall stone him to death.' It is noticeable that this action is required to 'purge the evil from your midst', placing stubborn rebellion against parents alongside rebellion against the LORD (13:5), the worship of other gods (17:7), murder (19:13), perjury (19:19) and adultery (22:22). When a child learns to rebel against their parents with impunity, it will have an impact upon the whole community.

The land must not be defiled (21:22-23)

Hanging was not the means of death (v. 22), but the body is hanged, presumably as a warning. Is this the stubborn son of the previous verses? As in 21:1-9 the issue is the desecration of the land.

Life must be positively valued (22:1-8)

We see in verses 1-4 that animals should not suffer in human disputes. In fact, here is a call to get proactively involved to prevent someone else or their animal from suffering. Three times, we are told not to ignore the stray animal (vv. 1, 3, 4). We are not to pass by on the other side (Luke 10:30-35) but offer help when it is within our power.

Verse 5 properly belongs in the next section (see Introduction).

In verses 6-7, life is not to be needlessly destroyed, and the supply of food in the land was to be preserved. Israel was allowed to take the young, but the mother was left to reproduce again.

Verse 8 is beloved of church health and safety officers everywhere! Israel was to take sensible precautions to prevent accidents.

From text to message

Getting the message clear: the theme

The section contains regulations for a messy world about the legitimate taking of life. The whole community is to be involved in preserving innocent life and punishing when required.

Getting the message clear: the aim

Ensure that the guilty are punished but that the innocent and vulnerable are protected.

A way in

Last week, a seventeen-year-old boy was murdered in broad daylight on Oxford Street, the UK's busiest shopping street in central London. Who is to blame?

One man stabbed him to death, but two others have been arrested for assisting an offender. Some articles have blamed a 'gang culture' or government policy that encourages it. Others blame his absent father for not being there to raise him.

At the risk of some lazy broad-brush comments, a 'right-wing' response might be that the individuals need to take responsibility; and a 'left-wing' response might be that the systemic problems need to be addressed.

Our passage here would suggest both are right. When it comes to the legitimate taking of life and the priority of protecting innocent life, the world is messy and we need to think carefully. Chapters 19–22 handle the judicial process in matters of life and death. They'll help guide us to know about what matters to the God of justice.

Ideas for application

- The whole community bears some responsibility for crimes committed. This is a striking feature of many of these rules, and we should bring out that corporate component at some point of application in the sermon.

- Life has value and wherever possible it must be protected. Sometimes this is best done through dramatic action which acts as a deterrent (19:18-19). It is striking how much effort is required from the whole community in response to a single human death (21:1-9).

- Family life must be taken seriously, whether it is protection of the family unit or the need to address a stubborn and rebellious child. This is not *merely* a matter for the immediate family; the whole community is affected. Paul reminds us that the command to honour parents is the first commandment with a promise (Eph. 6:2-3). All of us who are parents will give an account before the Lord for how we have carried out our role. More widely, the whole church must remember how highly the Lord values family relations in creating stable communities.

- We learn about just war practice. War is an inevitable feature of life in a world of sinful humans. Given that, Israel is given parameters to shape their conduct of war. The principles given in chapters 20–21 show that Deuteronomy

  ○ prefers non-violence when possible (20:10-11);

  ○ insists on negotiation before conflict (20:10);

  ○ shows an ecological restraint (in opposition to total war; 20:19-20);

  ○ demands humane treatment of female prisoners (21:10-14).

- There is a need to make atonement. There is an elaborate procedure to remove bloodguilt from the people in 21:6-9 and similar issues with avoiding defilement in 21:22. We may be shocked by the treatment of the stubborn and rebellious son in

21:21, yet the Christian knows that they are guilty of stubborn rebellion before the Lord and deserve the curse of verse 22. However, we look to the one place of atonement: the cross of Jesus, where he was hung on a tree as a curse for us (Acts 5:30; 10:39; Gal. 3:13).

Suggestions for preaching

It is impossible to handle all sections properly, so it is prudent to give a sentence on each section or at least enough to indicate what is meant; then in each chapter take one incident at greater length and apply it properly. (The next chapter will suggest a way of taking chapters 19–22 together with 22:9–23:18.)

How do we handle life and death in a fallen world?

- Establish guilt rightly (19:1-21)
- Wage war justly (20:1-20)
- Handle life's mess fairly (21:1-23)
- ⇨ Atonement must be made for you and me too.

Questions to help understand the passage

1. What is the issue in 19:1-13?

2. What are the key principles to shape Israel's response (19:10, 13)?

3. Why does 19:14 appear in a section all about matters of life and death?

4. What are the principles and what is the motive here (19:19-20)?

5. What do the three sections (beginning 'when') describe (20:1, 10, 19)?

6. How is Israel meant to treat differently the cities far away (20:10-15) from cities that are near (20:16-18)?

7. Why is Israel to destroy them? What will this prevent? (20:17-18)?

8. Why does it matter so much that the people don't ignore an unsolved murder (21:8-9)?

9. Whose rights are the concern in 21:10-14? What about in 21:15-17?

10. In 21:18-21, what is the problem highlighted with this delinquent young man?

11. What is the problem with leaving a man hanging on a tree (21:22)?

12. What holds (most of) these laws together (22:1-8)?

Questions to help apply the passage

1. What does God care deeply about (19:10, 13, 20)?

2. How easy is it to ensure that the guilty are punished and the innocent protected? Whose responsibility is it?

3. What did Israel really need to know when they were fearful (20:1-4)?

4. What do we learn about the importance of family structure (21:15-21)? Who else have we seen described as stubborn and rebellious in the book of Deuteronomy?

5. How do we make atonement for guilt (21:8-9, 22-23)?

14.
Protecting the Boundaries of Relationships
(Deuteronomy 22:9–23:18)

Introduction

Most commentators recognize this section as an outworking of the Seventh Word, 'Do not commit adultery.' If you are following the suggested series structure of taking this section together with 19:1–22:8, then you'll only really have time for 22:13-30. There are lots of apparently random verses within this section which don't immediately seem to flow from the Seventh Word. However, the overall theme that appears to tie all these topics together is 'maintaining appropriate boundaries' – between proper and improper sexual relations; between different types of seeds, animals and cloths; and between those who should and should not be allowed entry into the assembly.

It is a section concerned with protecting the integrity of the nation of Israel.

The cultural gap between Israel then and us now is starkly apparent in this section. In the twenty-first-century West, we really struggle with the fact that there is no room for private discretion in responding to a case of adultery.

We ask, 'Where is forgiveness?' Yet Deuteronomy views adultery and other sexual sin as an assault upon the family. And because the family is the basic building block of the nation, sexual sin is an attack against the whole community. It is viewed as an evil that must be purged.

Listening to the text

As is typical in chapters 19–26, although the structure seems determined by an amplification of the Ten Words, there are some verses which either introduce the next Word or seem a hangover from the last (see comments in the introduction to chapter 19):

- 22:5 appears to naturally fall within the subject matter of maintaining boundaries (between men's and women's attire)

- 23:15-16 seems to fall within the remit of the Eighth Word on theft

- 24:1-4 would appear to fall most naturally under the topic of 'no adultery'

This section has a dense repetition of the command 'You shall purge the evil from your midst' (22:21, 22, 24),[1] which reveals that Moses is not simply talking about personal sexual ethics but about how to maintain a healthy community. A little yeast can spread through the whole batch of dough.

It is striking how frequently the father is held to have responsibility for his daughter and what happens to her.[2] This is, again, quite foreign to our ears. At some points, it

---

1. See also 13:5; 17:7; 17:12; 19:19; 21:21; 24:7.

2. See 22:15, 16, 19, 21 (twice), 29 and 30.

is both mother and father who are responsible (22:15), but this was a culture where parents were viewed as responsible for their children (cf. 21:18-21). Perhaps the most helpful question to ask of all these laws is, 'Who is being protected?' Way before a '#metoo culture' there is, here, a pronounced concern to prevent the weak from being exploited.

Structure

Although it is possible to subdivide further, these are the most obvious divisions:

- Don't allow confusion of nature's distinctions (22:9-12)
- Don't allow sexual misconduct (22:13-30)
- Don't allow certain groups into the assembly (23:1-8)
- Don't allow uncleanness in the military camp (23:9-14)

Working through the text

Maintain boundaries in nature (22:5 and 22:9-12)

The text in 22:5 can be translated more simply as 'A woman shall not wear an item suitable for a man.' Whatever that looks like in a culture, it is not limited to clothing. This fits well with the overall idea of our section, of not crossing boundaries. The surprise is the vehemence with which this is denounced: it is 'an abomination'. The overwhelming use of this word in Deuteronomy refers to idolatrous practices,[3] and so it is possible that transvestite practices were found in Canaanite worship.

Verses 9-12 prohibit the mixing of different types of seeds, animals and cloth. Carmichael suggests that 'sowing'

---

3. See 7:25, 26; 12:31; 13:14; 17:4; 18:9; 18:12 (twice); 20:18; 27:15; 32:16 (the exceptions possibly being 14:3; 17:1; 24:4 and 25:16).

and 'ploughing' have sexual overtones to them,[4] which is why they are included. That is possible, but the theme of keeping separate things which should not be mixed would also fit easily into this section. The garment of verse 12 is used as something to cover modesty in Exodus 20:24-26, which is probably why it features here.

Maintain the boundaries to sexual activity (22:13-30)

There are different cases explored here, with the chief concern being to 'purge the evil from your midst'. Yet alongside that, the case studies lean towards the protection of the weaker party.

An accusation of premarital unchastity (22:13-21)

Verses 13-14 present the scenario: a husband accuses his new wife of not being a virgin when they get married. The language is somewhat heated here. The husband 'hates' her, and his accusation 'brings a bad name upon her'. There is then quite a disparity in the length given to the possible outcomes. Verses 15-19 show at some length how her reputation can be protected, while verses 20-21 more briefly deal with what happens if she is guilty.

The father and mother have the responsibility of defending their daughter and do so by presenting the bedsheets.[5]

---

4. Quoted in Olson, *Deuteronomy and the Death of Moses*, 101.

5. Here again is something we find bewildering, yet it remains a practice in some cultures. Years ago, while spending time in a town in the south of Morocco, I witnessed a wedding week when numerous couples married. There were different parts of the service held over three days, including on the third day the parading of the bloodied bedsheets of each couple for the whole town to see. It certainly made this Brit feel very uncomfortable!

The punishment for the husband, if he is shown to be lying, is surprising. We might expect him to fall under the judgment of 19:15-21 and be killed for his public lying. Yet it seems that his crime is viewed as an offence not only against his wife but against her parents too; hence, he is forced to pay them 100 shekels (twice a normal bride price of 22:29). The elders of the city are also to take him for the public humiliation of whipping (22:19).

We may be surprised at the concluding element of 22:19 – that divorce is now made impossible for the accusing husband. Yet the aim is for rehabilitation. When you are told that you cannot walk away, then there is an added incentive to actually make the marriage work by giving yourself to it. It also protects the wife, as being a divorced woman in that culture was a highly vulnerable situation.

On the other hand, if the husband's accusation is found to be true, then 'the men of *her* city shall stone her to death.' This judicial activity does not fall to the men of her husband's city but the city where she grew up – presumably the city where she was sexually active. Here is a public demonstration that her behaviour is 'outrageous'. The motive for the punishment is to 'purge the evil from your midst' and so prevent such behaviour from becoming normalized. Like many of the laws in Deuteronomy, we do not read of this being enacted. Presumably the law was quite a deterrent to false accusations against a vulnerable wife!

A simple case of adultery (22:22)

Perhaps the most striking element here is that both are found equally guilty. We might not expect that, given what we find in Israel's later history. When Jesus encounters the woman caught in adultery in John 8, there is no suggestion of the man also being stoned to death – but that is what Deuteronomy prescribed! We will consider below how Jesus protects the woman.

Sex with a woman who is betrothed (22:23-27)

Betrothal was a more significant commitment in that culture (and many cultures today) compared to a modern 'engagement'. Two different scenarios are outlined. The presumption in verses 23-24 is that the sex is consensual, otherwise when the woman cried for help, someone in the city would have heard (bearing in mind that a 'city' back then did not have the same vast anonymity as a megacity today[6]). Therefore the punishment is the same as verse 22; the woman is betrothed, so the crime is adultery.

In the second scenario of verses 25-27 it is considered a case of rape, so the man is killed while nothing is done to the woman. She is the one who needs protection and vindication before the law.

McConville helpfully observes that these laws are not meant to cover every single eventuality but rather provide principles by which judges could follow 'justice, and only justice' (16:20): 'The two laws almost certainly operate together to establish parameters within which wise counsel might prevail.'[7]

---

6. It's a disputed area of archaeology, but the varying estimates in *Biblical Archaeology Review* put the population of the city of Jerusalem at somewhere around 500–3000 when it was captured by Israel. We are talking a very different scale! (Hershel Shanks, 'Ancient Jerusalem: The Village, the Town, the City,' *Biblical Archaeology Review* (May/June 2016). Online: https://www.biblicalarchaeology.org/daily/biblical-sites-places/jerusalem/ancient-jerusalem.

7. McConville, *Deuteronomy*, 342.

Sex with a woman who is not betrothed (22:28-29)

Here again is a law we find shocking. Why does raping an unbetrothed virgin not receive the same punishment as raping a betrothed virgin? The answer seems to be that adultery is viewed as a 'great sin' (Gen. 20:9; 39:9). The Seventh Word is not 'No sexual immorality' but rather 'No adultery.' Adultery in a marriage is a picture of the unfaithfulness of God's people to the LORD. That seemingly is why it is highlighted above other sexual sin.

Why is the man commanded to marry her? Presumably the rape victim in a small community is less eligible to marry. Marriage is therefore a place of economic security. Again, the Mosaic law envisages rehabilitation. Once the man receives the notoriety for his crime, he has every incentive to demonstrate his repentance to the community by actually being a good husband to the woman he has wronged.

Verse 30 seems to connect the two chapters or sections, moving from sexual sin to issues of purity.

Maintain the boundaries to God's assembly (23:1-8)

While the restrictions here are stark, it is intriguing that they are not absolute. The commentators point to evidence that verse 1 may well have been a ritual mutilation in service to pagan gods. The forbidden union of verse 2 could be incestuous or marriage to a Canaanite (7:3).

Moab and Ammon in verses 3-6 follow naturally as two nations born of forbidden union (between Lot and his daughters in Gen. 19). They were located on Israel's eastern border. Two reasons are given for their exclusion in verse 4: (1) their lack of provisions when Israel was in need and (2) the attempt by Balak to have Israel cursed.

However, verses 7-8 introduce two groups that could eventually join – Edomites because of their kinship and Egyptians due to their hospitality (presumably a reference to the more positive time of Joseph than slavery in the time of Moses).

There may be something to McConville's suggestion that there is a progression through three different groups here:

Canaanite worshippers (vv. 1-2) => prohibited foreigners (vv. 3-6) => permitted foreigners

Two points are worth noting here:

- Here is another passage when it is assumed that the *herem* command to 'devote to destruction' is not absolute extermination, as Israel has to be warned to keep Canaanites out.

- Even at this stage of history, God's assembly was not limited to those of physical descent but was beginning to open up to those of spiritual allegiance (vv. 7-8).

Maintain boundaries to cleanliness (23:9-14)

Verse 14 reveals that a concern for cleanliness around semen emissions and excrement is primarily due to ritual impurity, not hygiene or moral behaviour. The assembly of God is a holy temple and these physical commands were to remind Israel of the spiritual truth of the difficulty of a holy God dwelling with an impure people.

Maintain boundaries to sexual behaviour (23:17-18)

Verses 15-16 will be taken in the next chapter, but the section concludes with two warnings:

- Prostitution is unacceptable in Israel (v. 17; cf. Lev. 19:29).

- The surrounding cultures allowed the use of shrine prostitutes if the fee was paid to the sanctuary, but that was unacceptable in Israel (v. 18).

From text to message

Getting the message clear: the theme

There are boundaries which we are not meant to cross – especially sexual boundaries.

Getting the message clear: the aim

Don't break sexual boundaries, as it will damage you and weaken the precious church community.

A way in

'What I get up to in my bedroom is none of your business.'

That sounds entirely reasonable to many in the twenty-first century, as long as there is consent between two adults. Yet we feel a little differently if it is our spouse having sex with someone else or our sixteen-year-old daughter having intercourse with her boyfriend on a first date. We will certainly feel differently if there is not consent and sex is coerced.

We all draw boundaries to what is appropriate in sexual ethics. We may disagree with where the Bible draws them, but we all draw them somewhere.

Ideas for application

▪ **Purging the evil**

The recurrent warning here (22:21, 22, 24) is a reminder that when we allow immoral behaviour to go unchecked it will affect the whole community. Paul makes the same point in the New Testament: a little yeast will leaven the whole

batch of dough (1 Cor. 5:13). If certain sinful behaviours
are ignored and not confronted, then they will become
normalised and increasingly common. The Bible has no
concept of private sin that does not affect others. That's
a truth more readily accepted in Eastern cultures than
Western ones and is a significant challenge for some of us.

Yet to state that positively, it is far easier to maintain
sexual purity within a church culture with a high view of
community, family and sexuality, than it is on our own. If we
are to maintain God's kind boundaries of sexual behaviour
then we need one another. We are vulnerable on our own
and stronger together. Certainly, within our church, men
and women have been trapped in porn addictions and affairs,
but honesty and accountability has brought transformation.

▪ Protecting the weak or vulnerable

The seventh commandment and its outworking can be
viewed as restrictive, or you can hear it as God saying, 'I
care deeply for you and your body. I want to protect you
from suffering harm.' In a #metoo era, here is the Living
God declaring that he cares so much for your honour, he
will not even permit lusting after you (cf. Matt. 5:27-30).
Certainly here in Deuteronomy 23, there is a concern to
protect the reputation of vulnerable women.

▪ Inclusion in the assembly of God

Deuteronomy 23 begins to indicate that other nations may
join God's people. That happens with an increasing pace
through the Bible as revelation progresses. In the days
when the judges ruled, even a Moabitess like Ruth can
join God's people. Strikingly, Isaiah predicts that when
God's salvation comes, foreigners and eunuchs will NOT
say, 'The LORD will surely separate me from his people'

(Isa. 56:3-8). In Acts 8, we meet a man who is both a foreigner and a eunuch who upon declaring his faith is instantly baptized into God's people.

- **There is forgiveness on offer**

Not every adulterer in the Old Testament is stoned to death. There is the obvious example of King David. After his adultery with Bathsheba, David is seemingly forgiven, although two things happen:

1. David's son Absalom copies his father and commits adultery. The evil was not purged.

2. Yet David's son dies of sickness. Is that a pointer towards THE Son whose blood is shed in our place so that we do not die for our adultery or lust?

In John 8, Jesus seemingly wants us to understand that none of us are innocent of adultery in our hearts. He does not condemn the woman caught (where was the man?) but goes on to offer a truth that will set people free.

Suggestions for preaching

Getting into the detail of some of these laws is unlikely to be greatly edifying for most congregations. Highlighting the most significant principles here and explaining how the New Testament applies them can, however, do a church family enormous good.

Don't cross boundaries which endanger you

- Protect the boundaries of marriage (22:9-30)
- Protect the boundaries of the assembly (23:1-14)

It is quite possible to preach chapters 19–23 in one sermon. Naturally, you will need to be more selective in the material you cover, but it is certainly possible to show the chief burden of the laws in each section.

Protecting God's precious community

- Protect the life of the innocent (ch. 19)
- Protect the boundaries of marriage (ch. 22)

Questions to help understand the passage

1. Can you break the text of 22:13-30 into different scenarios?

2. What is the phrase or command that occurs several times? What does that mean?

3. Who does the law seem most concerned to protect in 22:13-21?

4. What is the significant difference in the crimes of 22:23-24 and 22:25-27?

5. What is being protected in 23:1-8?

6. What is the reason for the instructions in 23:9-14 (see especially v. 14)?

Questions to help apply the passage

1. How does the New Testament take up the command to 'purge the evil from your midst' (1 Cor. 5:1-3)? What does that look like in your church?

2. How can we help one another to maintain God's boundaries in sex?

3. How does Jesus treat the woman caught in adultery (John 8)? What happens to her punishment?

4. Who can be included in the people of God now (cf. Isa. 56:3-8)?

15.

Be Open Handed, Not Tight Fisted

(Deuteronomy 23:19–25:16)

Introduction

I was once asked to preach a sermon on precisely this passage at a pastors' conference. I asked, 'Is that because you thought it was the most obscure part of the book and you wanted to demonstrate a point?' The simple response was 'Yes'.

This section covers the final three of the Ten Words: 'Do not steal', 'Do not bear false witness', and 'Do not covet.' More than in any other section, there is overlap here between the commandments: bearing false witness and coveting can often look like stealing.

It is worth observing that this is not 'pure law'. There are numerous little narrative and motivational phrases spread throughout – most commonly, to remember what the LORD had done for Israel in the past. This is a description of life lived in response to his gracious action.

Perhaps the most striking aspect of these laws is their concern for the community. To a Western culture steeped in capitalism and individual rights, it can be a disconcerting read. In Deuteronomy, economic activity is a key way of expressing mutual cooperation and the interdependent nature of the society. Israel must show righteousness to those who are socially and economically vulnerable. There is considerable overlap thematically with chapter 15.

We too need to remember the Lord who gives and the Lord who judges if we are to be generous as the Bible expects.

If I may borrow the rhyme of the English doggerel concerning Fireworks Night ...

> Remember, remember the fifth of November
> Gunpowder treason and plot.
> I see no reason why gunpowder treason
> Should ever be forgot.

... then the message of these chapters might be summed up like this:

> Remember, remember the Lord who redeemed
>   you;
> Without him you'd still be a slave.
> So, share what he gives you, with brothers and
>   sisters;
> You'll rejoice when you exit the grave.

Listening to the text

Structure

The challenge here is not so much dividing up the text into units but rather seeing what unites sections!

As we have observed previously, the division between each of the explications of the Ten Words is not watertight. However, though at points it is hard to discern, there seem good reasons to divide the section as follows:

- 'Do not steal' (23:19–24:7)
- 'Do not bear false witness' (24:8–25:4)
- 'Do not covet' (25:5–25:19)

This central section of law is concluded in 25:17-19 with the call to blot out the memory of Amalek, corresponding to the call of 12:2 and following to wipe out the Canaanites. A frame around the law is thus formed by the idea of God giving them 'rest from their enemies' (12:10 and 25:19).

The need to remember is a clear feature of the whole book of Deuteronomy (5:15; 7:18; 8:2, 18; 9:7, 27; 15:15; 16:3, 12) and is evident here:

- Remember your past.

    ○ 'Remember what the LORD your God did to Miriam' (24:9)

    ○ 'Remember that you were a slave' (24:18)

    ○ 'You shall remember that you were a slave in the land of Egypt' (24:22)

    ○ 'Remember what Amalek did to you' (25:17)

- Remember the LORD is judge.

    ○ 'It shall be righteousness for you *before the LORD your God*' (24:13)

    ○ 'Lest he cry against you *to the LORD*, and you be guilty of sin' (24:15)

Working through the text

Do not steal (23:19–24:7)

The Hebrew verb 'to steal' is found only in the Ten Words (5:19) and in this section (24:7), pointing towards this block of law coming chiefly under the rubric of 'Do not steal.'

No charging interest on loans to the poor (23:19-20)

This looks like quite a blow to capitalism! We should note that the parallel passages (Exod. 22:25; Lev. 25:35-37) say that you cannot charge interest on loans to the poor. I think the principle is 'no exploitative loans'. The point of the law is to prevent the poor within Israel from being exploited and taken advantage of. It is designed to prevent the hard-hearted from making a profit out of hard times for others. They were to give help to those in need, without it being a burden to them.

Some will be aware that Calvin gave qualified support to the legitimacy of interest in commercial loans and that certainly does seem different from the situation envisaged in these verses. Although it was not set within the people of God, an egregious example in the UK was Wonga – the payday loan company that charged up to 4000 per cent interest on loans to the vulnerable.

No withholding what you've promised to give (23:21-23)

The flow of the chapter suggests that the point is this: you should honour vows you've made regarding money. Promised a loan? Then make it. Promised to give a certain amount of money? Then give it.

No ruthless capitalism or abuse of kindness (23:24-25)

The assumption here is that landowners have not picked every grain and grape; they have deliberately left some behind (as in 24:19-22). So, if you're hungry, you can go and eat in the landowner's field. But don't take advantage of this generosity! Don't take a bag and fill it up; don't take more than you're allowed to.

There is a balance to these laws: be compassionate if life is going well for you, yet be respectful if you're a beneficiary.

No exploiting a vulnerable widow (24:1-4)

This is a tricky section and you'll need to read more widely to reach your own conclusions. Clearly, there is a desire to protect the woman from becoming a marital football passed back and forth. I'm persuaded that it makes most sense here if there is a profit motive, so Husband 1 has become interested because divorce from Husband 2 has left her wealthy. However, that is certainly not conclusive.

No depriving a new family of sound finances (24:5)

It's not just the prospect of absence in the army but rather any public duty that is precluded, so it seems that the concern is that the new family is able to build a solid economic foundation. Let the husband pour his energies into making an economic start for his new family. The opportunity for a child would also have been important for the family's economic well-being.

No withholding daily bread (24:6)

The mill was a crucial domestic device for grinding grain. The modern equivalent would be something like this: 'I'll lend you some money till the end of the day but take your oven, stove and microwave as collateral.'

No kidnapping for slavery (24:7)

This is serious! It is the only time the death penalty is invoked for theft. This is a crime that requires evil to be purged! The motive for stealing a brother and selling him would be financial profit.

So, the section closes on the starkest of warnings: Do not steal!

Don't bear false witness but be fair (24:8–25:4)

False witness is unacceptable (24:8-9)

Back in Numbers 12:10-15, Miriam and Aaron spoke against Moses. They claimed that they could speak for God just as well as Moses did. As a consequence, the LORD struck Miriam with leprosy. This is the only mention of skin diseases in the whole book (quite unlike Leviticus!), but the concern seems to be the importance of listening to your leaders. In this context, listen to the instruction of the priests at the central court (17:8-13).

You shall not rob a man of respect (24:10-13)

The concern here seems to be that you are not to humiliate another man by entering his house and taking back your pledge to him – allow him the dignity of bringing it out to you. Verse 13 suggests that some things are more important than being 'legally right'. If you are a man of righteousness then you will not deprive a poor man of his cloak at night, even if he has not repaid you. The LORD will see and judge what you do.

You shall not rob a man of his wages (24:14-15)

McConville notes that the language of poverty is confined to chapters 15 and 24 of Deuteronomy. Verse 15 offers a complementary truth to verse 13 – failure to treat the poor fairly is sin! (Note how, if the recipient is poor, it makes the failure to pay a wage worse.) 'If the creditor fails to show compassion, he may avoid the sentence of a court, but he will be "in the wrong" with Yahweh.[1] Here again, the LORD will judge what you do.

In court you pay for your own crimes (24:16)

This verse struggles more than most to fit into a section on not bearing false witness. Yet presumably the logic is that in court you pay for your own sins. We all know the temptation to blame others for our sins. An abusive husband could say that his behaviour was due to the way his parents neglected to love him. That may well have affected him, but he also needs to own his own sin. To blame it all on his parents is 'false witness' to the truth of the situation.

You shall not deprive the poor of sustenance (24:17-22)

Four references to the triplet of 'sojourner, fatherless and widow' unite this section. The law of gleaning is quite some way from modern society's benefits system. This is no hand-out but rather the poorest in society are to be given access to the wealth of the land and enabled to feed themselves through their labour. Those without a stake are to be given a very small stake to work. We see this at its best in the book of Ruth. The temptation to maximize your own accumulation is strong in humans though. Twice here (vv. 18, 22) Israel is told to remember where they have come from. Wright pithily summarizes the importance of remembering: 'When Israel forgot its history, it forgot its poor.'[2]

This is one section of the larger unit that is really worth focusing on in preaching, as it succinctly handles the issue

---

1. McConville, *Deuteronomy*, 362.

2. Wright, *Deuteronomy*, 261.

of ensuring righteous treatment for the most vulnerable, which in many ways is a good summary of chapters 23–25.

You shall not humiliate your brother (25:1-3)

The concern here is that the punishment of the guilty is proportionate (v. 2) and that the guilty party is not degraded (v. 3). This is justice, not retaliation. The aim, as with much of the sentencing in the law, is to see the guilty brother restored to fellowship.

You shall not deprive a worker of his wages (25:4; 1 Cor. 9:8-12; 1 Tim. 5:17-18)

Compassion even extends to animals working in Israel. Just as the poor should not be prevented from gleaning, so the livestock should not be prevented from feeding themselves either. Paul's references to this text stress the need to treat gospel ministers fairly. If God requires that in relation to animals, he surely does so for gospel workers.

Don't covet but be unselfish (25:5-19)

Have we moved on to the Tenth Word now? Did we do so at 25:4? Again, I don't think we are given precision. Life is messy and the laws blur into one another.

Don't selfishly neglect family obligations (25:5-10; 1 Tim. 5:3-8)

The concern here is to maintain the family line, preserve the man's name and keep property within the family (v. 6). The (presumably unmarried) brother of the deceased is evidently breaking convention by not marrying his sister-in-law.

The man is given a chance to repent as the elders talk to him (v. 8), but if he persists the punishment is intriguing –

it is not a legal sentence but a public shaming. This shame is designed to tarnish his reputation into the future (v. 10).

The welfare of the wider family is deemed more important than the man's personal desires. We should take obligations to our family seriously, as Paul argues even more strongly in 1 Timothy 5.

Don't angrily attack family continuity (25:11-12)

I leave you to chase down the various interpretations here, but the connection seems to be that, whereas in verses 5-10 a man withheld his private parts selfishly, here a woman grabs them aggressively (possibly damaging capacity to procreate?). The deterrent is certainly a strong one. Both laws are seeking to avoid chaos in the family.

Don't deceitfully trade with others (25:13-16)

Here is the final piece of social legislation in the book – honesty is commanded in transactions. This law and section conclude with a strong motivational appeal. Positively, honesty brought long life. Negatively, dishonesty made you an abomination to the Lord.

25:17-19

These verses close the section. The destruction of Amalek seems placed here to form a bracket with destruction of altars and high places in chapter 12. They are a similar exhortation to holy war. Why the Amalekites? Wright helpfully suggests that, in attacking Israel when they were vulnerable after the Exodus, they typify a merciless approach to the weak (those lagging behind) that is the antithesis of the laws of Deuteronomy.[3]

---

3. Wright, *Deuteronomy*, 268.

From text to message

Getting the message clear: the theme

Remember how God has treated you and so have a generous concern for others in Israel, not a selfish accumulation.

Getting the message clear: the aim

Have a concern for the welfare of the church community, not just yourself.

A way in

A young woman aged twenty-five at church is made redundant and can't pay her rent. She's been with the church for three years and is completely committed. Her parents live on the other side of the country. What do we do?

A guy at church aged thirty takes out a loan to pay for a master's degree but the bank's interest rate is crippling. Should the church do anything about that?

An asylum seeker in church is from Iran: she fled that country when she became a believer and feared for her life. She is being threatened with deportation and can't pay the legal costs to fight the case. She doesn't understand the UK asylum system. What is our responsibility?

Ideas for application

- God's blessing upon Israel was for the whole community to enjoy, so wealthy individuals were expected to share God's blessings with those in need. There is something in all of us which thinks, 'My money' or 'My house' or 'My car'. Deuteronomy would remind us that the hand of the generous God lies behind all possessions that we are blessed with (cf. 8:11-14).

This is seen in lots of ways in a church family – some people offer their car freely to anyone who needs it, while others organize holidays and take the lonely with them. We've had some church members take on the unemployed on a temporary basis until they can get another job; others have covered rent for individuals when they're struggling. In the wider culture, lots of people seem to eBay children's clothes to earn some money, but in a church, they get passed around to those most in need. All these are lovely applications of the principle.

- The vulnerable must be protected from exploitation. Everyone nods and agrees with this statement, but we should be asking how much of a reality it is within our own churches. The sin of partiality towards the wealthy is a temptation in every generation of the church (James 2:1-13). It seems in the last few years that the evangelical church in the West has had to face numerous cases of ignoring abusive patterns of behaviour by the powerful. Here are laws telling us we must ensure that the claims of mistreatment from those with the weakest voices are not ignored.

- Different might not be wrong. At some point, even if it's brief, there needs to be some comment on the fact that Israel's justice system was very different from ours. Most punishments were either financial or physical and they were immediate. I expect most people would view our current penal system as more compassionate or simply assert it as superior. While it is certainly not my area of expertise, I wonder if the high numbers of people incarcerated in the UK or US and the high levels of reoffending might make us pause before reaching that judgment. Some sanctions in Israel were undoubtedly more brutal, but individuals were able to move on quickly, rather than spend years incarcerated. We may well struggle with some of the sanctions here – and personally, I am no theonomist – but perhaps we need to be slow to insist our modern system is superior.

- It's good to remind congregations of the simple rule of thumb with Old Testament laws and promises: we should see how they are fulfilled in three places:

  1. In Christ: 'For you know the grace of our Lord Jesus Christ, that though he was rich, yet for your sake he became poor, so that you by his poverty might become rich' (2 Cor. 8:9).

  2. In the church: 'There was not a needy person among them, for as many as were owners of lands or houses sold them and brought the proceeds of what was sold and laid it at the apostles' feet, and it was distributed to each as any had need' (Acts 4:34-35).

  3. In the new creation: 'He will wipe away every tear from their eyes, and death shall be no more, neither shall there be mourning, nor crying, nor pain anymore, for the former things have passed away' (Rev. 21:4).

Suggestions for preaching

- Don't steal but be generous (23:19–24:7)
- Don't bear false witness but be fair (24:8 – 25:4)
- Don't covet but be unselfish (25:5–25:19)

Questions to help understand the passage

1. The Hebrew verb 'to steal' is found in Deuteronomy only in the Ten Words (5:19) and in 24:7. This suggests that the section 23:19–24:7 may come under a heading of 'Do not steal.' Try going through the section and asking in each case, What is stolen?

2. What is allowed and what is not (23:24-25)?

3. What happens if you deprive someone in Israel of their 'bread-maker' (24:6)?

4. Looking at 24:7, can you remember what other crimes in Deuteronomy received the death penalty (13:5; 17:7, 12; 19:19; 21:21; 22:21-24)? What seem to be the most serious offences in Israel?

5. Read 24:8–25:4. What is the motivation given for keeping this set of laws in 24:13 and 15?

6. Who is shown concern in 24:17-22? Why these three? What is the motivation (v. 22)?

7. In 25:5-10 what is the law's concern (v. 6)? What is the brother's concern (v. 8)?

8. What are the motivations given in 25:13-16?

Questions to help apply the passage

1. A young woman aged twenty-five at church is made redundant and can't pay her rent. She's been with the church for three years and is completely committed. Her parents live on the other side of country. What do we do?

2. A guy at church aged thirty takes out a loan to pay for a master's degree, but the bank's interest rate

is crippling. Should the church do anything about that?

3. An asylum seeker in church is from Iran: she fled that country when she became a believer and feared for her life. She is being threatened with deportation and can't pay the legal costs to fight the case. She doesn't understand the UK asylum system. What is our responsibility?

4. How do you see a concern for the financial and social welfare of others play out in your church?

16.

A People of Curse and
a God of Blessing
(Deuteronomy 26–28)

Introduction

There have been two tunes competing throughout Deuteronomy – one optimistic about Israel's future, the other expecting her to fail. In these three chapters the tragic tune swells to its loudest and almost completely drowns out any optimism. Yet, for those with ears to hear, the chapters still contain elements of God's grace. For the Christian reader, the relentless talk of curse in chapters 27–28 forces us to think of Galatians 3 where Paul quotes Deuteronomy 27:26 ahead of declaring that 'Christ redeemed us from the curse of the law by becoming a curse for us' (Gal. 3:13).

Moses brings his second speech to a close in 26:16-19 and with it closes the frame around the statutes and rules of chapters 12–26.

This is a difficult section for several reasons. First, it is difficult to define the structure and in particular how chapter 27 fits into it. Second, it is a long section and so a judgment must be made on how much to have read and actually to preach on. Third, and perhaps most obvious to the reader, the section is emotionally hard to cope with, as the LORD is described as the source of terrible curses, climaxing in the shocking phrase 'the LORD will take delight in bringing ruin upon you and destroying you' (28:63). This is not the passage to preach to a new or unknown congregation, nor the week to skimp on sermon prep!

If preaching an overview series, you would certainly not spend more than one sermon on this section and there is merit in just preaching on chapter 27 as representative of the whole here, with a few references from chapter 28.

Listening to the text

Structure

Chapter 26 is the concluding part of Moses's second speech (4:44–26:19), and chapter 27 is an interlude between speeches, with Moses referred to in the third person. Chapter 29 begins Moses's third speech (29:1–30:20). The fact that the text could run smoothly from 26:19 into 28:1 without any need for chapter 27 causes some commentators no end of spilt ink. However, most evangelical commentaries observe the following structural balance to the frame around the laws of chapters 12–26.

11:26-32	11:26-28 Blessing and curse announced in Moab	11:29-31 Ceremony on Gerizim and Ebal	11:32 Call to obey the commands
26:16– 28:68	26:16-19 Call to obey the commands	Ch. 27 Ceremony on Gerizim and Ebal	Ch. 28 Blessing and curse announced in Moab

There are several other pointers to chapters 12 and 26 forming an inclusio:

- References to the 'statutes and rules' appear in 12:1 and 26:16 (the term also wraps the inner frame at 5:1 and 11:32).

- Israel is to go to the place of worship to make offerings (12:5-7; 26:1-2).

Working through the text

Individual worship before the LORD (26:1-15)

Although we will want our congregations to understand the structure of the book, I don't think that many will preach a sermon on 26:1-15. Olson includes 26:1-15 within the Tenth Word as he thinks that these offerings are here as antidote to coveting. It's possible, but the chapter seems to focus on the *individual* recognizing and *declaring* the LORD's goodness. The laws of chapters 12–26 seem to give way to an act of worship which is very different in tone.

These verses are looking to the future: 'When you have come into the land ... and live in it' (v. 1).

- In verses 1-11 the individual (first person singular verbs in vv. 3, 5 and 10) is told to acknowledge how good the LORD has been and worship him. There is an obvious emphasis upon all that the LORD has 'given' to him:

  ○ the land (vv. 1, 2 ,3)
  ○ liberation from slavery (v. 9)
  ○ success in labour (vv. 10 and 11)

Although the individual relates the corporate history of Israel, it is still a personal declaration: 'I have come ... now I bring' (vv. 3, 10). More than a declaration, there is also a physical gift to the LORD who has given all.

- In verses 12-15, there is a reminder of the mutual obligations to other Israelites. This is not the annual tithe of 14:22 but the triennial tithe for the poor (14:29-29). The declaration is striking: not only is there a positive statement in verse 13 but also three negative affirmations in verse 14. Knowing that this verbal declaration was coming would no doubt have helped stiffen the resolve of individual Israelites to obey.

The call to obey the commands (26:16-19)

'This day' in verse 16 brings us back from the future to the present day (stressed three times in four verses). Moses drags Israel's attention back to the day of decision for this formal ratification of the covenant. Verse 16 contains a familiar Deuteronomy combination of

- 'the LORD your God commands you' (obedience is essential);

- 'you shall ... do them with all your heart and with all your soul' (an emotional engagement, not mere external conformity).

The most striking feature of verses 17-19 is the level of reciprocity in the two declarations:

Israel declares that the LORD is their God and	The LORD declares that Israel is his treasured possession and
○ that they will walk in his ways;	○ that they will keep his commandments;
○ keep his statutes, commandments and rules;	○ he will set them above all nations;
○ obey his voice.	○ they shall be holy as he promised.

So, this bookend of the legal code is a return to the exuberance of chapters 1–11, with a final emphasis on God's election of Israel and his appointing them to be an example to the nations (cf. 4:7-8).

Wright helpfully observes: 'Distortion of the law, whether towards legalism or toward antinomianism usually creeps in when God's people forget either the grace of God on which they stand or the glory of God for which they alone exist.' [1]

A commitment to avoiding God's curse (ch. 27)

The first question that strikes the Bible teacher is, What is chapter 27 doing here? The text could run seamlessly from 26:19 to 28:1-14, but chapter 27 interrupts the logic. Despite this being within Moses's second speech, the chapter names Moses three times in the third person (vv. 1, 9, 11). The curses in verses 15-26 also seem at first glance unnecessary, given the longer list of curses in chapter 28.

It seems that the placing of the chapter here begins to build the expectation that Israel is going to fail. That is reinforced by chapter 28 and made explicit in chapter 30. It is striking to note the following in this chapter:

- The stones of testimony and altar are set up on Mount Ebal, the mountain of curse – not on the mountain of blessing or even between the two mountains in Shechem.

- Although blessings are proposed in verse 12, the list in verses 14-26 contains only curses.

A witness against you and a means of atonement (27:1-8)

We are told that Moses *and the elders* commanded the people – presumably because this is outlining a covenant

---

1. Wright, *Deuteronomy*, 273.

renewal ceremony to take place at Shechem soon after Israel has entered the land, a point when Moses will not be with them.

The first thing they are to do when they cross the Jordan is to erect these large stones. While commentators argue over whether it really was the whole of Deuteronomy written on them, the phrase 'all the words of this law' (vv. 3 and 8) is also used of the whole of Deuteronomy being written in a book as a witness against Israel (31:24). It seems likely that these stones fulfil the same purpose: they are a witness against Israel. Barker observes, 'The placement of the stones of the law on the mountain of curse suggests that at least one function of the law is to expose the sinfulness of Israel and bring it under the curse of the law. The expectation is that Israel will disobey.'[2]

However, we must not ignore verses 5-7! Even in a chapter which predicts failure, there remains the possibility of forgiveness and reconciliation through sacrifice. 'At the very place of curse, Yahweh provides a means of avoiding such a sentence. The altar and the instruction for burnt offerings are a gracious provision of a means of atonement to a sinful people.'[3]

Two types of offering are prescribed:

1. The burnt offering was made to secure atonement seemingly in a general sense rather than for specific sins. The whole animal was consumed by fire (Lev. 1:4; 6:8-13; 16:24).

2. The peace (fellowship) offering symbolized fellowship with God; the people were having a meal with him.

---

2. Paul Barker, 'The Theology of Deuteronomy 27,' *Tyndale Bulletin* 49.2: 288.

3. Barker, 'The Theology of Deuteronomy 27,' 297.

It was a celebration of being in right relationship with him (Lev. 3; 7:11-36).

Having the two types of offering seems to emphasise both that atonement will be necessary and that dwelling in God's company is possible.

It is also worth noting that the place of this ceremony is Shechem. We are meant to remember that this is where the promises were first made to Abraham (Gen. 12:6-7), where Jacob bought land (Gen. 33:19) and where his bones were buried (Josh. 24:32). As Wright observes: 'Even in physical symbolism, the law is surrounded in grace.'[4]

So, embedded in a chapter which implicitly expects Israel to fail, there is the hope of grace held out. Falling under the curse of the law need not be the final word.

Back to the decision of today (27:9-10)

Whereas verses 1-8 had looked ahead to arrival in the land, Moses and the Levitical priests now pull the people back to the decision of *that* day. It is striking that Moses is again sharing the speaking duties. He is about to exit the stage and will be replaced by the Levites bringing the law to bear on Israel.

The call to 'keep silence' is a mark of the solemnity of the moment. The declaration that 'this day you have become the people of the LORD your God' is not suggesting that they were not beforehand. Rather, it means that they are being declared so again, in the context of a covenant renewal ceremony. However, in line with the thrust of the appeals to 'today' throughout the book, every generation does have to choose whether they will live out their calling as the people of God.

---

4. Wright, *Deuteronomy*, 276.

A public commitment to avoid curse (27:11-26)

Moses introduces the ceremony to take place when they have crossed into the land (seen in Josh. 8:30-35). The most obvious feature here is that, despite the announcement of blessings in verse 12, the ceremony of chapter 27 has none! Again, the implication seems to be that Israel's future is, without doubt, one of curse. [5]

The chief difference between these and the curses of chapter 28 is that here the focus falls upon the nature of the *offences*, whereas in chapter 28 the focus is upon the nature of the *curses*. Chapter 27 declares what actions will lead to curse, and chapter 28 describes what the curse will be.

There is also a particular focus upon 'secret sins' in verses 15 and 24. It is not enough to present external moral conformity to the community. There needs to be obedience in your heart and in your home when no one else can see. McConville suggests that this emphasis upon secret sins shapes the placement here: it is designed to purge the evil from among the people at a crucial stage of the book.[6] That is true, yet we should not downplay the overwhelming note of failure either – we are being told to expect that.

Perhaps the purpose of this section is most easily understood when it is read aloud. The twelve-times-repeated pattern has the effect of each Israelite committing publicly to resist sin:

1. 'Cursed be ...'

---

5. Although that purpose seems relatively clear, how this ceremony fits with chapter 28 is less so. Block suggests, 'The movement from verses 12-13 to 14 suggests that the ritual of verses 15-26 is intended as a response to the blessings and curses recited.' (*Deuteronomy*, 632). Yet if that is the case it is not obvious why it is not recorded that way.

6. McConville, *Deuteronomy*, 392.

2. … anyone who commits this particular sin

3. '… and all the people shall say, "Amen."'

The design is for each man and woman to feel the weight of essentially calling down a curse upon themselves if they break the covenant – even if in secret, when no one but God knows. Block finds a chiastic structure[7] but it is perhaps simpler to think of the curses as being for

- idolatry (v. 15);
- dishonouring parents (v. 16);
- hurting the economically vulnerable (vv. 17-19);
- crossing sexual boundaries (vv. 20-23);
- violence and murder (vv. 24-25);
- general disregard of torah (v. 26).

The final curse is expressed negatively and seems to function as a catch-all.

I don't think this passage can be taught well without being effectively read, perhaps even with the congregation joining in with the 'Amens'. (Although it would need a little interpretative explanation first. We are not Israelites in Shechem!)

Unlike Israel, we are not publicly binding ourselves to the law. But we do publicly bind ourselves to Jesus. There is some value in publicly committing to a certain pattern of behaviour and holding one another accountable, but in the end we will always need to go back to the place of atonement, which for us is the cross.

Four curses and a blessing (ch. 28)
We can't help but be struck by the imbalance here – fourteen verses of blessing and fifty-three verses of curse. As

---

7. Block, *Deuteronomy*, 633.

readers, we are being implicitly told to expect Israel's failure. Yet for Moses's first audience the purpose was to plead, cajole and even scare them into obedience with the impassioned language of verses 20-68. It is always better to be motivated by the love and grace of God, but Jesus also is not averse to warning of judgment to motivate believers to keep going.

Despite the difference in length, there is an obvious symmetry to the two sections:

vv. 1-2	If you will/will not obey the voice of the LORD your God ... be careful to do ... that I command you TODAY ... then all these blessings/curses shall come upon you and overtake you		v. 15
vv. 3-6	Six times: 'Blessed shall you be'	Six times: 'Cursed shall you be'	vv. 16-19
vv. 7-14	Detailed explanation of blessings and curses		vv. 20-68

However, there is a danger that we might give the impression that blessings are earned by obedience and curses earned by disobedience. We must remember that curses for forsaking the LORD are earned whereas blessings are not. Israel was being given the land of blessing and lived in it because of the LORD's gracious gift (9:4-6). No sinner ever earns God's blessing, but we can enjoy living within it.

The blessings of loyal obedience to the LORD (28:1-14)

A few limited observations:

- The first blessing for faithful obedience is that God will 'set you high above all the nations of the earth'. In the biblical narrative, this is so that Israel will be a blessing to others (Gen. 12:3; Deut. 4:6-8). The section declares that Israel will 'lend to many nations' (v. 12) and that she will influence and lead them in international relations (v. 13).

- Verses 3-6 emphasise the 'beatitudes' of domestic life, whereas verses 7-14 focus upon Israel as a people. There is abundant prosperity in families, crops and herds, with the especially appealing image of verse 12: 'The LORD will open to you his good treasury.'

- The blessings are clearly conditional: 'The LORD will establish you ... IF you keep the commandments' (v. 9) and 'the LORD will make you the head ... IF you obey ... and IF you do not turn aside' (vv. 13-14). Yet these are also grounded in the patriarchal promise 'as he has sworn to you' (v. 9).

- The section concludes with the common Deuteronomy observation that disobedience is epitomized by going after 'other gods' (v. 14) (see Introduction).

The curses for forsaking the LORD (28:15-68)

Again, some limited observations:

- Structurally, the curses fall into three sections. There is a division at verse 45, whereby verses 45-46 summarise verses 20-44 and then verses 47-48 introduce verses 49-57, which seem to escalate the horror of what will take place. Verse 58 has a new conditional clause introducing a section which is less specific but emphasises the reversal of salvation history.

- The LORD is the subject of all the verbs. He sends, causes, strikes, brings disaster. Although there are secondary causes, it is clear that he is actively punishing Israel.

- At several points, there are reminders of *why* this taking place:

    ○ 'on account of the evil of your deeds, because you have forsaken me' (v. 20)

    ○ 'because you did not obey the voice of the LORD your God, to keep his commandments' (v. 45)

    ○ 'because you did not serve the LORD your God with joyfulness and gladness of heart' (v. 47)

    ○ 'because you did not obey the voice of the LORD your God' (v. 62)

- The length and relentless cycle of the warnings with their assault of lurid detail is designed to permanently ingrain the consequences of disobedience in the hearts and minds of Israel. This *is* tough to read or hear, and there is no prospect for relief in the litany of curses.

- In a pattern we'll see repeated in chapter 32, there is a correspondence between their sin and God's punishment:

    ○ Because you chose to serve other gods (v. 14) … you shall be forced to serve other gods (v. 64)

    ○ Because you did not serve God (v. 47) … you will serve your enemies (v. 48)

- Taken together, the curses completely undo all of the blessings that the LORD has bestowed upon Israel. Although the descriptions of suffering in warfare are some of the hardest to read, the curses end with an unravelling of God's blessings in verse 62 ('Whereas you were as numerous as the stars of heaven, you shall be left few in number') and climax in a return to Egypt (v. 68).

From text to message

Getting the message clear: the theme

Israel is commanded to obey the Lord so that they continue in his blessing, but they are warned of the horrific curses that they will deserve for disobedience.

Getting the message clear: the aim

The aim for them was that they serve the Lord with joyfulness and gladness because of his abundant generosity in the gift of the land – and so avoid his curse.

The aim for us is that we serve the Lord with joyfulness and gladness because of Jesus's curse-bearing death that saves us from the horror of God's judgment.

A way in

Have you ever had the experience of being at a large Christian conference and feeling a great spur towards Christian living? You make fresh resolutions with your friends and determine that you're going to hold one another accountable for your behaviour going forward. Your new commitments are possibly unrealistic, but in the moment you are overcome with zeal.

Have you ever done that? Have you ever known the crushing failure that comes a few weeks afterwards when you mess up? It's that sort of scenario we have in chapter 27.

Ideas for application

- **Warnings are a sign of a God who cares.** The blessings and curses urge, encourage, coax and threaten with powerful and horrific imagery and language. This is a deliberate attempt to shock and shake people out of a lethargic response. One thinks of Jonathan Edwards' preaching of 'Sinners in the Hands of an Angry God' or Martyn Lloyd-Jones:

  > I am not afraid with being charged, as I frequently am, with trying to frighten you, for I am definitely trying to do so. If the wondrous love of Jesus Christ and the hope of glory is not sufficient to attract you then such is the value that I attach to the worth of your soul that I will do my utmost to alarm you with a sight of the terrors of hell.[8]

  Yet we must not flatten God's plan of redemption. The New Testament expects a born-again Christian with the indwelling Spirit to respond to God's warnings and flee from his judgment in a way that an Israelite would not. Notwithstanding the possibility of sacrifice embedded in 27:5-7, the overwhelming weight of the passage suggests that Israel's failure is inevitable.

- **Corporate commitment is a good thing.** Israel was going to fail because she did not have a heart to understand what Moses was saying (29:4), but that does not negate the fact that the very public and corporate nature of the commitment made

---

8. Quoted in Iain Murray, *D. Martyn Lloyd Jones: Volume 1 (The First Forty Years, 1899–1939)*, (Edinburgh: Banner of Truth, 1982), 216.

in chapter 27 (similarly in ch. 29) is a good thing. While it was ineffective for Israel it can be effective in the life of a born-again church. That's why we are to 'exhort one another every day, as long as it is called "today", that none of you may be hardened by the deceitfulness of sin' (Heb. 3:13).

- **There is grace amidst failure.** It must have been overwhelming to be an Israelite and hear the curses of chapter 27 that you were going to have to corporately declare and promise to avoid. Surely the sensitive Israelite believer who did love the LORD would be forced to turn and look towards the altar on Mount Ebal and think, 'That is my only hope – in a sacrifice that can bring me atonement.'

  The Christian is one who knows that they fall short: 'Cursed be anyone who does not confirm the words of this law by doing them' (27:26). Yet they rejoice that Paul quotes this verse in Galatians 3:10-14 as a prelude to the gospel that 'Christ redeemed us from the curse of the law by becoming a curse for us ... so that in Christ Jesus the blessing of Abraham might come to the Gentiles, so that we might receive the promised Spirit through faith.' We receive the blessings (described in agricultural terms) of chapter 28 while Jesus took the curses.

  A helpful confession in a church service when preaching on this could be the following:

  > As we kneel at your cross help us to see the stark reality of our sin,
  > and the wonderful measure of your love for us in Christ Jesus.

He was cut off from God
that I might be welcomed and adopted
He was punished
 that I might be blessed
He was made sin and curse
 that in him I might be declared righteous
He was put to death
 that I might enjoy eternal life
He entered darkness
 that I might have eternal light
He groaned in anguish
 that I might have endless song
He wore a crown of thorns
 that I might wear a crown of glory
He endured hell
 that I might enjoy heaven.

Infinite is the evil of our sin,
greater still is the worth of Christ's precious
blood, which has bought our ransom and
washed away our guilt. Amen.

Suggestions for preaching

There is certainly enough material to preach three sermons on chapters 26, 27 and 28, but I would suggest one on the whole section. Chapter 27 allows you to bring out the themes of the section, especially if you read out a representative section or two from chapter 28.

A curse you deserve and a blessing you don't (Deut. 27:1-26)

- The law means atonement is needed ... (vv. 1-8)
- ... for despite a commitment to obey ... (vv. 15-25)

- ... none can escape God's curse (v. 26; Gal. 3:10-14)

Questions to help understand the passage

1. What are the two things to be built when Israel crosses into the promised land (vv. 2-4 and vv. 5-7)?

2. What is the purpose of these two things?

3. What is meant to happen in verses 12-13? So, what is missing in verses 15-26?

4. How does Paul quote and apply 27:26 in Galatians 3:10-14?

Questions to help apply the passage

1. What impact does it have when you stand up with a group of people and declare your commitment together?

2. Israel is told to set up stones to write the law on and to be an altar as a place of atonement. What should have been the impact of the law and the altar?

17.

Beware a Poisonous Root and Bitter Fruit

(Deuteronomy 29)

Introduction

Chapters 29–30 compose a single speech of Moses – his third in the book to the whole people assembled. If chapters 27–28 gave the impression that the curse was highly likely, these chapters reveal that it is inevitable. Yet beyond that, there is hope in God's grace.

It is possible to preach the two chapters in one sermon – and in an overview series that makes sense – but it will take some skill to do so clearly. We will consider a method for that in the next chapter. However, chapter 29 is fascinating in its own right, with helpful warnings for Christians which find echoes in the New Testament, especially Hebrews 12.

Listening to the text

Structure

Within Moses's third speech, it is possible to discern the following structure. Most commentators have some variation on this. Crucially, 30:6-8 sit at the centre; Israel's hope depends upon the LORD's gracious initiative.

A The importance of obedience (29:2-28)

  B The law is clearly revealed (29:29)

    C *You* will return to the LORD and obey him wholeheartedly (30:1-2)

      D The LORD will again prosper Israel (30:3-5)

        E The LORD will circumcise Israel's heart to love him wholeheartedly, and Israel will turn and obey him (30:6-8)

      D' The LORD will again prosper Israel (30:9)

    C' *You* will return to the LORD and obey him wholeheartedly (30:10)

  B' The law is clearly revealed (30:11-14)

A' The importance of obedience (30:15-20)

For chapter 29, Nelson highlights helpfully that three paragraphs begin with 'You':[1]

- *You* have seen ... all that the LORD has done in the past (vv. 2-9)

- *You* are standing ... and you're all in this together (vv. 10-15)

- *You* know ... that following 'turd-gods' (see notes) will bring God's wrath (vv. 16-28)

This seems to provide a sensible structure to the chapter (accepting that verses 1-9 are framed by 'the words of the covenant').

---

1. Nelson, *Deuteronomy*, 337.

- The language of covenant is prominent in the chapter (vv. 1, 8, 11, 13, 20, 24)

- The language of curse is also frequent: the Hebrew word *'alah* appears four times, although it is translated variably:

  - 'sworn' in verses 12 and 14

  - 'curses' in verses 20 and 21

The suggestion seems to be that Israel is taking onto herself the curses of the covenant – solemnly declaring that they will have deserved them if they fail in their faithfulness. As McConville suggests: 'The key to understanding chapter 29 is the proposition that every curse written in the book of the law is effective for every member of the people of God; that is what they are entering into today.'[2]

Working through the text

It's not immediately obvious what the referent is for 'the words of the covenant' (v. 1). Yet, rather than referring to what comes next (which is quite limited in content), they seem to be referring to all that has come in chapters 5–28. This covenant in Moab is 'besides' the covenant at Horeb. McConville observes that 'the relationship of the Moab covenant to the Horeb covenant is not one of clean distinction, but rather a new realization.'[3] I found the illustration of it being similar to a 'software update' a helpful one.[4]

---

2. McConville, *Deuteronomy*, 413.

3. McConville, *Deuteronomy*, 409.

4. Andrew Shead, in conversation.

You've seen but you do not see (29:2-9)

The exegetical challenge here is what to make of verses 2-4. Israel has *seen* all the LORD did in Egypt and their eyes *saw* the signs and wonders – 'but to this day the LORD has not given you a heart to understand or eyes to *see* or ears to hear.' (See comments on the heart in Introduction and on chapter 30.)

It is clear that something more than physical sight is required. The parallelism between heart and eyes is a frequent feature in Deuteronomy (4:9; 11:18; 15:9; 28:65, 67). Israel has not seen with 'the eyes of their heart' (Eph. 1:18).

Who is responsible? Despite all they observed, Israel has not responded with faith – they are culpable. Yet, the LORD has not given them this heart to see – Israel requires the miracle of grace that will be described in 30:6.

Daniel Block argues that the expression 'to this day' in verse 4 suggests that from this time onwards the LORD *has* given them the heart to understand.[5] However, this seems unlikely as Moses declares in 31:27-29 that this generation is just as stubborn and will act corruptly in the future. The nation as a whole was still waiting for the promise of 30:6 to be fulfilled. Paul alludes to 29:4 in Romans 11:8 to state that Israel still lacked the heart to understand 'down to this very day'. That is evidently and wonderfully not true for every individual.

This does appear to be a verdict upon Israel as a nation: they *corporately* lacked the heart to understand. (The promise of Ezekiel 36 also has a corporate emphasis.) This does not deny that some *individuals* within Israel

---

5. Block, *Deuteronomy*, 676.

had the heart to understand: presumably, as a minimum, we would put Joshua and Caleb in the category of those who had hearts that understood. Later, the LORD does a work in the heart of Josiah (2 Kings 22:19). A failure to distinguish between Israel corporately and individuals within the nation would turn the great appeal of 30:15-20 into a cruel deception from the LORD.

Yet here in 29:4, this truth should have created a great sense of longing within Israel for the heart that can respond rightly. While the LORD is sovereign, Israel is held responsible. They should have done all within their power to pursue this right response from the heart.

Moses's review of Israel's history has similar notes to chapter 8 – especially in verses 4-5 where it mentions the miraculous provision of clothes and shoes that did not wear out. He returns to themes of chapter 2 in the conquests described in verses 7-8. This review stresses that Israel *is* responsible and should have responded with faith. The application comes in verse 9: 'Therefore keep the words ... and do them.'

You're all in this together (29:10-15)

There is a stress on the events of 'today' here (five times in vv. 10-14), but what is most striking is the inclusive nature of the list – the greatest to the least are identified in such detail (the wood-cutter and water-carrier) as to stress that the whole community is involved.

Verse 13 connects back to the patriarchal promise. The covenant being sworn in Moab was a fulfilment of the promise made to Abraham. The next generation is referenced to stress that decisions made today will affect their future.

You know that your heart will be tested (29:16-28)

29:16-21

Moses first addresses the danger of an individual's heart turning away. In a passage reminiscent of the 'heart murmurs' in chapters 7–9, Moses warns against a deceitful heart. The temptation will be idolatry, described in vivid language in verse 17 where 'their idols' could literally be translated 'pieces of excrement' or 'sheep poo'. That is what they are worth.

Israel is warned of the potential for this person to be a bitter root that could cause others to become defiled (Heb. 12:15).

Perhaps the most terrifying thing here in verse 19 is that, in the very moment when the individual hears the words of the covenant spoken in the assembly, he declares: 'I shall be safe, though I walk in the stubbornness of my heart.' While the end of verse 19 is difficult to understand, in the flow I think it makes most sense to see the comparison as this: just as a plant disease will destroy watered plants and dry plants, so the man or woman who commits some secret offence could cause the guilty and innocent to suffer.

Moses is clear in verses 20-21 that the LORD sees. Being part of a faithful community will not excuse the stubbornness of the individual. The only specific mention of forgiveness in the entire book of Deuteronomy – and it is negative! Verse 21 is a striking verse in emphasizing individual accountability. Our sins will find us out and we must give an account for them.

29:22-28

These verses turn back to the theme of collective rebellion. There is an incredibly dense section on God's anger with six different terms used. It seems here that Israel's failure is inevitable and that the curses will fall. The question is asked, 'What caused the heat of this great anger?' It is idolatry. As throughout Deuteronomy, it is always idolatry that produces the strongest response of great wrath, fury and jealousy from the LORD. (The same question and answer is also given in Jer. 22:6-9.) The strength of the language reminds us that this is no *mere* judicial sentence. The LORD is furious.

Wright vividly describes verses 22-29 as a kind of photographic negative of 4:5-8.[6] Whereas in chapter 4 the nations ask, 'What great nation is there that has a god so near to it as the LORD?' Here they ask: 'Why has the LORD destroyed their land?'

It is worth observing that, in 1 Kings 9, after the messianic promise that there will always be a descendant of David upon the throne of Israel, Solomon adopts the language of Deuteronomy 29:24-28. Solomon taught Israel not to rip Moses out of the line of promise from Abraham through to David.

Verse 29 seems to function as a transitional verse. Moses switches from addressing Israel to the first person plural. If it is right to see this verse as paralleled with 30:11-14 (see 'Structure' above), then it is stating that God has revealed everything necessary to know him and obey him. While Israel's failure will come, individuals like Joshua and Caleb know enough that they can trust the LORD.

From text to message

Getting the message clear: the theme
Here is a warning that, although the nation of Israel lacked the heart to understand the LORD, they were responsible

---

6. Wright, *Deuteronomy*, 288.

for responding. They were to 'keep the words of this
covenant' (v. 9) and watch out for individuals ruining the
whole community, or the anger of God would be terrible.

Getting the message clear: the aim

'Beware lest there be among you a root bearing poisonous
and bitter fruit.' Even members of the church today, with
our far greater privilege of having had the eyes of our hearts
opened, need to watch out for those who are stubborn of
heart.

A way in

'We win as a team and we lose as a team.' How true is that
in the Christian life? How responsible are we for our own
sins and how far are we responsible for allowing the sin of
others to affect us?

I think the preacher has a choice. You could (1) introduce
the differences between Israel and the church early on
(we *do have* the heart to understand and eyes to see). Or
(2) you could preach it more flatly as a sermon to Israel
and, having created tension, conclude with the longing for
further mercy and grace which comes in chapter 30 (e.g. we
read this and want to cry out, please Lord, give us a heart
to understand and eyes to see – he answers that promise!).

Ideas for application

- 'See to it that no one fails to obtain the grace of
  God; that no "root of bitterness" springs up and
  causes trouble, and by it many become defiled'
  (Heb. 12:15). While there is a strong emphasis on
  individual accountability in 29:19-21, the injunction
  in verse 18 is to watch out for individuals corrupting

the community. The same (you plural) appeal is found in Hebrews 12. Allowing sin to go unchecked will have a devastating effect on a community. In Deuteronomy 29, it is the next generation that suffers (vv. 22 ff.).

- Verse 19 is a terrifying reminder that our capacity for self-delusion is vast. At the very moment of being in church and hearing a sermon, an individual can assure themselves that their stubborn sin is fine and so harden their own heart (Heb. 3:13: 'Exhort one another every day ... that none of you may be hardened by the deceitfulness of sin.')

- 'The LORD will single him out' (v. 21). This was a warning ignored by Achan (Josh. 7) and Ananias and Sapphira (Acts 5) – we must remember that our sin will not be hidden or just buried along with other people's.

- We need mercy! If you preached a sermon just on chapter 29, it would be perverse to end with the anger of God from verses 20-28 because, in Moses's complete sermon of chapters 29–30, anger is not the final word! It is a chapter that leads us into confession – and then thanksgiving that there is mercy! In chapter 30, grace will triumph!

Suggestions for preaching

- 'You've' seen but you need God's grace to see (vv. 1-9)
- 'You're' all in this together when temptation comes (vv. 10-21)
- 'You'll' face God's curse because of idolatry (vv. 22-28)

(One could replace the 'yous' with 'Israel' and say, 'Israel had seen', etc., but my own view is that you are then in danger of giving a lecture rather than a sermon with exhortation.)

Questions to help understand the passage

1. What are all the things that Israel has seen the LORD do in verses 2-9? What is the application of this in verse 9?

2. What is the problem in verse 4? What does this mean, given the three parallel sentences in the verse?

3. Who is gathered there in verses 10-15? Why such a long list?

4. What is the nature of the temptation in verses 16-18?

5. What specifically must Israel beware (vv. 18-19)?

6. Why will the LORD destroy the land (vv. 22-28)?

Questions to help apply the passage

1. In what way are Christians in a very different place to Israel in verse 4?

2. How does verse 18 apply practically? How can we make sure that there is no one turning away who could influence others?

3. What does verse 19 teach us about the deceitfulness of sin? Are you shocked that someone could be so self-deluded?

4. How do verses 22-28 help us understand more deeply how the Lord views idolatry?

18.

Choose Life

(Deuteronomy 30)

Introduction

Chapter 30 rhetorically serves as a climax to the book of Deuteronomy, particularly in the choice set before the people in 30:15-20. It is a crucial chapter in the book, as it explains how God will overcome the persistent disobedience of the Israelites.

The central command of the book in 6:5 is to 'love the LORD your God with all your heart and with all your soul and with all your might.' In 10:16 the Israelites were told to 'circumcise their hearts'. Yet in 29:4, Moses explained that 'to this day the LORD has not given you a heart that understands.'

In chapter 30 Moses explains God's resolution to this problem: he will circumcise their hearts. Although Deuteronomy takes it for granted that the nation as a whole will fail, the promise of a circumcised heart was a real possibility for individuals in every generation. 'Heart' appears fifty-one times in the book. The greatest concentrations are four times in chapter 4 and chapter 6 – yet eight times here.

There are some difficult interpretative issues to resolve in chapter 30, and they are crucial for how you read the book as a whole. However, the preacher must not lose the rhetorical force of chapter 30. Moses is imploring the people to 'Choose life' and to make that choice 'today'. We must be equally urgent in our preaching if we are to do justice to this text. It's not enough to give a Bible overview on new hearts.

Listening to the text

Structure

We are still in the outer frame to the law (where chapter 4 has verbal links with chapters 29–30). Deuteronomy repeatedly embeds the law within a narrative – it only makes sense in the context of who God is and what he has done. From chapter 31:1 the book returns to narrative.

4:44 'This is the law'
5:1   'Moses summoned all Israel and said'

    12:1   'These are the statutes and rules that you shall be careful to do'

    26:16 'This day the LORD your God commands you to do these statutes and rules'

29:1 'These are the words of the covenant that the LORD commanded'
29:2 'Moses summoned all Israel and said'

There are three clear units in the chapter:

- Verses 1-10 are a promise/appeal for repentance.
- Verses 11-14 are an assurance that the obedience called for in Deuteronomy is possible.
- Verses 15-20 are the climactic call of the book to 'choose life' not death.

There is a delicate balance in verses 1-10 between what we do and what the LORD does. He grants a new heart but we repent. Preachers need to ensure that this balance is kept and not be too quick to impose systematic categories upon the text.

Working through the text

I am personally averse to the attempt to find chiasms everywhere in the Old Testament, but in verses 1-10 it is impossible to ignore the structure and language of the text:

A When *YOU* return with all your heart and soul (30:1-2)

  B The LORD will return your fortunes (30:3-5)

    C The LORD will circumcise your hearts (30:6-8)

  B' The LORD will turn back in delight (30:9)

A' When *YOU* turn to the LORD with all your heart and soul (30:10)

This balanced structure reveals that although the syntax ('when … then') suggests that the LORD's action follows Israel's repentance, the centre of the passage falls on verses 6-8. The LORD's work in their hearts is what causes Israel to respond with their heart and soul.

In verses 1-10 the word 'return' (*ŝûb*) is the key term and appears seven times. It expresses both the turning of Israel to the LORD (vv. 1, 2, 8, 10) and the turning of the LORD to Israel (twice in v. 3 and once in v. 9).

A. Return to the LORD with all your heart (30:1-2, 10)

The outer frame is marked by the language of Israel turning back to the LORD with their heart and soul.

Moses is describing events in the future. In verses 1-5,
'these things' is a reference to the words of blessing and
curse in the covenant (29:1; 29:9). Here is a time after the
Israelites have entered the promised land and after they
have enjoyed its blessings AND after they have failed to
love God – so the Lord removes his blessing and they're
driven out of the promised land. It has very close verbal
and predictive links to 4:27-30.

There is a decision to be made about how to translate
the Hebrew word *kî*. The logic suggests that it is best
taken as a temporal clause: 'when you return' rather than
a conditional clause, 'if you return'. Verses 7-8 make most
sense if they are Moses describing a future event rather
than commanding people in the future who are not present
before him. The NIV is inconsistent in its translation. It
opts for 'when' in verse 2 but 'if' in verse 10. This is unlikely
because if *kî* is a conditional clause, there will normally be
a 'when' following it. Verse 10 lacks this.

Moses declares that Israel will fail, but that after that
they'll recall the words of Deuteronomy and return to the
Lord. They will repent or turn around. Verse 2 is not
predicting perfection but a new fundamental loyalty (see
the parallel between verse 16 and verse 17 below).

B. Then he will delight to prosper you (30:3-5, 9)

The second level of the chiasm is marked by the Lord's
activity in turning back to Israel.

When the people return to the Lord (v. 3), three things
happen:

1. The primary action is that *the Lord turns* back to his
   people. It's not that he has walked off anywhere, but he
   turns back in blessing: he will 'restore your fortunes'.

2. *He will gather* from all nations (v. 4). By the time of
   Daniel and Esther, Israel was banished to the distant
   land of Persia. They were scattered and alone.

3. They will return to the *promised land* – the place of
   security and bounty.

Verse 9 makes very similar points to these three but undoes
the curse language of chapter 28. Whereas under the curse
Israel's wombs, beasts and land would be barren (28:30),
now they will be fruitful. Whereas in 28:63 the LORD would
be delighted to destroy them, here he is delighted in them.

C. When he has circumcised your heart (30:6-8)

Here is the meat at the centre of the passage. Here is how
permanent change is made. 'The LORD your God will
circumcise your heart ... so that you will love the LORD your
God with all your heart and with all your soul' (v. 6). The
very thing expected and commanded of the Israelites is only
possible when the LORD changes their hearts. The LORD's
action comes first. His work in their hearts enables the right
response. Grace would triumph in the end – the people would
be faithless, but God would be faithful. Some generations
would suffer in exile, but God never abandoned his people.

Moses reveals that the only way to have a circumcised
heart – that is, a heart with all the moral and spiritual
barriers to true devotion removed – is if God does it. The
only way for Israel to have undivided love and obedience
is if God acts to change them internally.

Verse 6 is the first time in the book when love is not a
command but a statement. It is enabled by the LORD. No
one in Israel (and no one today) can take the initiative for
a restored relationship with the LORD. He must act first.

Overall in verses 1-10, it seems as if the writer has deliberately created a balance between the LORD's work and Israel's response. Although his work is prior, human responsibility and divine action fit together. It is not either/or. This strengthens the rhetorical appeal to return. It is when the exiles return to the LORD that they discover that he has been at work in them, granting them the hearts that they needed.

The command is possible (30:11-14)

It is striking that the most negative assessment of Israel in verses 1-10 (the curse has come upon them) is followed by the most positive in verses 11-14. You could frame the question: 'So, was keeping the law possible for Israel or not?' However, this is misleading. The optimism of verses 11-14 derives from the circumcision of the heart by the LORD in verse 6. The word is placed in the heart by the circumcision of the heart. So, a less misleading question would be, 'How can Israelites have the word in their hearts?' Answer: 'If the LORD has circumcised those hearts.' You cannot get the word in your heart by obeying chapters 12–26. You need circumcision of the heart before you can obey as verses 11-14 describe.

While scholars overwhelmingly agree that verses 1-10 have a future reference and verses 15-20 have a present urgent force to the people in the plains of Moab, there is some debate about verses 11-14. Are these verses describing a future state of affairs after exile or was this a possibility for Israel then?[1]

---

1. Among those suggesting that vv. 11-14 are not addressed to Moses's initial audience but to the exiles are Paul Barker and Steven Coxhead ('Deuteronomy 30:11-14 as a Prophecy of the New Covenant in Christ,' *WTJ* 68.2 (2006): 305-320). Among those arguing that vv. 11-14 address

While both options are linguistically and exegetically possible, it is most sensible to take verses 11-14 as addressed to the people in Moab. In the immediate context, the pleading of Moses to keep the commandment in verses 15-20 becomes cruel if the Lord knows full well that, even though he says it is not too difficult, in fact it is beyond them. It renders the rhetoric of Moses's speech meaningless.

Furthermore, throughout Deuteronomy, the law is given alongside repeated references to the promises given to Abraham (here in v. 20) and to a people who have been redeemed. I am sympathetic to Wright's comment: 'The idea that God deliberately made the law so exacting that nobody would ever be able to live by it belongs to a distorted theology that tries unnecessarily to gild the gospel by denigrating the law.'[2]

Verses 11-14 are NOT saying that Israel could obey the Lord on their own. They are saying that the obedience of faithful loyalty is possible after the Lord has placed the word in the heart of an individual. The 'yous' of verses 11-20 are all singular. He is addressing individuals here.

Verse 11 literally refers to 'the commandment', singular. This singular term sometimes denotes the entire covenant text – that is, all the stipulations in 12–26. Yet, given that it follows from verse 10, it is best understood as the call to 'Love the Lord your God with all your heart and with all your soul.'[3] The emphasis on achievability is repetitive:

- not too hard for you (v. 11)
- we may ... do it (v. 12)

the Israelites in Moab are McConville and Robson. Moo and Schreiner take this latter position in their Romans commentaries.

2. Wright, *Deuteronomy*, 290.

3. See comments in Introduction, page 15.

- we may ... do it (v. 13)
- you can do it (v. 14)

The two terms of verse 11 suggest two slightly different emphases. 'Not too hard' suggests that it is clear. Not 'far off' stresses that it is near. Israel could keep the law – not in their own strength, but if they trusted in God's promise of a transformed heart.

It is clear

The verb behind 'too hard' gets used in 17:8 of law cases that *are* too difficult to judge. In other words, there are some cases where you sit there as a judge and you don't know the right thing to decide. NOT SO the commandments. When God says 'Do not steal,' it's obvious what to do.

The same point was made just before chapter 30 in 29:29. God doesn't tell us everything, but what he does tell us is straightforward to understand. While Bible scholars are a great blessing to the church, you don't need a PhD in theology to understand the main message of the Bible.

It is near

Moses says that we don't need spiritual heroics to be believers. We don't need to ascend to heaven or cross the sea. All we need is the word in our heart (v. 14). If it is in our heart, then it will be in our mouths, because out of the abundance of the heart the mouth speaks (Matt. 12:34). How does the word get into our hearts? God puts it there when he gives a new heart (v. 6). Moses is not saying that an Israelite could keep all the commandments of chapters 12–26. He is saying that they could trust the God who has promised to save them and give them new hearts.

Although Israel as a nation will fail, there would be a remnant of faithful Israelites who did have circumcised hearts. Their responsibility was, by faith, to trust God's promise of forgiveness.

Paul confirms this as the meaning of Deuteronomy 30 when he quotes these words in Romans 10. In the context there, he is explaining that the greatest need of any human is to have righteousness. That's the only way to spend eternity with God. Paul contrasts two responses to the law of Moses. First, there is the response of unbelieving Jews:

> But the people of Israel, who pursued the law as the way of righteousness, have not attained their goal. Why not? Because they pursued it not by faith but as if it were by works. (Rom. 9:31-32 NIV)

The law was never to be pursued by works, as if by keeping it they could attain righteousness. The law was never meant to be kept as a ladder to heaven. It was meant to be kept by trusting in the God who promises to save. The Israelites should have grasped that Christ was the goal, the terminus, the purpose of the law. Jesus is the fulfilment of the promise of Deuteronomy 30:

> Christ is the culmination of the law so that there may be righteousness for everyone who believes. Moses writes this about the righteousness that is by the law: 'The person who does these things will live by them.' (Rom. 10:4-5 NIV)

Paul takes up Leviticus 18:5 as typifying the legalists of his day. In its original setting, Leviticus 18:5 is describing obedience in response to faith – that is, if you're a believer you'll bear fruit (cf. John 15:5-6). So Paul is quoting Leviticus 18:5 as Pharisees would have taken it, not as Moses intended. He contrasts it with Deuteronomy 30.

Then Paul describes the second response – the one that Israel should have had and Christians now have – which is faith:

> But the righteousness that is by faith says: 'Do not say in your heart, "Who will ascend into heaven?"' (that is, to bring Christ down) 'or "Who will descend into the deep?"' (that is, to bring Christ up from the dead). But what does it say? 'The word is near you; it is in your mouth and in your heart,' that is, the message concerning faith that we proclaim: If you declare with your mouth, 'Jesus is Lord,' and believe in your heart that God raised him from the dead, you will be saved. (Rom. 10:6-9 NIV)

Paul applies Deuteronomy 30 by saying that you don't have to perform spiritual heroics to be a Christian:

- No one made Jesus came down. He came down voluntarily. No one rose Jesus from the dead – that was God's work (Rom. 10:7).

- What is the word that is near, according to Paul? It is the message of faith (Rom. 10:8).

- What is the word that can be in your mouth? That Jesus is Lord (Rom. 10:9).

- What is the word that should be in your heart? That God raised Jesus from the dead (Rom. 10:9).

Jesus is the one who pours out his Spirit so that people can have transformed hearts. This promise was for a small remnant in Israel, but now it is for the vast church of Christ this side of his cross, resurrection and ascension. Again, I can't see that it makes sense of the chapter to have Moses saying, 'Israelites, you can't really keep this, but one day Christians will do so.' The rhetoric of the passage pushes us to conclude that Moses was saying, 'You Israelites *can* do what the law requires by faith in Christ (you don't know his name but can trust in God's promises which terminate upon him).'

An Israelite could not keep the law by the spiritual heroics of climbing to heaven or crossing the sea. They could not keep the law, confident of sinless perfection. But an Israelite could have their sin exposed and cry out to God for mercy on the basis of his promise. We are in the far better position of being able to see clearly what Mr and Mrs Israelite could only see in shadow. We see Jesus and all of God's promises fulfilled in him. We have a far clearer word to trust in.

Choose faith in the saviour, not your own gods (30:15-20)

Moses is very obviously setting before them a choice:

- 'See, I have set before you today' (v. 15)
- If … then (v. 16)
- If … then (vv. 17-18)
- 'I call heaven and earth to witness … that I have set before you … ' (v. 19)

When preaching this, we'll need to capture the force of the appeal in verses 19-20: 'Therefore choose life!' This is a choice that must be made today (vv. 15, 16, 18, 19) and every day.

The outcomes of the choice are stark:

- life or death, good or evil (v. 15)
- live and multiply or perish (vv. 16-18)
- blessing or curse (v. 19)

We are of course not longing for the land of Canaan but the promised land of the new creation.

But what does the choice practically look like?

Good option 1 in verse 16 is:	**Bad option 2 in verse 17 is:**
• obeying the commandments of the LORD; • loving the LORD your God; • walking in his ways; and • keeping his commandments and his statutes and his rules.	• your heart turns away; • you will not hear; • you are drawn away to worship other gods and serve them.

The two options are not, Will you keep the law or not keep the law? Will you pass God's exam or fail it? Rather, verse 17 makes clear that the bad choice is not primarily about morality and it is not foremost about external deeds. The bad choice is that your heart is drawn away. It is that you worship other gods and serve them. 'It is not a simple choice to obey. Rather Israel is being asked to choose Yahweh and his grace which will enable obedience.'[4]

Overall, the choice is: Who will you worship?

- Will you place faith in the LORD or follow other gods?

- Will you love him in your heart or resent him?

- Will you use your talents and gifts to serve him or will you serve yourself and your man-made dreams?

---

4. Barker, *The Triumph of Grace*, 212.

- Will you choose faith in him (the promise of a new heart) or assert your own righteousness?

Verse 20 concludes the chapter with a reminder of the LORD's faithfulness to the patriarchal promises. You really can trust this God, so choose him.

Intriguingly, we are not told Israel's choice (unlike in, say, Joshua 24), perhaps to force the choice upon us the readers.

The appeal to us today is: Choose Jesus! Choose to trust in his work for you. Choose to have God transform you. That choice is seen in worshipping him, loving him rather than worshipping other gods and loving our own desires.

From text to message

Getting the message clear: the theme

When the Lord has done his work of circumcising the heart, you can turn to him and follow him with loyal obedience (not perfect, but a fundamental allegiance). Salvation is God's work, but there is human responsibility. We need to repent. We need to choose him.

Getting the message clear: the aim

Confident of God's work in you, choose to trust Jesus, not your own works and not other gods. Choose him every day.

A way in

Don't you long for change? The government sets up 'nudge departments' to try and make people behave differently. In the end, there's only one way to live a transformed life.

Ideas for application

- **Repent.** The Lord still says in the twenty-first century, 'Return to me and I will prosper you.' We need to make sure that this is rightly understood though. The call is still to repent – to turn around and stop walking away from God. However, we don't have to wait until we find ourselves exiled in Persia or Iran if we trust that Jesus took the curse for us and love him.

- **The benefits of repentance.** He'll prosper you. The same three things highlighted in the text still happen today. *He turns back to you* – our relationship with the Lord is restored. *He gathers nations to himself.* People from every tribe and nation can become Christians. In the church where I minister, we have believers from Iran, the Philippines, China, Australia, America, France, Germany, Malaysia, Singapore, Hong Kong, Egypt, England, Scotland, Ireland and Wales! We are no longer scattered and alone. The church is an exceptional place of support and fellowship. We don't yet possess – but we are looking forward to – the *promised land* of heaven where all the work of our hands will prosper.

- **Only God can do this.** The picture of a circumcised heart highlights how serious our problem is. The physical parallel is of some use here. If you needed a heart transplant you can't do that yourself. If you were incredibly brave and resilient you might be able to amputate a finger or two off your own hand, but you can't replace your own heart. During a heart transplant you are incredibly passive. Your life is in the hands of the surgeon. It is God's work to enter into the heart of an unbeliever and give them new life, to bring conversion. As the Bible's revelation unfolds, we understand that this is the gift of the Holy Spirit. Following the death and resurrection of Christ, he pours out his Spirit to bring new life. Wonderfully, when God gives you a new heart it's a permanent change – he has given you the faith to trust in him and obey him. For Israel in the Old Testament, there were times of obedience but never lasting loyalty. The story of the Old Testament is the recurrent faithlessness of the people. When God grants a new heart, it produces a fundamentally new loyalty. I think it's always worth making the point that there is no other way to be a Christian. It's not that God tinkers with us a little. It is not a repaired heart that we need but a NEW heart.

- **Obedience.** The new heart means you WILL obey the Lord (v. 8). Once we have received the gift of a new heart, it enables us to live very differently. We CAN love the Lord our God with all our heart and soul in a way we had no desire for before.

- **Daily choice.** Each and every day will be one when we choose to trust Christ rather than our own righteousness. Each and every day we must resolve to follow him rather than other little gods that have appeal for us.

Suggestions for preaching

I think that this chapter is so important for an understanding of Deuteronomy that it could be a good thing to slow right down and preach it in two or three sermons (vv. 1-10; vv. 11-14; vv. 15-20). For the unconverted church member or young Christian, it is also a great passage for teaching on

God's work of new birth. However, it is possible to preach it in one and there is real value in helping people see how the whole chapter holds together. Chapter 29 and verse 4 could be used in the introduction to explain the problem that has loomed over the whole book.

Choose Life (Deuteronomy 29–30)

- There's a problem in the heart (29:4)
- The LORD must change your heart (30:1-10)
  - You will return (vv. 1-2, 10)
  - Then he will prosper you (vv. 3-5, 9)
  - When he has circumcised your heart (vv. 6-8)
- You must choose to trust him (30:11-20)
  - The word of faith was near them (vv. 11-14)
  - Choose faith in the saviour, not your own gods (vv. 15-20)

Questions to help understand the passage

1. What was the great command of Deuteronomy 6:5 and what has been the main problem for Israel throughout Deuteronomy (29:4)?

2. What is the wonderful promise here (30:6)? (Look up also Jer. 31 and Ezek. 36:26.)

3. In verses 1-10, what does the LORD do and what does Israel do?

4. What are the promises of verses 3-5 and verse 9?

5. What is said about the commandment to love the LORD in verses 11-14? Is it impossible to achieve?

6. Look up Romans 9:31-32 and 10:6-9. How does Paul interpret these verses from Deuteronomy?

7. What actually is the choice Paul presents to the Israelites in verses 15-20? Fill in this little table:

	Good	Bad
The choice in verses 16-17		
The outcomes in verses 15-19		

8. What does Moses emphasise about the LORD as he concludes his speech in verse 20?

Questions to help apply the passage

1. What must God do for every sinner before they can repent (cf. John 3:3-8)?

2. How do the promises of verses 3-5 and verse 9 apply to the Christian?

3. What is the outcome of having a new heart (v. 8)?

4. What is the fundamental choice that every human must make? How does a Christian keep choosing that 'today'?

5. How is this wonderfully encouraging to us?

19.

A Faithful God and a Faithless People
(Deuteronomy 31:1–32:47)

Introduction

The text returns to narrative at this point and exhortation is dialled down after the climax of chapter 30. It would almost be possible to skip over chapters 4–30 and read 1–3 and then 31–34 as one continuous narrative. The last four chapters do seem to act as the outer frame corresponding to chapters 1–2; however, whereas at the start of the book Moses looked back, here he is looking forward.

The section from 31:1–32:47 is dominated by the Song of Moses, and if you preach this as one sermon, the focus will be upon the song. However, chapter 31 is clear that as Moses dies, Israel actually needs three things in his place: a new leader, the torah, and a song to sing. It is entirely possible for a mini-series in these two chapters.

The song is fundamentally about God's faithfulness and the people's faithlessness. Most of the song condemns the incomprehensible stupidity and ingratitude of Israel in turning from the LORD to other gods. It is frank that apostasy will come and yet … the final word will be compassion and atonement.

The New Testament quotes the song frequently and applies it to the world today. So we'll see that its warning against ingratitude is a timeless message for the world and in a secondary sense for the church.

Listening to the text

There are some recurrent thoughts:

- The death of Moses (31:2, 14, 16, 27) is the occasion for a written law, a new leader and – dominating these chapters – a national song.

- 'A witness against Israel'. This is the function of
    - the song (31:19, 21);
    - the torah (31:26);
    - heaven and earth (31:28; 4:26; 30:19).

- In the song, the LORD is most frequently described as the 'Rock' (32:4, 15, 18, 30, 31b).

- The fundamental problem is the turning to other gods (31:16, 18, 20; 32:16, three times in 17, 21, 37, 39). This is important in the development of the rest of the Old Testament and also for understanding that the essential call to loyalty, the call to choose life in Deuteronomy, is to choose Yahweh over false gods. Obedience to individual laws is an indicator as to whether that has been done.

- When we get to the song in chapter 32, it is striking what is *not* there. Although it is a history of Israel, it is written in vague and somewhat ambiguous terms. We would expect references to redemption from Egypt, but there are none. Similarly, there is no reference to the patriarchs or to being brought into the promised land, to the covenant at Sinai/Horeb or that in the plains of Moab. The emphasis is upon God's generosity in creating, sustaining and protecting. As such, it is a song which is very easy to appropriate for later generations of humanity, as we will see the New Testament does.

Structure

Chapter 31 alternates between the three elements which will replace Moses, with perhaps a chiastic structure:

Words to Israel and Joshua (31:1-8)

> Words about the torah (31:9-13)

> > Words to Joshua (31:14-15)

> > > The giving of the song (31:16-22)

> > Words to Joshua (31:23)

> Words about the torah (31:24-27)

Words to Israel (31:28-29)

Chapter 32 is a song with a 'chorus' in verses 4-5 and then five 'verses' to sing:

- God is a Rock of faithfulness (32:7-14)
- Israel are children with no faithfulness (32:15-18)
- God rejects his people who desert him (32:19-25)
- God rejects 'no people' for their pride (32:26-35)
- God will vindicate his people when they're humbled (32:36-43)

Working through the text
The succession plan (ch. 31)

The LORD himself will go before you (31:1-8)

The drumbeat of Moses's death sounds continually through these last chapters. This would naturally have been unsettling for Israel, but the important truth they need to hear is 'The LORD your God *himself* will go over before you' (v. 3). Joshua will be the new leader, but crucially the LORD is with them, and it is his activity that matters:

- 'He will destroy' (v. 3)
- 'The LORD will do' (v. 4)
- 'And the LORD will give them over to you' (v. 5)

Israel and then Joshua are commanded, 'Be strong and courageous' (vv. 6, 7, 23) and also told 'Do not fear' (vv. 6, 8). Both admonitions are grounded in the truth that the LORD will 'not leave you or forsake you' (vv. 6, 8; v. 23 is also similar). It's still a truth Christians need to hear (Heb. 13:5).

The law will go with you (31:9-13, 24-27)

There would be a natural flow of thought from verse 8 into verse 14, yet verses 9-13 are very deliberately inserted here. You must decide whether you think 'this law' refers to the whole Torah or just to Deuteronomy. It's hard to be dogmatic, but the latter seems a more natural reading. Moses commands them to do three things:

- Read the law every seven years (in a context of celebration)
- Assemble all the people (so that they hear and fear the LORD)

- Let their children hear it (as they may never have done so)

It is striking that the context for reading the law was celebration (v. 10). It is to happen in the year of release, when people were liberated from slavery and debt to commemorate the liberation from Egypt (ch. 15). It is to take place at the Feast of Booths when Israel was celebrating the harvest (16:14-15).

We are told a second time that Moses's words were transferred to a written text in verses 24-27. A note of pessimism rings out clearly, in that the law – like the song – is a witness against Israel, and in particular her rebelliousness. The emphasis on Moses's words being written is loud and striking. Block observes: 'More than any other text in the Old Testament, chapter 31 binds Moses to a written document more tightly than any of the prophets who follow in his train.'[1]

The LORD will be with Joshua (31:14-15, 23)

The text shows Moses's exiting the stage in the progression of the three references to Joshua:

- Moses summons Joshua (vv. 7-8)
- The LORD summons Moses to call Joshua (vv. 14-15)
- The LORD commissions Joshua (no mention of Moses)[2] (v. 23)

This song will be with you (31:16-22)

This long introduction to the song binds these two chapters together. There are numerous verbal similarities:

---

1. Block, *Deuteronomy*, 735.

2. Olson, *Deuteronomy and the Death of Moses*, 134.

- milk and honey (31:20; 32:13-14)
- heaven and earth (31:28; 32:1)
- provoke to anger/jealousy (31:29; 32:16, 19, 21, 27)
- 'hide my face' (31:17, 18; 32:20)

In preaching Israel's rebellion, it will be important that we capture the sense of outrage and incredulity at their ingratitude. They 'whore' after foreign gods (31:16), 'forsake' the LORD (31:16) and 'despise me' (31:20).

The introduction does contain references to the breaking of the covenant, in a way that the Song of Moses itself does not. Yet the great difference between the introduction to the song in chapter 31 and the song itself is that the final 'verse' of the song ends with hope. God's faithfulness will triumph over Israel's unfaithfulness.

It is striking that the song is to be put in their mouths (31:19, 21), just as the law was to be placed there (30:14). It seems that the song *is* sung torah.

A song of ingratitude (ch. 32)

Introduction (31:30–32:6)

Moses addresses the whole nation, and the solemnity is reinforced by heaven and earth being summoned as a witness (cf. 4:26; 30:19; 31:28).

He encourages Israel that this song can do you a great deal of good (v. 2): it is rain, dew and showers in a dry land. If you're feeling dry, it can bring life; if you're feeling stagnant, it can bring growth.

Verse 3 tells us in parallel clauses what Moses is about to do in the song: proclaim the name of the LORD and ascribe greatness to our God. We must ensure the tone of our sermons on chapter 32 does precisely that.

Verses 4-6 introduce the theme of the song, which is then explored at greater length. The essential contrast is between the faithful God (v. 4) and foolish and corrupt Israel (vv. 5-6).

The idea of God being 'the Rock' is one of the dominant metaphors of the song and worth dwelling upon. In a dangerous land, a rock provides shelter and protection. It is a picture of strength, refuge and stability. Verse 4 emphasises the unchanging and consistent nature of God by being verbless. A more literal, if clumsy, reading is 'The Rock: perfect works, just in all ways, faithful, no wrong, upright and just.' There are no verbs of change because God is always and maximally these things; there is no improvement in his work, ways or character.

The contrast comes in verses 5-6. In contrast to all the wonderful descriptions of God, Israel is corrupt … blemished … crooked … twisted. We are meant to hear and feel the utter incredulity of verse 6: 'Is *that* how you repay the LORD's generosity?'

In the song, God is described as the father (v. 6) who bore them (v. 18). Israel are described as his children. It is worth being clear that this is not in a legal sense, like the New Testament concept of being adopted into the family. Rather it is part of the extended metaphor of God being their creator – the one to whom they owe everything: he 'created you … made you and established you' (v. 6).

In Philippians 2:14-15, Paul quotes Deuteronomy 32:5, taking a verse about Israel and applying it to humanity in general. Christians are to live as 'children of God, without blemish, in the midst of a *crooked and twisted generation*'.

Repaying the Rock with senseless ingratitude is a timeless sin and not unique to Israel!

God is a Rock of faithfulness (32:7-14)

The song's 'chorus' of verses 4-6 is now expanded upon, with more detail on how God treated Israel. His character is seen here in his actions.

Israel is commanded to 'remember' (v. 7), which is the only imperative in the song until we get to verse 43. As elsewhere in Deuteronomy, the key to obedience is remembering what God is like and what he has done for us.

He is the one who allocated lands to the nations (v. 8), yet above all chose Israel as his 'portion'. Verse 10 is a highly evocative scene. It evokes the picture of a baby dying of exposure in the howling waste of the wilderness. Yet the king comes across the child and makes them his greatest delight. He should be too busy to care, but it's as if he personally feeds the child, protects them, reads them stories, brings them into maturity. The commentators argue over whether the desert land in verse 10 is Egypt or more simply a picture of wilderness, similar to Ezekiel 16. The latter seems more likely to me.

Verse 11 is a parallel picture, with the LORD like a vast golden eagle with a wingspan of more than 2 metres. The eagle hovers over the young (just like the Spirit of God in creation – Genesis 1 is the only other time in the Pentateuch that this verb is used). If you're in need, this eagle will feed you; if you fall, he will catch you; if anything threatens, he will protect you.

He did this work alone (v. 12), for he has no rivals. Verses 13-14 stress how wonderfully well God treated them. His generosity was so bountiful that luxurious honey oozed from rocks and necessities such as oil did too (v. 13). They received the finest cuts of meat and the best sparkling wine (v. 14).

God took this vulnerable people from dying of exposure (v. 10) to living in the lap of luxury (vv. 13-14).

Israel are children with no faithfulness (32:15-18)

But Jeshurun (or Israel) was a fathead (v. 15)! When they grew strong and powerful, they forsook God.

In a timeless crime, they declared, 'We're impressive and we don't need you.' There is an extraordinary variety of terms used for the false gods in verses 16-17:

- strange gods (v. 16)
- abominations (v. 16)
- demons (v. 17)
- no gods (v. 17)
- unknown gods (v. 17)
- new gods (v. 17)

Either side of this pagan list we are told in parallel phrases that:

- Israel 'forsook God … and scoffed at the Rock' (v. 15)
- Israel was 'unmindful of the Rock' and 'forgot' God (v. 18)

What a contrast between the ever-faithful Rock and the new, strange, unknown and abominable demons! We're meant to feel the pain of verse 18 as they reject the one who gave birth to them and provided them with all that they have.

It is an act of wickedness but also utter madness. We might imagine a six-year-old child declaring one day to their parents, 'I don't need you. I don't want you. I'm moving out and you won't hear from me again.' The parents would naturally ask, 'Where will you live? How will you

eat? How will you stay warm?' For the child to persist
and say, 'I'm healthy and strong. I no longer need you,'
would be gross ingratitude but also senseless stupidity.
They cannot survive that way. How did Israel reach such
a stupid conclusion? They had failed to 'remember' (v. 7).
Craigie expresses it very well: 'Israel abandoned the source
of its creation and scorned the basis of its salvation, acts of
incredible folly – but the incredible becomes the credible
when God's people forget the source of their blessing.'[3]

God rejects his people who desert him (32:19-25)

The big idea here is that the punishment fits the crime. The
LORD will treat Israel as they have treated him:

They forgot the Rock (v. 18)	The LORD spurned them (v. 19)
They made him jealous and angry (v. 16)	He'll make them jealous and angry (v. 21)
They followed 'no god' (v. 21)	They'll be conquered by 'no-people' (v. 21)
They were foolish (v. 6)	They'll be ruled by a 'foolish' nation (v. 21)

Again, the description of Israel is deeply unflattering. They
are guilty of provocation (v. 19), they are perverse (v. 20)
and they have no faithfulness (v. 20).

Given that they had rejected him, the LORD will 'hide
his face'. That is the opposite of the Aaronic blessing of
Numbers 6:25. It is a picture of revulsion and sorrow.[4]

---

3. Craigie, *The Book of Deuteronomy*, 382.

4. Jeffrey Tigay, *The JPS Torah Commentary: Deuteronomy* (Philadelphia: Jewish Publication Society, 1996), 308; Craigie, *The Book of Deuteronomy*, 383.

Blessing is withdrawn and therefore Israel will return to the condition of verse 10, dying in the howling waste. Whereas Israel enjoyed luxury at God's hand (vv. 13-14), she will now experience hunger (v. 24).

Alongside withdrawal, there is also language of active punishment. The LORD is provoked to anger (v. 21). Not of course a 'flying off the handle' anger but, in John Stott's helpful phrase, a 'steady, unrelenting, unremitting, uncompromising antagonism to evil in all its forms and manifestations'.[5]

The LORD will send numerous 'arrows' against them (vv. 23-24):

- wasting hunger
- plague and pestilence
- teeth and venom of beasts
- invasion and destruction by the sword

Verse 25 contains numerous merisms – outdoors and indoors, man and woman, nursing child and a man with grey hair. The point is that no one will escape.

Here, fully revealed, is the madness that comes from turning away the Rock who is your creator, provider and source of protection. If you forsake the Rock, he will forsake you. It's hard not to hear the echoes of Romans 1: 'God gave them over'.

God rejects 'no people' for their pride (32:26-35)

There is a pause in God's judgment of Israel in verse 26. God would have wiped out Israel, except that would have led another group to arrogant pride.

---

5. John Stott, *The Cross of Christ* (Leicester: IVP, 1986), 173.

The 'enemy' in verse 27 is the same group as 'no people' and the 'foolish nation' of verse 21. They made the timeless and arrogant claim of humanity throughout the centuries: 'Our hand is triumphant, it was not the LORD who did all this.'

The modern accent may say, 'This is humanity's great achievement, for there is no god,' but the sentiment is the same: '*Our* hand is triumphant.'

God tells us what he thinks of this claim in verses 28-29. They are foolish. Verse 30 is what they *should have* said. 'No nation' should have realized that there is no way they could have defeated Israel unless the LORD, the Rock had given them up.

Verse 31 returns to commentary upon their fate. They are cut from the same cloth as Sodom and Gomorrah in their poisonous arrogance.

We should notice here *how* God works – Israel's punishment came at the hand of a foolish pagan nation, who were then destroyed by another one. There's no message in the sky, with God saying, 'This is my doing.' His justice looks like the events of world politics – aggressive nations and natural forces.

In some ways, the crime of 'no people' is very similar to that of Israel. It is an arrogant rejection of the creator. Whereas Israel said, 'We no longer need God,' 'no nation' has declared, 'We have no need for God. Our hand is triumphant.'

Verses 34-35 remind us that God operates to a different timescale. His judgment of 'no nation' may be sealed up for a long time. Yet the time of calamity and vengeance will come in due time.

God will vindicate his people when they're humbled (32:36-43)

The LORD will relent or show compassion on his servants 'when he sees their power is gone' (v. 36). When his servants have reached their limits, when they have no hope but God, no source of strength but him, then he will show compassion. When people abandon their false gods and brittle rocks (vv. 37-38), then they will know compassion. In other words, when they have returned to him or repented (30:2).

Verses 39-42 are a staggering assertion of the LORD's uniqueness. As we trace the I's in this section, we may feel like Job facing the whirlwind: it is an overwhelming passage on the utter sovereignty of God. This is still the tender father and protector of verses 10-11, but abandoning him is utter folly.

We may instinctively feel that verses 40-41 are brutal, but at times, in order to defeat evil, you have to fight. We should remember that vengeance in the hands of the Rock whose work is perfect and just in all his ways is not like human vengeance; it is entirely fitting and judicial punishment.

In literature, when good King Richard returns to England to vindicate Robin Hood and take vengeance against bad King John, we cheer. In *The Lord of the Rings*, when King Théoden is woken from his strange sleep and then vindicates his niece and nephew and takes vengeance against Gríma Wormtongue, we cheer.

It is against this backdrop of vindication and vengeance that the call comes in verse 43 to rejoice. This joy is in justice and vindication, yet also in cleansing (atonement).

Intriguingly, this cleansing is of the land, as the sin of the people has polluted the land of promise. It needs to be cleansed, along with God's people.

Given Paul's adoption of this in Romans 15:10, it seems most sensible to take this as a call for the nations to rejoice. Rejoicing is caused by justice, vindication and atonement.

It's worth pausing to ask how the song is quoted in the New Testament as this certainly helps clarify some of the timelines here. The song depicts events in the life of the nation of Israel, and yet the New Testament is clear that they find their fulfilment in later generations too.

- *'A crooked and twisted generation'* (32:5)
  Paul declares in Philippians 2:14-15 that this is true of the whole of humanity. Christians are to live distinctively amongst those who have senselessly rejected their creator.

- *'I will make them jealous'* (32:21)
  Romans 10:19 says that this is happening now. People from every nation and ethnicity across the globe are becoming Christians, and in part it is to make those of a Jewish background jealous – so they turn back to God.

- *'Vengeance is mine'* (32:35)
  In Romans 12:19, God says that justice will come on all in humanity who say, 'Our hand has triumphed; there is no God.' That future certainty of vindication and vengeance liberates the Christian from retaliating today.

- *'Rejoice, you nations, with his people'* (32:43 NIV)
  Romans 15:8-12 says that this is happening now – nations are rejoicing because they know that God

has made atonement for his people through Jesus Christ.

- *'The Rock, his work is perfect, for all his ways are justice'* (32:4)
  Revelation 15:3 reveals the saints singing the Song of Moses in heaven. We may as well learn the words now!

Conclusion (32:44-47)

There is a question over what precisely is meant by 'all these words' in verse 45. It could refer to the whole of Moses's speeches in Deuteronomy, or, in context, it could refer to the song. The latter understanding strengthens the idea of it being 'sung law' – a summary of all that they are meant to know, a national anthem designed to witness to the essence of what is required of them.

From text to message

Getting the message clear: the theme

God is faithful and humanity is faithless. His faithfulness means that judgment must come and yet also that atonement is possible.

Getting the message clear: the aim

Sing of the greatness of God! Remember all he has given you and don't be foolishly ungrateful.

A way in

In Gulliver's travels, Jonathan Swift gives us his view of ingratitude in the laws of the Lilliputians: 'Ingratitude is reckoned among them a capital crime; for they reason that whoever makes ill return to his benefactors must needs be a common enemy to the rest of mankind ... And therefore such a man is not fit to live.'[6]

Golly, is ingratitude really such a terrible thing? In the face of God's vast and abundant generosity, yes.

Ideas for application

- **The ingratitude of idolatry.** What is the nature of Israel's failure? What actually did they get so wrong? They broke the fundamental commandment to love the LORD with all their heart. Rather, they chased after other gods. Idolatry is the great crime of Deuteronomy, as it remains throughout Israel's history. Block observes: 'Whereas echoes of the Decalogue, the basic covenantal document, are rare in the Old Testament, echoes of the Song embedded in Deuteronomy 32 are ubiquitous.'[7] So be wary of saying, 'My/Our hand has triumphed.' As chapter 8 warned us, when life goes well and we feel 'stout and sleek' there is a danger that we can fall into the madness of forgetting that we owe everything to our creator. King Lear is by no means a model father, yet Shakespeare gave him words of timeless truth when he is betrayed by two of his daughters:

  > Ingratitude, thou marble-hearted fiend,
  > More hideous when thou show'st thee in a child
  > Than the sea-monster!

  > How sharper than a serpent's tooth it is
  > To have a thankless child![8]

---

6. Jonathan Swift, *Gulliver's Travels*, Part I, Chapter VI

7. Block, *Deuteronomy*, 770.

8. William Shakespeare, *King Lear*, ed. Louis B. Wright and Virginia A. LaMar (New York: Washington Square Press, 1957), 1.4.259-261 and 290-291. References are to act, scene and line.

- **The stupidity of idolatry.** Alongside the pictures of God's anger, the song is clear on what an appalling act of self-harm it is to reject the Rock of our salvation. John Bunyan wrote, 'He that forgets his friend is ungrateful unto him; but he that forgets his Saviour is unmerciful to himself.'[9] It's such a foolishly damaging thing to do.

- **The judgment upon idolatry.** The punishment fits the crime. If people reject God, he will reject them. He abandons them to their stupidity (Rom. 1:24, 26, 28). Ultimately, he rejects forever, in hell. The song reminds me of G. K. Chesterton's observation: 'Hell is God's great compliment to human dignity. A compliment? Yes, because God is saying to us, "You are significant. I take you seriously. Choose to reject me – choose hell if you will. I will let you go."'[10]

- **A song?** As Moses prepares to leave, God's people are given a leader, the written word of God and a song. I wonder if the third is a surprise to some of us. We value good leadership in our churches, we hold the word of God to be central, but songs are not viewed as especially important – indeed, some hold that they could be dangerous if they distract from the word. That doesn't seem to be God's view here; he wants Israel to sing the torah too. We would be wise to recognize the fact that songs have a unique ability

---

9. John Bunyan, *Pilgrim's Progress: From This World to That Which Is to Come* (Oak Harbor, WA: Logos Research Systems, Inc., 1995). Part II, the Second Stage.

10. Quoted in Lee Strobel, *The Case for Faith* (Grand Rapids: Zondervan, 2000), 169.

to affect and shape us. Maybe we need to encourage more songwriters to write biblically saturated lyrics and put them to good tunes. Perhaps, in particular, we would benefit from songs which tell the whole Bible story, so that we in turn are shaped by that story.

- **He has made atonement.** The Christian reads the expressions of God's anger in the song and gives thanks that Jesus has made atonement, reparation and amends. Taking verse 39, we must pause upon the wonder that he was put to death so that we could have life. He was wounded so that we could be healed. He was slain so that we could be restored. He was treated as an enemy of God so that we could become his people.

Suggestions for preaching

If preaching an overview series of Deuteronomy, then these chapters will be taken together. It is quite natural to do so. The challenge then is what to include and what to leave out. To preach one coherent sermon will require a brief explanation of what happens in chapter 31 before focusing on the song.

Singing the law (chs. 31–32)

- A faithful God (32:1-14)
- Faithless people (32:15-19)
- A fitting response (32:20-35)
- A cause for rejoicing (32:36-43)

If you are preaching through the book in sections (as opposed to one series), then there is more than ample material to preach a helpful series of three. This gives the space to press the points home that are made in the song, rather than perhaps just stating them.

Build your life upon the Rock I (31:1-30)

- The LORD himself will go before you (and Joshua) (31:1-8, 14-15, 23)
- The law will go with you (31:9-13, 24-27)
- This song will be with you (31:16-22)

Build your life upon the Rock II (32:1-25)

- A faithful God (32:3-4, 7-14)
- Faithless people (32:5-6, 15-18)

Build your life upon the Rock III (32:19-47)

- He rejects his people who desert (32:19-25)
- He rejects 'no people' who are proud (32:26-35)
- He atones for his people who are humbled (32:36-43)

Questions to help understand the passage

Chapter 31

1. What is the great encouragement in 31:1-8? Who is going to do most of the work?

2. What are both the people and Joshua commanded (31:6 and 7)? What are the grounds for their being able to keep these commands?

3. When is the whole law to be read (31:9-13)? Who is to be there? What is the context? What is the aim?

4. What will Israel do after Moses's death (31:14-20)? What is the chief accusation against them (vv. 16, 18, 20)?

5. What will witness against Israel (31:19, 26, 28)?

Chapter 32

1. What is God like (32:4)? What is Israel like (32:5-6)?

2. What did God do for Israel? (Work through 32:8-14.)

3. How did Israel respond to God's generosity, protection and care (32:15-18)?

4. In particular, what did they turn to (32:16-17)?

5. How would a parent feel if they had been treated as God was by Israel (32:18)?

6. Look at verse 21. What is the connection between how Israel treated God and how he responds to them?

7. What happens when Israel rejects the protection of God (32:23-25)? What change has there been in their condition between verses 13-14 and verse 24?

8. What stopped the Rock from wiping Israel out according to verses 26-27?

9. What do we learn about this nation that conquered Israel (32:28-29)? What should they have realized (v. 30)?

10. When will they be punished (32:34-35)?

11. When will the LORD have compassion on his people (32:36)? What state are Israel in?

12. What is stressed about the LORD in 32:37-42?

13. What causes rejoicing in 32:43?

Questions to help apply the passage

1. Philippians 2:15 ascribes the idea of a 'crooked and twisted generation' to the whole of humanity. So, what do we learn about God's treatment of humanity in general?

2. What do we learn about humanity's response to the generosity and protection of God? How sensible is it?

3. What tends to happen when we forget that God has given us all that we have? How do we view ourselves?

4. Is it okay to cheer when evil is defeated and good vindicated?

5. How does Paul interpret 32:39-43 in Romans 15:8-12? When should we be singing this song?

20.

Happy Are You ... a People Secure in the Everlasting Arms
(Deuteronomy 33–34)

Introduction

How to end an extraordinary book like Deuteronomy? The final two chapters are, chiefly, a hopeful reminder that Israel is loved by the LORD who is the source of great blessing. The era of the great Moses is over, but they still have his words and the LORD.

These chapters certainly alter the mood on which the book ends. In meteorological terms, we have been under cloudy skies with the certainty of thunderstorms since chapter 27. Although there was the brief promise of future sunshine in chapter 30, chapters 31 and 32 have returned to thunder and lightning. Yet now, we have two chapters where the clouds part and the sunshine breaks through. Deuteronomy concludes with two chapters of hope and positivity (if also a longing for another prophet).

This does matter for our overall reading of the book. Although failure and judgment was certain for Israel, and salvation and grace lay beyond that, they were still

347

presented with a choice of trusting the LORD today. He is good and the source of all blessings.

Listening to the text

It is best to include 32:48-52 with these chapters rather than the song of chapter 32. There is a sense in which the whole book is framed by the death of Moses. It was mentioned three times at the start (1:37; 3:23-29; 4:21-22). Here we have it in 32:48-52 as well as the whole of chapter 34.

It seems as if the text is edited in such a way as to force the question, 'Now Moses is gone, what will you do?'

Structure

There are three obvious sections, with chapter 33 being far longer and structured around the twelve tribes. Amongst those, Levi and Joseph have far longer blessings than the other tribes.

- The death of Moses the 'faith-breaker' foretold (32:48-52)
- The final blessing of Moses the 'man of God' upon Israel (ch. 33)
- The death of Moses the 'unrivalled servant' of the LORD (ch. 34)

Working through the text

The death of Moses the 'faith-breaker' foretold (32:48-52)

Deuteronomy makes us ask the simple question: Why did Moses die?

- In the references in chapters 1–4, the emphasis is that he would die without entering the land *because of the people's sin.* Yet it would be a mistake to view this as being vicarious, even as a foreshadowing of Christ, because …

- … Moses broke faith with the LORD at Meribah and did not treat the LORD as holy (32:51). This is the same double reason that was given in Numbers 20:10-13. Moses was clearly a great leader, but he remained a sinner.

As mentioned in notes on 3:23-29, it is quite possible that both of the points above are true. Yet it is striking that in the final chapter of the book neither the people nor Moses himself are blamed. The death of Moses is stated as a fact, but the concluding picture of him borders on hagiography. The overall impact is that, while we can be clear that Moses is a sinful human, we see also that he was a remarkable man of God, servant of the LORD and unique prophet – we need one like him.

The final blessing of Moses the 'man of God' upon Israel (ch. 33)

Here is an extraordinary contrast to the previous verses: Moses is described as 'the man of God' and we see him bestowing a glorious blessing upon the tribes of Israel. Whereas the song of chapter 32 was a witness *for* the LORD and *against* Israel (e.g. 31:19), this is a blessing *for* Israel. It has obvious echoes of the patriarchal deathbed blessing of Genesis 49 as Moses works his way through all the tribes. The first and last books of the Pentateuch conclude with the blessing of the chief patriarchal figure from outside of the land.

It is possible to work through the chapter verse by verse, but I would lean towards highlighting the frame's emphasis upon the LORD's protection and then zooming in more briefly on Levi and Joseph, which receive far longer blessings than the other tribes.

Safe in the hand of the king (33:2-5, 26-29)

The blessing is framed in vv. 2-5 and 26-29 by twin pictures of the LORD as a warrior for his people.

This frame provides the dominant theme of the chapter. Divine protection and the conquest of enemies is stressed in the blessing of numerous tribes (vv. 7, 11, 12, 17, 20, 25).

Verse 2 is a fairly overwhelming picture of the LORD coming with flaming fire and what appears to be an army of tens of thousands of angels. Yet he uses this power to demonstrate his love for his people, kept safe in his hand (v. 3). The people respond with obedience.

Verses 5 and 26 both contain the idea of God as king (surprisingly only occurring elsewhere in the Pentateuch at Exod. 15:18 and Num. 23:21-23). He is king of 'Jeshurun' (meaning 'straight') – the ironic pet name for Israel.

Verses 26-27 are quite wonderful and it's natural for the preacher to dwell on these pictures. God's people need to know that:

- he rides across the heavens to help them;
- he is their dwelling place;
- he is beneath them with everlasting arms; and
- he is before them to give them victory.

The consequence is that 'Israel lived in safety … in a land of grain and wine, whose heavens drop down dew.' This double blessing of verse 28 is not a bad summary of the blessings listed in Moses's words to the twelve tribes. The conclusion in verse 29 returns to the dominant theme of the chapter: the Lord is a shield and sword. Enemies will come fawning.

Very practically for believers, the great comfort *here* is not the promise of a life of comfort and ease, but that in the midst of battles and enemies, God's people can know the everlasting arms of God are beneath them.

Faithful Levi shall teach the people and make the Lord smile (33:8-11)

The blessing upon Levi is the most distinctive. Given their lack of land, this is possibly unsurprising, but it does mean that along with length, the content of the blessing stands out. Two things are stressed here: Levi's loyalty to the Lord and the twin task given to the tribe.

Levi is to be given the Thummim and Urim. While no commentator is absolutely confident on what they are, it appears that they were to be used to discern the Lord's will in binary decisions (Ezra 2:63; Num. 27:21). They are awarded to Levi for their faithfulness (v. 8) and their love of the Lord ahead of their family (v. 9).

The two tasks are outlined in verse 10: they are to (1) teach God's law to the people and (2) make offerings to the Lord. They will (translating literally) 'put incense in your nostrils', expressing the pleasure that the sacrifices offered in faith bring to God.

Yet, even for faithful Levi, there is no guarantee of spiritual health. Moses asks the Lord to bless his substance (Levi has no land to be blessed) and accept the work of his hands (v. 11).

In a chapter which highlights that Israel is safe in the hand of the Lord, here is a reminder of what is required to keep them there! Faithful teaching and regular sacrifices provided by Levi. They are the priests (18:1-3) and preachers (27:9-26) as well as, here in chapter 33, teachers of the law.

Joseph receives the choicest of gifts (33:13-17)

Joseph is described in language reminiscent of Genesis – he is a prince among his brothers (v. 16).

Yet the accent here falls on the blessing upon the land. The LORD is the source of all good gifts, not any pagan fertility god. And what gifts! Five times we are told that these are the choicest or best gifts (vv. 13, twice in 14, 15, 16) using the same Hebrew word each time: *meged*, which is also translated 'rich yield and abundance'. Israel will have the best gifts of heaven ... the sun ... the months ... the mountains ... the hills ... the earth. This comes along with the 'favour of him who dwells in the bush'.

The death of Moses the 'unrivalled servant' of the LORD (ch. 34)

The events (34:1-6)

The text would read quite naturally if it flowed from 32:52 to 34:1, but the insertion of chapter 33 has already begun to alter the readers' concluding thoughts on Moses from the negative assessment of 32:48-52 to the far more positive one here.

The events of Moses's death are presented in a somewhat matter-of-fact fashion. He is passive and the LORD is the chief actor: 'The LORD showed ... said to him ... buried him'.

It is hard for us to really grasp the poignancy of this moment. Moses has been looking forward by faith to the land for forty years. It has been a key subject throughout the three final sermons of Deuteronomy and so verses

1-3 allow us to see Moses taking a slow panoramic look across the whole land. Yet he cannot enter, as the LORD had spoken. Despite this, there are obvious privileges here: Moses is described for the first time in the book as 'the servant of the LORD' (although this has been used in the Pentateuch in Exod. 14:31 and Num. 12:8), and, in a highly personal phrasing, we are told that the LORD buried Moses, albeit outside the land.

His vigour (34:7-9)

It is unclear quite what to make of the comment that although he was 120 years old when he died, Moses's 'eye was undimmed and his vigour unabated.' Certainly, it reinforces the idea that his failure to enter the land was not due to old age but was God's judgment upon Moses's breaking faith at Meribah.[1] Yet possibly, it also leads into the assessment of his incomparability. Of course, his death causes great distress as the people weep and mourn for thirty days. They do have Joshua but he is not Moses. The LORD had told Moses to 'invest him with *some* of your authority' (Num. 27:20). Things were never the same again.

His incomparability (34:10-12)

The final stress is that Moses is the prophet without equal in two particular ways. First, in intimacy or knowledge of God: the LORD knew him face to face (cf. 5:4 for the expression used of hearing God speak at Horeb). Second, there was 'none like him for all the signs and the wonders' he was sent to do. These are amplified as 'all the mighty power and all the great deeds *that Moses did*', which is

---

1. Gen. 6:3 would suggest that Moses has lived a full life as the LORD declared that a maximum.

striking as throughout the book God has been the one who performed 'signs and wonders'.[2] Clearly, Moses is only the vehicle for the LORD's power, but verse 12 emphasises his role greatly.

It is somewhat unclear when these last few verses have been written. The use of 'since' in verse 10 suggests a much later perspective.

As suggested, the overall impact of concluding the book with such an exalted view of Moses seems twofold:

- So, Israel, what will you do now? Moses has left you the word of God and the Levites to teach you and offer sacrifices. Will you trust the sovereign King who fights for you and brings blessing?

- It would be wonderful to have a prophet like Moses who performed signs and wonders but who did not break faith with the Lord, so that we need never weep and mourn at his passing.

From text to message

Getting the message clear: the theme

The LORD is an irresistible warrior who loves, blesses and protects his people. He gave them Moses, the servant and unrivalled prophet. His death is a tragedy and great loss; we need one like him but greater.

Getting the message clear: the aim

Rejoice that we have a prophet like Moses who brings us God's blessing and wonderfully will never die.

---

2. See 4:34; 6:22; 7:14; 11:3; 26:8; 29:3. A point made by Olson (*Deuteronomy and the Death of Moses*, 172).

A way in

Do you think that you tend to leave church encouraged or challenged?

It's a silly question, really. Often, we will feel both as a result of meeting with God's people and hearing from the Lord.

Yet no matter how much challenge, rebuke or warning we've heard, there is always hope.

Even for Israel.

We come to the end of Deuteronomy where there has been an enormous amount of warning and indeed discussion of the inevitability of Israel's failure, and yet it concludes with hope and optimism for that generation stood on the borders of the promised land ...

Ideas for application

- **There is always hope when the eternal God is your dwelling place.** After chapters of warning about eviction from the land and a looming sense of failure, Israel is left with a clear vision of their glorious Lord who is the source of all blessing. There is none like him and no enemy can stand before him. If our God is for us, who can stand against us? Even though Israel was about to face many battles, they could know that the eternal God was their dwelling place. Christians can know that in the midst of struggles he is still our dwelling place and will ensure that we reach the promised land of heaven.

- **We are greatly blessed to be the people of God.** There are familiar truths warmly expressed in chapter 33 – we are secure in the Lord and we require the law to be taught to us and sacrifices offered. Part of the preacher's task is to bring these truths home with the same warmth that the passage does. Here is a chapter to cause us to delight in the Lord! The blessings here are very earthy and real and while recognizing that *our* land still awaits us in glory, Jesus would still want us to know that in this life we are truly blessed and not lacking. (See especially Mark 10:29-30 where it says, 'There is no one who has left house or brothers or sisters or mother or father or children or lands, for my sake and for the gospel, who will not receive a hundredfold *now in this time*, houses and brothers and sisters and mothers and children and lands.')

- **There has not arisen a prophet in Israel like Moses.** Next time we see Moses, he is on another mountain (where else?), alongside Elijah and Jesus. One is the only other comparable prophet of the Old Testament. The other is the one who supersedes him. The people wept when Moses died. Christians are those who will shed no more tears when they are united with their great prophet. Jesus is the prophet who ensures we will know the blessings of chapter 33, rightly understood in the church and in the new creation.

Suggestions for preaching

Trust the king who brings blessing (ch. 33)

- Secure in his arms (vv. 2-5, 26-29)
- Still needing his priests (vv. 8-11)
- Enjoying his blessing (vv. 13-17)

Celebrate the prophet like Moses (ch. 34)

- There was none like him
- Yet there is one better

Questions to help understand the passage

1. What impression do you get of Moses from 32:48-52? Then what impression do you get of him from 34:1-12? What are we meant to think when we put these together?

2. What is highlighted in the beginning and conclusion of Moses's final blessing (33:2-5, 26-29)? So, what tone or impression are we left with as the book ends?

3. Which two tribes are highlighted?

4. What is highlighted about them (33:8-11, 13-17)?

Questions to help apply the passage

1. What does it mean to you that the Lord is your eternal dwelling place (corporately) – that he is underneath you and before you?

2. The Levites had two main jobs (33:10-11). Who does those jobs today?

3. What impact does the delightful listing of blessings in 33:13-16 have?

4. When do we next see Moses in the Bible? What does this tell us about his status as the incomparable prophet (i.e. does he point us elsewhere)?

5. What do you *really* want to remember and be changed by through your study of Deuteronomy?

About The Proclamation Trust

The fundamental conviction underlying the work of The Proclamation Trust is that when the Bible is faithfully taught, God's voice is clearly heard. We are ambitious for the spread of the gospel – and of expository preaching and teaching in particular – in the UK and beyond.

There are three strands to our ministry:

First, we run the Cornhill Training Course in London, a flexible, multi-year, part-time course for anyone who wants to handle and communicate God's Word more faithfully and effectively.

Second, we run a range of conferences to equip, enthuse and energise senior pastors, assistant pastors, students, ministry wives, women in ministry and church members in the work God has called them to. We also run the Evangelical Ministry Assembly each summer in London, which is a gathering of over a thousand church leaders from across the UK and from around the world.

Third, we produce an array of resources, of which this book in your hand is one, to assist people in preaching, teaching and understanding the Bible.

For more information, please go to www.proctrust.org.uk

Christian Focus Publications

Our mission statement –

STAYING FAITHFUL

In dependence upon God we seek to impact the world through literature faithful to His infallible Word, the Bible. Our aim is to ensure that the Lord Jesus Christ is presented as the only hope to obtain forgiveness of sin, live a useful life and look forward to heaven with Him.

Our books are published in four imprints:

CHRISTIAN
FOCUS

Popular works including biographies, commentaries, basic doctrine and Christian living.

CHRISTIAN
HERITAGE

Books representing some of the best material from the rich heritage of the church.

MENTOR

Books written at a level suitable for Bible College and seminary students, pastors, and other serious readers. The imprint includes commentaries, doctrinal studies, examination of current issues and church history.

CF4•K

Children's books for quality Bible teaching and for all age groups: Sunday school curriculum, puzzle and activity books; personal and family devotional titles, biographies and inspirational stories – because you are never too young to know Jesus!

Christian Focus Publications Ltd,
Geanies House, Fearn, Ross-shire,
IV20 1TW, Scotland, United Kingdom.
www.christianfocus.com
blog.christianfocus.com